THE
GOOD
WALK

Creating New Paths on
Traditional Prairie Trails

MATTHEW R. ANDERSON

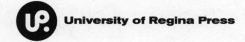

University of Regina Press

Printed and bound in Canada. The text of this book is printed on 100% post-consumer recycled paper with earth-friendly vegetable-based inks.

COVER AND TEXT DESIGN: Duncan Noel Campbell
COPY EDITOR: Dallas Harrison
PROOFREADER: Rachel Taylor
COVER IMAGE: Between Chimney Coulee and Eastend, Saskatchewan, July 31, 2015.
Photo by George Tsougrianis, courtesy of Overtime Studios

Library and Archives Canada Cataloguing in Publication

TITLE: The good walk : creating new paths on traditional Prairie trails / Matthew R. Anderson.

NAMES: Anderson, Matthew R. (Matthew Robert), author.

DESCRIPTION: Includes bibliographical references and index.

IDENTIFIERS: Canadiana (print) 20230552250 | Canadiana (ebook) 2023055234X | ISBN 9780889779686 (hardcover) | ISBN 9780889779655 (softcover) | ISBN 9780889779662 (pdf) | ISBN 9780889779679 (EPUB)

SUBJECTS: LCSH: Trails,—Prairie Provinces. | LCSH: Trails,—Social aspects,—Prairie Provinces. | LCSH: Prairie Provinces,—Description and travel. | LCSH: Hiking,—Prairie Provinces. | LCSH: Hiking,—Social aspects,—Prairie Provinces. | LCSH: Prairie Provinces,—History. | LCSH: Prairie Provinces,—Ethnic relations,—History. | LCSH: Indigenous peoples,—Prairie Provinces,—History.

CLASSIFICATION: LCC FC3234.3 .A53 2024 | DDC 796.5109712,—dc23

10   9   8   7   6   5   4   3   2   1

University of Regina Press

University of Regina, Regina, Saskatchewan, Canada, S4S 0A2
TEL: (306) 585-4758 FAX: (306) 585-4699 WEB: www.uofrpress.ca

University of Regina Press is located on Treaty 4 Territory, the traditional lands of the nêhiyawak (Cree), Anihšinapêk (Saulteaux), Dakota, Lakota, and Nakoda Nations, and the homeland of the Métis peoples.

We acknowledge the support of the Canada Council for the Arts for our publishing program. We acknowledge the financial support of the Government of Canada. / Nous reconnaissons l'appui financier du gouvernement du Canada. This publication was made possible with support from Creative Saskatchewan's Book Publishing Production Grant Program.

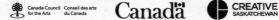

THE
GOOD
WALK

CONTENTS

For Hugh Henry

Between Chimney Coulee and Eastend, Saskatchewan, July 31, 2015.
Photo by George Tsougrianis, courtesy of Overtime Studios.

A gift begets a gift; a story begets a story; motion begets motion.
—NIIGAAN JAMES SINCLAIR[1]

The stories we tell today will inform those of tomorrow.
—TASHA HUBBARD AND JADE TOOTOOSIS[2]

---

1   Niigaan James Sinclair, email to the author, October 22, 2019.

2   Tasha Hubbard and Jade Tootoosis, "Preface," in *Storying Violence: Unravelling Colonial Narratives in the Stanley Trial*, Gina Starblanket and Dallas Hunt (Winnipeg: ARP Books, 2020), 13.

A THANKSGIVING
by Richard Kotowich

MY OPENING WORDS FOR THIS BOOK ARE MEANT to respectfully communicate Indigenous ways of knowing, seeing, and guiding behaviour in the world for both individuals and collectives. They are a modification and an abbreviation of a traditional address; they are informed by my Métis lived experience of walking across the Canadian Prairies in pilgrimage, and they draw from my everyday reflections on living life.

Imagine that you have just crawled out of your sleeping bag and exited your tent into the morning light. The nylon fabric is beaded with droplets from an overnight shower. The air is heavy with moisture, and everything smells new and fresh. The prairie grass, blade by blade, is similarly bejewelled by raindrops. In the bushes all around, various birds are chirping as they go about their busy daily work of survival. The sun, already risen, has climbed behind a dense shroud of grey cloud overhead, but a band of bright blue sky along the western horizon promises a warmer day. Around the camp your fellow pilgrims are stirring. You hear them talking to one another in low tones and short phrases punctuated by the soft clatter of pots and dishes as they make their breakfasts or dis-

Photo of Richard Kotowich, by the author, August 8, 2017,
Otter's Station, Saskatchewan.

mantle tents. There is occasional quiet laughter. Another day of
walking lies ahead. Another day of rhythmic crunches underfoot
while treading gravel roads or the swish-crunch of crossing grass
and sage-clumped fields and pastures. Another day of being aided
by friends while dropping to the ground to carefully roll under
barbed-wire fences, barriers that demarcate private properties on a
once-not-so-very-long-ago untamed grassy landscape. Another day
of sights to be seen, mounting fatigue to deal with, and guaranteed
weariness and relief upon arrival at its end. But for now the aches
and pains that greeted you upon awakening have already begun to
ease as you stand erect and stretch your arms skyward. It seems
like a good time to pray, like a good time to earnestly and humbly
say words of thanksgiving and petition to all Creation and your
fellow pilgrims.

Ekosi! Let's walk on!

Richard Kotowich,
Regina

INTRODUCTION: A NEW STORY

Be aware of your histories, of your stories, and then figure out what it means to take responsibility for those histories.

—GINA STARBLANKET AND DALLAS HUNT[1]

CANADA NEEDS NEW STORIES. MANY OF US HAVE discovered that the narratives about this country that we learned in school were at best half-truths. Sometimes they were outright lies. Gina Starblanket and Dallas Hunt point out that, if Canadians hope to change the cycles of violence that we inflict on the land and its Indigenous Peoples, then we need to begin with *honest* retellings of the past and assessments of the present. "Denial is the handmaiden of violence," Métis lawyer and activist Bruce McIvor writes.[2] Many of the "facts" about our history that we thought we knew are falling like dominoes. They're being proven time and again as false, incomplete, or both.

Meanwhile, Indigenous Peoples are telling new stories. From mapping and recovering children's graves carried out by First Nations at the sites of former residential schools, to drawing widespread attention to militarized police actions on their territories,

1 Gina Starblanket and Dallas Hunt, *Storying Violence: Unravelling Colonial Narratives in the Stanley Trial* (Winnipeg: ARP Books, 2020), 16.

2 Bruce McIvor, *Standoff: Why Reconciliation Fails Indigenous People and How to Fix It* (Gibsons, BC: Nightwood Editions, 2021), 110.

to Water Walkers protesting pollution and climate change, to the joyful renaissance of Indigenous cultural production in visual art, writing, music, journalism, and more, Indigenous artists, writers, activists, and communities are creating new narratives.

Like them, Canadians also need to create better narratives about this land and our place, past and present, in it. We Canadians need new stories that reinforce humility, tell the truth about the past, learn from it, and open us up to the rebirth that will come with more responsible treaty relations.

This is one of those stories.

From his nêhiyaw, or Cree, perspective, Dwayne Donald has written about how walking is one way to arrive at a "new story."[3] That has certainly been my experience. What follows is the tale of some unusual—and very long—walks across the prairies. Working with the Saskatchewan History and Folklore Society (SHFS), I trekked with other settler-descended Canadians as well as Métis and nêhiyaw participants. The journeys that we took, and that SHFS groups are still walking, are meant to revive historic paths, especially on Treaty 4 and Treaty 6 territories.

For over a thousand kilometres, we journeyed footsore on land that Indigenous Peoples have walked for millennia. We learned about ourselves and the land through our feet. "If you want to understand yourself," writes David Robertson in his memoir *Black Water*, then "take the initiative to seek out what came before you."[4] We did. What we started has since become a modest ongoing movement.

The paths that we walked and the people whom we met ended up educating us in ways that we hadn't expected. Harold Johnson talks about the mistaken and harmful stories that one family, Canadians, have told about another family, the Indigenous Peoples with

---

3   Dwayne Donald, "We Need a New Story: Walking and the wâhkôtowin Imagination," *Journal of the Canadian Association for Curriculum Studies (JCACS)* 18, no. 2 (2021): 53–63.

4   David A. Robertson, *Black Water: Family, Legacy, and Blood Memory* (Toronto: HarperCollins, 2020), 62.

whom treaty put Canadians in relation.[5] On our walks, we were taken aback by the evidence of how savage colonialism has been and how pervasive it still can be. At the same time, we learned about the vitality—the art and music, the scientific and environmental knowledge, the poetry and ceremony, the friendliness, and the laughter—of our Indigenous fellow walkers and of the Indigenous communities that we encountered.

We also experienced the warmth and welcome of many non-Indigenous farms and communities. We discovered the hidden treasures—some old, some new—of the Saskatchewan hamlets and small towns where we stayed, places too often forgotten by more urban centres.

By chance more than by design, each of our first three journeys across the prairie led us to a different kind of learning. Our initial trek across southern Saskatchewan was exploratory. We asked ourselves, "Can this even be done?" When it was finished, we realized that it had been largely about remembering prairie settlements long gone and about complicating colonial history in new ways. Our second pilgrimage, heading north along the western edge of the province, evolved into a witness to present-day colonialism. In the fraught months before the Stanley trial and its verdict, this second walk took us through Mosquito–Grizzly Bear's Head–Lean Man First Nation, close to where Colten Boushie's life had been taken by Gerald Stanley. The third long journey documented in this book was in many ways the easiest: a large and mixed Indigenous–settler-descended group walked together in a spirit of decolonization that set the tone for biennial prairie pilgrimages since.

One of the best things about healthy new stories is that they can replace problematic older ones. My hope is that this might happen with this tale. It's not that the narratives that many of us grew up hearing were always wrong. But they were incomplete. The stories told to me as a child concerned pioneers and frontiers, railways stretching across continents, land and horses "broken," and empty

---

5 Harold Johnson, *Two Families: Treaties and Government* (Saskatoon: Purich, 2007).

country filling up with hard-working immigrants.[6] Those stories inevitably ended with prosperous, and very white, communities. The few nêhiyaw, Anihšināpēk (Saulteaux), Nakota, and Niisitapi[7] characters in the stories that I heard growing up played minor and tragic roles. They were brought in for supporting parts and soon ushered off stage.

Even before becoming an adult and reading works by Indigenous authors—many of whom had their fingers on the pulse of western Canadian culture better than I did—I had already figured out some of the problems with the bright and shiny pioneer narratives. Driving through the country where I was raised, I noticed that many of the supposedly successful small towns were boarded up, nearly abandoned, their grain elevators torn down. Newcomers had helped to revitalize some of these communities, but they still struggled. The world of my grandparents, and even of my parents and aunts and uncles, was clearly gone, along with the farmsteads and rural churches and community halls increasingly plowed under by agribusiness. I could sense my relatives' regret, as weathered and palpable as the grey boards on an abandoned farm building. I witnessed how their memories of the 1930s to the 1950s, written with love into the small-town anniversary books that they had worked so hard to compile, sat forgotten in family basements or nursing home shelves.

I grew up selling popcorn and cola in spectator stands filled with my neighbours during Swift Current's Frontier Days. My earliest memories are of my parents going to dances and funerals in Simmie township's Pioneer Hall. Those words—*frontier*, *pioneer*, *settler*—surrounded my childhood. They defined my parents' generation and in turn affected my own.

---

6   Starblanket and Hunt, *Storying Violence*, 30–47.

7   The names for Indigenous groups throughout this book follow the primary guidance of Gregory Younging, *Elements of Indigenous Style: A Guide for Writing by and about Indigenous Peoples* (Edmonton: Brush Education, 2018), with secondary input from the University of Regina's Office of Indigenous Engagement and Canadian Association of University Teachers (CAUT) practice.

Words such as *pioneer* and *frontier* hold incredible power over our relationships with the land and its original peoples. Aileen Moreton-Robinson has shown how the enduring legends of the pioneer, "the battler" who struggled to survive and triumph, have served above all to legitimize myths about ownership.[8] In my life, *pioneer* was an adjective applied to everything from margarine containers to motor oil. It defined where I and my family came from. I thought that it was only because of the "pioneers" that I was growing up in Swift Current, Saskatchewan, a small city that I did not realize held such a troubled history.

Like a substratum of glacial gravel beneath both the loam of settler enterprise and the clay of settler regret sat a deeper narrative that I rarely heard. This was and remains the land's original and ongoing story—a story of the Indigenous Peoples so conspicuously absent from the coulees, hills, rivers, and even streets and neighbourhoods around me, to which they had given names. It was a story about treaties that I had barely heard of, even though those treaties were the charters that gave my family its roots.[9] These stories were not being told. They are stories that until recently have not just been forgotten but actually suppressed.

Even though it describes our long, unsettling pilgrimages, on a deeper level this book is really about the stories that we Canadians tell ourselves about why and how we are here in this land. What follows could be called settler-descendant, or aware-settler, writing.[10] It tells how people like me must take time and care to find out who we are in relation to Indigenous Peoples and what our responsibilities are toward them. *Responsibility* is one of those "pioneer" words that's still useful, even if we now need to apply it in new ways.

---

8   Aileen Moreton-Robinson, *The White Possessive: Property, Power, and Indigenous Sovereignty* (Minneapolis: University of Minnesota Press, 2015), 3.

9   See Raymond Aldred and Matthew R. Anderson, *Our Home and Treaty Land: Walking Our Creation Story* (Kelowna: Wood Lake Books, 2022).

10   See Matthew R. Anderson, "'Aware-Settler' Biblical Studies: Breaking Claims of Textual Ownership," *Journal for Interdisciplinary Biblical Studies* 1, no. 1 (2019): 42–68.

The Good Walk is a here-to-there account of journeying many hundreds of kilometres by foot across arid, often scorching, terrain. The book takes its title from a teaching given to our little group at the outset of the first pilgrimage by a Lakota Elder at Wood Mountain First Nation. After smudging us, he sent us off with the instruction to "Go, walk the good walk."

My mother and father grew up, lived, and died in southwestern Saskatchewan, not far from where that Lakota Elder greeted us, and within a short drive of the Cypress Hills, where we ended our first trek. My final visits with them took place during hard months that happened to coincide with planning and walking these pilgrimages. I would fly from Montreal to Regina, pick up a car, and drive to nursing homes at Gull Lake, Swift Current, and Herbert. My father would whisper advice about the trails from his hospital bed. In ways that I never would have guessed when I started writing and researching, my parents and I were participants in the ongoing history of Treaty 4 territory. I was to discover that my parents' two families played roles in some of the dramas that I was documenting. I'd thought that we had almost nothing to do with the big picture of Canadian colonization. I learned that exactly that assumption is often part of the problem.

My mother died while I was preparing to walk from Wood Mountain to Cypress Hills. My father died during our planning of the route from Swift Current to Fort Battleford. In addition to everything else, then, this is also the story of two funerals and the long prairie walks that followed them.

Chapter 1
WALKING

As for mortals, their days are like grass; they flourish like a flower of the field; for the wind passes over it, and it is gone, and its place knows it no more.

—FROM PSALM 103[1]

He carried my grandfather's stature,
leaned into the land
his ancestors bought for ten dollars in
1912.
—SKY DANCER LOUISE BERNICE HALFE[2]

NEW PATHS ON TRADITIONAL TRAILS

NO ONE WALKS ACROSS THE PRAIRIE.[3] AT LEAST, almost no one walks any distance unless their vehicle has broken down or they're one of those solitary athletes crossing the country for some cause and sticking to

---

1   Read at the funeral for my mother, Shirley Yvonne Anderson, née Golling, June 19, 2015.

2   Sky Dancer Louise Bernice Halfe, *The Crooked Good* (Regina: Coteau Books, 2007), 54.

3   There are rare exceptions. Indigenous scholar Tasha Beeds, together with a group of primarily Indigenous Water Walkers, walked over a thousand kilometres across the Prairies along the North Saskatchewan River, and

the Trans-Canada Highway. On each of our hundreds-of-kilometres journeys across the Prairies,[4] the most common reactions among passersby were offers of help. Farmers and ranchers usually assumed that we'd had a mechanical problem.

For most people, and most of human history, walking has been the only means of transport. That makes it ironic that, in richer nations, it's now considered an elite activity. The virtue—tied to the cost—of long-distance walking is that it takes time.

That time is important. It allows our bodies an opportunity to learn things that our minds haven't or won't. While we walk at four kilometres an hour, the world expands, and we notice the western kingbird flitting away from the ditch as we approach, the smell of prairie mint and sage, the badger waddling along the fenceline ahead, the feel of cool damp in the air before a rain. Details of weather, landscape, and plant and animal life that escape us when we're racing down a road at high speed press themselves intimately on the walker. Just the *physicality* of walking makes us feel distance in a bodily way. Writer, walker, and human geographer Yi-Fu Tuan wrote that "the feel of a place is registered in one's muscles and bones."[5] Walking turns out to be a particularly effective way

on to Lake Winnipeg, in 2021 and 2022 See N.C. Raine, "Walking the Line," *Eagle Feather News*, September 19, 2022, https://www.eaglefeathernews.com /health/walking-the-line. Non-Indigenous Saskatchewan plains walkers who have written about their treks include Ken Wilson, "Wood Mountain Walk: Afterthoughts on a Pilgrimage for Andrew Suknaski," *International Journal of Religious Tourism and Pilgrimage* 7, no. 1 (2019): 123–34; Trevor Herriot, *The Road Is How: A Prairie Pilgrimage through Nature, Desire, and Soul* (New York: Harper Perennial, 2014); and Norman Henderson, *Rediscovering the Prairies: Journeys by Dog, Horse and Canoe* (Victoria: TouchWood Editions, 2010).

4   In this book, I use lowercase "prairie" to denote the terrain typical of southern Saskatchewan/Treaty 4 and capital "Prairies" (plural) to denote the political entity of western Canada, specifically the provinces of Manitoba, Saskatchewan, and Alberta.

5   Yi-Fu Tuan, *Space and Place: The Perspective of Experience* (1977; reprinted, Minneapolis: University of Minnesota Press, 2001), 183–84.

of applying what is called "embodied" learning to land and our history and place on it.

On one of our treks, a rancher laughed out loud when I described what we were doing. "It takes a professor from Montreal to come up with the crazy idea of walking across Saskatchewan," he said. That was only partially true. It takes someone who grew up in the province smelling sage and marvelling at the bright stripe of the Milky Way hanging low over the pastures on a cold, dark prairie night, so low that you swear you could reach up and touch the stars. It takes someone who grew up watching hawks circle and dive above a treeless expanse. It takes someone who first learned to swim in the Swift Current Creek, to shoot cans off a post with a .22 rifle, and to drive a stick-shift grain truck following ruts through the fields.

In *Unsettling Spirit*, Denise Nadeau points out that a necessary first step for those of us who are settler descendants and wish to engage in solidarity with Indigenous Peoples is to begin by decolonizing our presence on the land.[6] To that end, notice how often we use imagery of a journey to conceptualize learning. For instance, I hope that this book puts you "on the road" to some new insights. Realizing that what we've been taught about Canadian history isn't accurate is "a necessary first step." Reading a book about it might place us on a learning "curve." We can "arrive" at fresh understandings.

For me, the path has been literal. It led across Treaty 4 and Treaty 6 territories.

Henry Kelsey was probably the first European to see the Great Plains. He left his canoe when his guides brought him to the grasslands of what is now south-central Saskatchewan.[7] In the summer of 1690, the Nakota[8] and nêhiyawak who guided Kelsey travelled overland

---

6   Denise M. Nadeau, *Unsettling Spirit: A Journey into Decolonization* (Montreal and Kingston: McGill-Queen's University Press, 2020), 5.

7   Bill Waiser, *A World We Have Lost* (Saskatoon: Fifth House, 2016), 10.

8   There is some debate in the literature about whether Kelsey left Fort York with Nakota directly or with Cree who then transferred him to the Nakota farther south.

on foot,[9] as did the Gros Ventre, the people whom he was trying to contact.[10] Pierre Gaultier de La Vérendrye and his sons, travelling westward from Quebec, walked on the prairie. During the next century, the 1700s, the use of horses spread to the northernmost Great Plains, and the Niisitapi, Anihšinápēk, Shoshone, Piikuni, and nêhiyawak who followed the bison north and south had horses.[11] But most still walked.

At the end of the nineteenth century and the beginning of the twentieth century, many of the first settlers striking out north and south from the Canadian Pacific Railway (CPR) line toward their quarter-section land claims walked, even if their possessions came by wagon. When my pregnant grandmother realized that it was time for her to give birth, she walked almost five kilometres across fields to the only farmer in the area who had a car and could drive her to the hospital. The child born later that day was my mother. The same land that seems to be so inhospitable to walking now is the terrain across which, for millennia, most human travel was on foot.

The prairie is still the prairie. It is we who have changed.

The previous century brought a revolution in human movement. At the same time, it changed our perceptions, and our language, concerning movement. We don't think the same way about direction, terrain, and time as did people of the past. In the 1940s, my parents and their friends travelled on foot or by horseback to Burns and Thring schools—long-disappeared rural schoolhouses. Their way was marked by natural features: stone piles, sloughs, coulees (the Michif word for prairie ravines),[12] and rare patches of cottonwood

---

9   Bruce Greenfield, "'Now Reader Read': The Literary Ambitions of Henry Kelsey, Hudson's Bay Company Clerk," *Early American Literature* 47, no. 1 (2012): 34, 40. On Kelsey's travels by foot, see 41.

10 Kelsey refers to them as the "Naywatame Poets." Greenfield, "'Now Reader Read,'" 41–42.

11 Henderson, *Rediscovering the Prairies*, 129–31, describes the spread northward of the horse from failed Spanish colonies.

12 Trevor Herriot, *Towards a Prairie Atonement* (Regina: University of Regina Press, 2016), 30.

or caragana. If for some reason those features were covered by snow or obscured by ice haze, as long as one could see the sun, the way could be deduced. Or the horses would know it. Travel was talked about in terms of terrain and distance: it was over three kilometres to school across country, farther if you kept to the road.

Now Canadians—and many Indigenous people—tend to think of travel in terms of vectors and of time. It's not uncommon to define the distance from Montreal to Ottawa, or from Regina to Saskatoon, in terms of hours—about two and a half hours—instead of referring to the actual distances. "Perceived space emerges out of spatial practices."[13] Because they follow largely predetermined routes, journeys by air almost force us into the mindset of trajectory. Winnipeg to Edmonton is a short-haul flight, whereas Vancouver to Montreal is long enough to take an overnight "red eye."

The clearest examples of seeing travel in terms of vectors are schematic maps. Think of London's iconic Tube map, which dates from the 1930s.[14] You can find the familiar multicoloured schematic on coffee mugs, T-shirts, and keychains. The graphic is a powerful representation of London, even though it makes little reference to physical sites.

The Tube map is the archetype for "vector travel": it doesn't bother with geography at all. Instead, it shows stations in relation to one another. For the traveller underground, it doesn't really matter if the distance from Paddington Station to King's Cross is half a kilometre or twice that. What matters is which line you are on and where you transfer.

More and more, in fact, our methods of travel isolate us from physical terrain. Once we're in a vehicle, even travel in rural Canada comes to be thought of in terms of what has been called "time-space."[15]

---

13 Sherene H. Razack, "When Place Becomes Race," in *Race, Space, and the Law: Unmapping a White Settler Society*, ed. Sherene H. Razack (Toronto: Between the Lines, 2002), 9.

14 John Tauranac, "Subway Maps: Getting from A to D," *Focus* 41, no. 4 (1991): 30.

15 Peter Merriman et al., *The Routledge Handbook of Mobilities* (London: Routledge, 2014), 195.

Whereas not much longer than a century ago it was the Eagle Hills, or Six-Mile Creek, or the availability of fresh water from a spring that marked distance, now it might be the time between fill-ups, electric recharging stations, or coffee shops. Speed leads to a different way of seeing land. More accurately, perhaps, speed has resulted in a new way of *ignoring* land.

Human geographers such as Tim Cresswell distinguish between *locale*—the set of coordinates that fixes a specific spot, like Global Positioning System (GPS) coordinates—and *place*, not only a more familiar but also a more indistinct definition. "Experience is at the heart of what place means," Cresswell insists.[16] For some theorists, "place" includes things such as feelings, emotions, attachments, and histories. Thus, places are made up not only of what is physical and can be touched but also and equally of much that is unseen. A place is a place because someone lives in it, works in it, has memories of and hopes for it, or is in some kind of relationship with it. For instance, 336 10th Avenue Northeast, Swift Current, Saskatchewan, is just an address. It's a space. What makes it a *place* for me are my memories of growing up in that house by the creek. "Space becomes a place when it is used and lived," Cresswell writes.[17] Place is never just about location. It's about experience.

This is a point that Indigenous writers and scholars have been making for a long time. Leanne Betasamosake Simpson notes that in Indigenous systems "meaning is derived from context, including the depth of relationships with the spiritual world, elders, family, clans, and the natural world."[18] On our walks, Sky Dancer Louise

---

16   Tim Cresswell, "Place," in *International Encyclopedia of Human Geography*, vol. 8, ed. Nigel Thrift and Rob Kitchen (Oxford: Elsevier, 2009), 170. Note that such use of the term is a generalization: these distinctions between "space" and "place" have been nuanced and complicated by subsequent scholarship. See Ken Wilson, "Place and Space in Walking Pilgrimage," *International Journal of Religious Tourism and Pilgrimage* 8, no. 1 (2020): article 3.

17   Cresswell, "Place," 170.

18   Leanne Betasamosake Simpson, *Dancing on Our Turtle's Back* (Winnipeg: Arbeiter Ring, 2011), 91.

Bernice Halfe and Métis fellow walker Richard Kotowich taught the rest of us about the importance of making relations and practising wâhkotowin (Cree for "kinship") with the prairie, the rivers, the animals of the prairie, the wind, and each other.

Importantly, the opposite is also true. Depending on how we live in and move through the landscape, we can *lose* our relation to the land. We can lose it precisely in the senses of "place" that I just outlined. If a locale is intentionally emptied of distinctive features, as in some shopping malls or airport terminals (or large sections of land cleared for cultivation), then these spaces can become "non-places" or "junk spaces."[19] The rendering of place into space in this case has a commercial goal. In malls or airport terminals, it tries to make us into consumers by giving us only one set of familiar symbols to which we can attach ourselves: product logos or store names.

At high speed, we tend to experience the inside of whatever vehicle we're in, not the environment outside it. In fact, vector- and time-based movement such as in a car or truck at 110 kilometres an hour, with the windows up and the air conditioning on, can easily render the meaning-filled *place* of the northern Great Plains, or of the Canadian Shield, or of the south shore of the St. Lawrence River into meaningless *space*. In contrast, for those fortunate enough to be able to do it, walking is an entirely natural way to create, reinforce, or remember *place*.

From Wood Mountain to Fort Walsh (2015), from Swift Current to Fort Battleford (2017), from Mortlach to Gravelbourg (2018), and in treks almost every year since, we've now walked across many kilometres of "places" on the prairies and parklands. Robert Macfarlane, the author of *The Old Ways*, writes that "there are memories of a place that only feet can recall."[20] One thing is sure: we walkers have experienced the treaty territories in a way that we never had before. We've slept under the immense dome of sky, emptied the short-grass

---

19   Adrian Parr, *Hijacking Sustainability* (Cambridge, MA: MIT Press, 2009).

20   Robert Macfarlane, *The Old Ways* (London: Penguin, 2013), 161.

soil from our shoes, and grasped handfuls of chokecherries to chew while we walked.

One evening in August 2017 the group of us making our way from Swift Current to Fort Battleford camped at an abandoned farmyard in the Bad Hills near Fiske, north of present-day Elrose. Unfortunately, fallen-in houses and derelict yards are a dime a dozen. The old boards and wild hedges are reminders of the economic winds of the past seventy-five years that once again, but in a far less violent fashion than in the late 1800s, have emptied the countryside of so many inhabitants.[21]

When we arrived, we set to work putting up tents in the long grass and a gazebo against the mosquitoes. Locals who visited that evening told us something about the farmstead. It was a sad story. Decades before, the farm had belonged to a young couple who had just had their first baby. There had been some good years but then more years of drought. They might have been weathered, except that tragedy struck. The young child died in an accident. Heartbroken, the couple buried the child, plowed in the house, and left the area.

That night we were unusually solemn. At various points in the evening, most of us wandered over to look at the remains of the house, and to visit the almost-forgotten grave, a wooden stake tucked away amid the caraganas. Richard and others put down tobacco and spent some time in prayer.[22] I tried to imagine the life that was once so vibrant, not far from our tents. I pictured the yard as it must have looked, with the two parents sitting on the stoop playing with their little one. I imagined the music from a radio, the linoleum on the kitchen floor, the warmth of coffee, the sounds of laughter.

---

21 Alan B. Anderson, *Settling Saskatchewan* (Regina: University of Regina Press, 2013), 386–87. On the complicated relationship among soil, geography, and farming in the so-called Palliser Triangle, see Waiser, *A World We Have Lost*, 426–30.

22 For more on the use of tobacco in ceremonies, see Kathleen E. Absolon (Minogiizhigokwe), *Kaandossiwin: How We Come to Know* (Winnipeg: Fernwood, 2011), 120.

The story of that farmstead is rich, but it's not unique. All over the west are similar abandoned yards and equally layered stories. Beneath and around those abandoned farmsteads are evidence from even earlier homes, rings where tents were erected for millennia. Their family histories also speak from the earth. That night, because of our walk, we were briefly touched by this part of the land and its history. Because we saw that place and honoured that memory, place was recreated from space. We were connected with one story, however briefly.[23]

Those of us who grew up as the children and grandchildren of prairie settlers had the land everywhere we looked. Yet most of us were blind to its life and its history. We had the sounds of Indigenous life and culture constantly in our ears. Yet most of us were never told, or bothered to learn, what we were hearing. The voice of our studies was English or French, our music was American, and our news was from Toronto (or increasingly from the United States). We were Canadians "ten thousand miles from Cree."[24] But it was never far from us. "Each day the inhabitants of Saskatchewan make these sounds. They are heard in the southeast, in the southwest, then on to the north and the northwest. They are the sounds of the Cree language. They are in the names of many of the towns, villages, and cities, in the names of the lakes, rivers, and landmarks, and in the names of streets."[25]

The heavily militarized actions of the Royal Canadian Mounted Police (RCMP) in recent years against the Wet'suwet'en, Mi'kmaq,

---

23 Ironically, the words of Duncan Campbell Scott were true, not of "the Onondaga madonna," but of a settler one: "And closer in the shawl about her breast, / The latest promise of her nation's doom, / Paler than she her baby clings and lies." Duncan Campbell Scott, "The Onondaga Madonna," in *Selected Poetry of Duncan Campbell Scott*, ed. Glenn Clever (Ottawa: Tecumseh, 1974), 14.

24 Sky Dancer Louise Bernice Halfe, *Burning in This Midnight Dream* (Regina: Coteau Books, 2016), 17.

25 Jean L. Okimâsis, "As Plain(s) as the Ear Can Hear," in *Plain Speaking: Essays on Aboriginal Peoples and the Prairie*, ed. Patrick Douaud and Bruce Dawson (Regina: Canadian Plains Research Center, 2002), 23.

and others, the fact that until recently our Canadian governments were still going to court to block claims on behalf of Indigenous children, and the shock of many Canadians at the "discovery" of unmarked residential school graves that survivors have always said were there have caused most Indigenous people to question the term "reconciliation." As Bruce McIvor notes, far too often so-called reconciliation has taken place "at the end of a gun."[26] Speaking of (or, worse, *claiming*) reconciliation has become a way for Canadian politicians and bureaucrats to sound virtuous without engaging in the hard work of living up to treaty obligations. Such language is taken too often as a shortcut to forgetting, and a quick fix, when the hard work of recognizing sovereignty and responsibility is what is needed.[27] Words are not enough.

Poet and Elder Sky Dancer Louise Bernice Halfe began walking with SHFS groups on the trails in 2018, when we trekked from Mortlach to Gravelbourg. She brings this warning to life in sometimes uncomfortable ways:

> *kahkiyaw, iskwêwak, nôtokwêsiwak,*
> *câpânak, êkwa ohkomipanak.*
> All Women. Grandmothers and Eternal
> Grandmothers, they scold with a wind
> that shakes leaves.[28]

If we Canadians really want to make a difference, then we can begin by allowing ourselves sometimes to feel awkward, ashamed, and unsettled. We can demand real change of our governments without so desperately trying to escape the discomfort that comes from the question, "What does it mean to be non-Indigenous and

---

26   Bruce McIvor, *Standoff: Why Reconciliation Fails Indigenous People and How to Fix It* (Gibsons, BC: Nightwood Editions, 2021), 90–93.

27   Aubrey Jean Hanson, *Literatures, Communities, and Learning: Conversations with Indigenous Writers* (Waterloo: Wilfrid Laurier University Press, 2020), 25.

28   Sky Dancer Louise Bernice Halfe, *Blue Marrow* (Regina: Coteau Books, 2004), 54.

on this land?" We need to lean into a time of what I call unhomeness. I am adapting the term from Freud, who used the German *unheimlich* to talk about "the uncanny" or the "unhomey."[29] I have proposed that the term "unhomeness" can be used not only in terms of questioning previous emotional attachments to a "homeland" but also as a statement of where decolonization leaves settlers, almost literally. This stage of alienation is a necessary step in decolonizing ourselves.[30] Before we can feel at home in a proper way, by treaty, on this land, we need to go through some cognitive dissonance concerning previous beliefs and allegiances regarding our country's taught histories, its stories, and its ongoing policies.

Between the lines, one can already read the uneasy feeling that I describe in the journals of writers such as Wallace Stegner, W.L. Morton, Rudy Wiebe, and others.[31] The feeling reflects a mismatch that afflicts anyone whose literature and television and pop culture are imports from Toronto or England or New York and Los Angeles. If that's where we get our identity from, and only there, then something doesn't fit the land, and the wind, and the feelings at the end of the sidewalk where the prairie begins (or the Canadian Shield, or the Great Lakes, or the marsh and muskeg).

Unhomeness is a first step toward decolonizing ourselves as Canadians and learning where we are truly from. It is learning that our identity is wrapped up not just in the *past* appropriation of Indigenous lands but also in an *ongoing* dispossession of those lands.

---

29 For a new English translation of Freud's classic writing on this, see Sigmund Freud, "The Uncanny," in *Dialogues in Philosophy, Mental and Neuro Sciences* 11, no. 2 (2018): 84–100.

30 Eva Mackey, *Unsettled Expectations: Uncertainty, Land and Settler Decolonization* (Winnipeg: Fernwood, 2016), 37. See also Raymond Aldred and Matthew R. Anderson, *Our Home and Treaty Land: Walking Our Creation Story* (Kelowna: Wood Lake Books, 2022), 119–28.

31 Jeremy Mouat, "'The Past of My Place': Western Canadian Artists and the Uses of History," in *Making Western Canada: Essays on European Colonization and Settlement*, ed. Catherine Cavanaugh and Jeremy Mouat (Toronto: Garamond, 1996), 261.

Nor is it just Indigenous lands that suffer from ongoing colonial acts; it is also Indigenous bodies, as the arrests and abuses of Indigenous protesters shows.

If we Canadians can tolerate a period of feeling that we do not *automatically* belong here, a time of unhomeness, then awareness of new truths will follow.[32] They include learning about what happened to Indigenous people in a past not that long ago. In my case, for example, I needed to learn why I grew up knowing of the town Assiniboia but not knowing of any Assiniboine (Nakotan) people.

During this time of unhomeness, walking is a good way of re-inscribing new identifications into our lives and of learning new truths about the land. It is slow, it is deliberate, and it brings new learning into us through our feet and our breath. "Pilgrimage" with others (in its largest sense, as spiritually motivated walking) is one way of seeking home once you've lost it.

When you give yourself to places,
they give you yourself back.

—REBECCA SOLNIT[33]

OFTEN, GETTING TO the start of a voyage takes longer than the journey itself. So it was with our first prairie pilgrimage, the 350-kilometre Traders' Road, also known as the North West Mounted Police Patrol Trail (NWMPT).

The crazy notion of trekking across southwestern Saskatchewan had been percolating for years. While a student at the University of Saskatchewan, I had spent a couple of summers working for

32 Chris Hiller, "Tracing the Spirals of Unsettlement: Euro-Canadian Narratives of Coming to Grips with Indigenous Sovereignty, Title, and Rights," *Settler Colonial Studies* 7, no. 4 (2017): 417.

33 Rebecca Solnit, *Wanderlust* (New York: Penguin, 2000), 13.

the telephone utility on what was called a plow crew. All through rural southern Saskatchewan, six days a week, ten or more hours a day, I shovelled, carried, and fetched along a long line of backhoes, caterpillar tractors, and trucks that dug in coaxial cable. Although I had spent a lot of time on our family farm, and had trekked coulees hunting deer with my father, those summers were my first taste of travelling long distances on foot across the land. It was walking. It was exhilarating. But it wasn't always pleasant carrying a short spade, wearing steel-toed boots, and having a foreman constantly shouting at me and the other summer workers.

Later I discussed prairie hikes with some friends from Montreal with whom I had done trails in Vermont and New Hampshire. Despite knowing some farmers along the route, none of us had any idea if it was even possible to walk east from Cypress Hills. All of us were at busy stages of life, some juggling careers, others babies. It seemed like an interesting but impractical idea, and we dropped it.

A decade or two later still, I found myself flying west from Montreal more and more often to help my brother and sister care for our declining parents. During those trips, my father was in the mood to talk about his early years. The land south of Swift Current, where as a youth he had trapped and hunted and farmed and courted my mother, became more and more vivid through our conversations.

Despite his wheelchair, a few times we manoeuvred my father into the car and drove south. Those were joyous experiences. I would drive, and he would point this way or that. In a whisper necessitated by his advanced Parkinson's—he was so quiet that I'd have to lean all the way across from the driver's side to hear him—he would tell me about walking to Gull Lake at three in the morning from the Pioneer Hall or about the whiskey still that his friend, my mother's brother, kept in a coulee east of their farm. He told me how the soil to the west of the highway could be so marshy in places that farmers had to use horses to pull out machinery mired up to the axles.

After I'd spent many years in the city, the land had lost some of its familiarity for me. With each new story, though, some part of it returned to life. This coulee was where my father as a preteen had faced a coyote that wouldn't leave him alone on the trapline. That hedgerow was where a British family had lived but given up during the late 1950s and moved back to England. My father reminded me that my first years were on the Anderson family farm, how I'd climb up onto the machinery or run down the path for cookies to the shack where my Norwegian grandparents spent their summers. We visited abandoned yards where the grey boards hinted at once-busy "home quarters."[34] Once or twice I drove my father farther south to put flowers on the grave of an infant sister whom I had never known, who died before I was born, but whose loss is very much part of this story.

On those drives, my father's memories filled the land with neighbours and parties and vibrant mid-twentieth-century villages no longer there. Each kilometre seemed to contain more and more stories. Guided by them, I began to see the land or, more properly, to *recognize* it. What I didn't know was that this recognition of land through story existed before my father—and before his father and mother—and that such recognition has always been the way. I hadn't yet learned the stories of the people who had lived on the same territory for so many generations before my grandparents. Stories that they told, and continue to tell, including of making treaty to share the land from which they were then removed by starvation and government policy, forcing them out of the way in preparation for my grandparents' arrival.[35]

Back in Montreal, I was called into the office by the chairperson of Concordia University's Department of Theological Studies, Dr. Pamela Bright. There I was asked—or rather told—to teach a class on pilgrimage and to take a group to walk the Camino de Santiago, a ninth-century pilgrimage through northern Spain.[36] Dr. Bright was

---

34   A "home quarter" was the quarter-section of land reserved for the farmer's (often homesteader's) house and other buildings. The term remained in use in Saskatchewan even for farms that were not homesteads.

35   Aldred and Anderson, *Our Home and Treaty Land*, 25–32.

36   One of the best non-specialist but still critical and academic introductions to the Camino is Nancy Louise Frey, *Pilgrim Stories: On and Off the Road to Santiago* (Berkeley: University of California Press, 1998).

a former nun who strategized like a Jesuit; I still have no idea why she approached me for this task. I was a historian, a New Testament scholar, and a Lutheran minister. I don't believe that I'd ever expressed any interest in pilgrimage. But when she set her mind on something, there was no refusing it. So, with my colleague Sara Terreault, I found myself designing our department's first course on pilgrimage and then taking a small group to Spain. Like many others who have taken that route, my weeks there hooked me on pilgrimage. I was fascinated and at the same time mystified by the people whom I met along the Camino Frances, the so-called French Way that extends from St-Jean-Pied-de-Port, France, to Santiago, Spain.

The following year, on a grant from the Concordia University Part-Time Faculty Association, I went back with a camera and a sound mic. This time I trailed a group of pilgrims over the Pyrenees Mountains and across the French-Spanish border. I asked anyone who would stand in front of the camera, "Why are you doing this?" The result was my first documentary, *Something Grand*.[37] In 2013, I walked the St. Olav Trail in Norway with a group of friends who, like me, were of Scandinavian background.[38] A month later I tracked the St. Cuthbert Trail from Melrose, Scotland, through the Borders region, to Holy Island in northeastern England. In the following years, I walked portions of St. Hilda's Way in the North York Moors, the Via Nova in Austria, the Whithorn Way in Scotland, and several pilgrim routes in Ireland, including the National Famine Way, St. Kevin's Way, and a part of St. Declan's Way. Once I joined a group of Icelanders on a trail from the first monastery in Iceland, at Bær í Borgarfirði, to Skalholt, one of the island country's oldest cathedrals.

By this time, I was also actively lecturing on, researching, and writing about pilgrimage. Meanwhile, Canada's Truth and Reconciliation Commission (TRC) was holding its final hearings. The TRC

---

37   See https://somethinggrand.ca/radio-drama/.
38   Matthew Anderson, "Walking to Be Some Body: Desire and Diaspora on the St-Olaf Way," *International Journal of Religious Tourism and Pilgrimage* 7, no. 1 (2019): 62–76.

had been set up in 2008 as part of the Indian Residential Schools Settlement Agreement reached after class-action lawsuits were filed against the Canadian federal government and various church bodies on behalf of over seventy thousand former Indian residential school survivors.[39] For five years, the commission held hearings across the country. The hearings resulted in significant media attention and what was *supposed* to be permanent public awareness of the abuse and death at the schools.

At the time, the revelations struck many of us as significant. However, our country's quick and easy amnesia became apparent when Canadians later claimed to be shocked and surprised as the survivors' stories were borne out by the thousands of unmarked and demarked graves that First Nations began to recover their children from in 2021.

Half a decade earlier the TRC's mandate had already included "Calls to Action" for Canadians. Responding to these calls, Sara Terreault and I, together with Christine Jamieson (Boothroyd-Nlaka'pamux First Nation) and other colleagues, planned a conference for 2014 titled Beyond Dreamcatchers. It featured nêhiyaw, Kahnawakehró:non, Mi'kmaw, and other Indigenous scholars, artists, and speakers.

The TRC gave universities in particular the twin tasks of decolonizing the curriculum to provide safer spaces for Indigenous students and educating Canadians about suppressed histories of oppression against Indigenous peoples. When the final TRC Calls to Action were published, Call to Action 62 read thus: "We call upon the federal, provincial, and territorial governments, in consultation and collaboration with Survivors, Aboriginal peoples, and educators, to . . . integrate Indigenous knowledge and teaching methods into classrooms."[40]

---

39 For more on the TRC, see Paulette Regan, *Unsettling the Settler Within: Indian Residential Schools, Truth Telling, and Reconciliation in Canada* (Vancouver: UBC Press, 2011), 10–13.

40 Available online but also in Bob Joseph, *21 Things You May Not Know about the Indian Act: Helping Canadians Make Reconciliation with Indigenous Peoples a Reality* (Port Coquitlam, BC: Indigenous Relations Press, 2018), 150.

To my mind, that Call to Action is not just a challenge to governments but also to those of us who teach. We are to open our classrooms to Indigenous knowledge and paradigms.[41] Sara, Christine, and I wondered which links could be drawn between the work that we were doing on pilgrimage, and Indigenous protest marches, fasts, and other traditional journeys, including those of the Water Walkers, as well as Indigenous Catholic pilgrimages such as the large pilgrimage to Lac Saint Anne.

Later that summer Sara and I presented at a conference at the University of York, England. There we listened to scholar after scholar from North America give presentations on pilgrimages in Europe. We wondered why none of us from North America was talking about trails back home. Could it have been an ambivalence about our history?[42] Gradually, we realized that our academic reluctance to talk about pilgrimage and journey in North America came from a discomfort—an unhomeness[43]—that had to be faced with what the final TRC report calls an "awareness of the past, acknowledgement of the harm that has been inflicted, atonement for the causes, and action to change behaviour."[44]

Sociologists Mollie McGuire and Jeffrey Denis studied why some Canadians begin to change their attitudes positively in relation to Indigenous Peoples. They concluded that several factors help, including (1) unsettling lessons learned about residential

---

41   There are many good books on Indigenous pedagogical approaches. An early, and still good, treatment is Margaret Kovach, *Indigenous Methodologies: Characteristics, Conversations, and Contexts* (Toronto: University of Toronto Press, 2009). See also Absolon, *Kaandossiwin*.

42   See Emma Battell Lowman and Adam J. Barker, *Settler: Identity and Colonialism in 21st Century Canada* (Winnipeg: Fernwood, 2015), 46.

43   On the positive but fearful implications of properly understanding this unhomeness, see Mackey, *Unsettled Expectations*, 167–69.

44   Truth and Reconciliation Commission, *Honouring the Truth, Reconciling for the Future: Summary of the Final Report of the Truth and Reconciliation Commission of Canada*, 6, http://publications.gc.ca/collections/collection_2015/trc/IR4-7-2015-eng.pdf.

schools and other colonial realities; (2) meaningful intergroup contact; (3) witnessing social injustice in Canada or abroad; (4) prior social justice activism; (5) personal experiences of marginalization; and (6) the influence of role models.[45] Many of these factors certainly made a difference for me. Through the testimonies of the Truth and Reconciliation Commission, reading Regan's *Unsettling the Settler Within*, and attending some meetings in Montreal at which survivors gave testimony, I had begun to experience the unsettling of which McGuire and Denis speak.

Sara and I decided that, if we could study and perhaps design pilgrimages in Canada, with the guidance of Indigenous Peoples, then such walks would make excellent embodied learning experiences for us and our students. Eventually, two initiatives came from our discussions: we began planning the first Old Montreal to Kahnawà:ke walk for our students, and I started thinking, once again, about a long trek on the Prairies.

AS WRITER AND walker Robert Moor points out, the terms that we tend to use interchangeably to describe walking routes can actually mean very different things. "Paths," "trails," "traces," "tracks," "treks," "roads," "ways"—all say something about mobility and terrain. Yet no two of them describe quite the same phenomenon. A path is something that we make, a trail something that we follow. For instance, there is a big difference between lying down in the *path* of a charging elephant and lying down in its *trail*.[46] In discussions of walking, such differences are often covered over or ignored.

---

45   Mollie C. McGuire and Jeffrey S. Denis, "Unsettling Pathways: How Some Settlers Come to Seek Reconciliation with Indigenous Peoples," *Settler Colonial Studies* 9, no. 4 (2019): 507.

46   Robert Moor, *On Trails: An Exploration* (New York: Simon and Schuster, 2016), 60.

Our focus in walking can be local. "If the day is fine, any walk will do," begins Annie Dillard in *Pilgrim at Tinker Creek*.[47] Her writing and walking are brilliant explorations of the plant and animal life around her neighbouring creek and island. Her writing points out the importance of paying attention to places that we might think we already know. In the spirit of Dillard, poet and writer Thelma Poirier writes in *Rock Creek* about her explorations on foot through geography and memory along the hills and creeks of Wood Mountain,[48] the starting point for our first pilgrimage. In 2015, Poirier took quite a bit of time with us, explaining to me the maps, pemmican caches, and trails of our Traders' Road walk and then visiting us along the trail.

When Poirier uses the term "trails," she is thinking about terrain that tends toward wilderness, whereas the term "track" connotes an even rougher way. For most, the term "path" brings the gentle English countryside to mind or perhaps even walks with the dog through a city park. The tracks that we walked across in Treaty 4 and Treaty 6 territories were not well marked. As anyone from the Prairies knows, they had none of the soft sentimentality of an English garden path.

The point is that the same paths can be described in very different ways. Definition is important. Descriptions of or stories about a path become as much a part of that path's nature as its physical terrain. In 2015, we walked the Traders' Road or the North West Mounted Police Patrol Trail. Which of those two names one chooses for this route is important. Similarly, I faced some gentle opposition in calling our trek a pilgrimage. Early on, one of the other walkers took me aside: "For you, this may be a pilgrimage, but it isn't one for me." When I pressed him on what the path meant to him, he was less sure. "I'll find out in the walking," he responded.

In the years since, that trekker found his definition of the trail in his *telling* about our walk. Eventually, he called it a pilgrimage

---

47   Annie Dillard, *Pilgrim at Tinker Creek* (New York: Harper and Row, 1974).

48   Thelma Poirier, *Rock Creek* (Regina: Coteau Books, 1998).

in honour of the changes that it brought to his life. This brings me back to Moor's book. I have come to believe that the *narration* of our experiences is the crucial moment in framing them. That works whether what we walk is (or is called) a pilgrimage, a trail, a groundbreaking path, a therapy walk, or a plain old hike.

Land comes with stories. So do the trails across it. Perhaps a version of the undergraduate philosophy class question "If a tree falls in the forest, but no one is there to hear it, does it make a noise?" could be put, tongue-in-cheek, to our walks: if the story of a trail is forgotten, then can a settler-descended society get away with pretending that the trail never existed? I believe that this is part of the reason that the nineteenth-century "starvation treks" made by Mistahimaskwa (Big Bear),[49] Payepot,[50] and the many Indigenous men, women, and children who walked with them were all but extinguished from Canadian memory.[51] Perhaps unconsciously, Canadians have tried to erase the guilt by expunging the stories and plowing over so many of the trails. They have not been forgotten in Piapot, Mosquito, and other First Nations.

Hikers say that the walk makes the walker. But in an interesting twist, the walker also defines the walk. Although the North West Mounted Police were hardly the first to use the Traders' Road north of the Canada-U.S. border,[52] the trail's Saskatchewan section eventually took their name. Perhaps this is because a good trail is almost always related to a good story, and the story of Sitting

---

49 Rudy Wiebe, *Big Bear* (Toronto: Penguin Books, 2011).

50 Dan Kennedy (Ochankugahe), *Recollections of an Assiniboine Chief*, ed. James R. Stevens (Toronto: McClelland and Stewart, 1972), 57. Note that Payepot's name is sometimes spelled Piapot. Piapot First Nation uses the spelling Payepot for the nineteenth-century figure.

51 Until the appearance of the academic bestseller written by James Daschuk, *Clearing the Plains: Disease, Politics of Starvation, and the Loss of Aboriginal Life* (Regina: University of Regina Press, 2013).

52 See the map of the Traders' Road in Garrett Wilson, *Frontier Farewell: The 1870s and the End of the Old West* (2007; reprinted, Regina: University of Regina Press, 2014), 218–19.

Bull's relationship with NWMP Inspector James Morrow Walsh was so strong.

Inevitably, we human beings cannot help but tell stories. Every walk or pilgrimage that I have been on was surrounded by stories long before we took our first steps, and it is no different with the three walks described here. In documentaries and interviews, in social media posts, and in telling our friends and families about our adventures, we added our own narratives. We were like the ants, or cattle, or mice that Moor describes as adding their footsteps to an existing path, forging a shortcut here, lingering longer there, and thus changing the path and reinforcing it at the same time.

It is still somewhat rare for decolonizing to be connected to long-distance walking. But that connection is what made our walks what I called pilgrimages even if not all my fellow walkers agreed at first. Walking was how we moved from the unhomeness that I described earlier toward a new understanding of how this place might again be our home.

I hope that the story of our walking these prairie trails will inspire others to follow us. I hope that they (perhaps you) come carrying packs, as we did, or perhaps driving on the nearby roads and reflecting on the history and the present-day communities.[53] These were foot, travois,[54] cart, and wagon trails long before we walked them. My hope was that they could be reinscribed in a new way in Saskatchewan and Canadian perception, if only we could walk them again in the twenty-first century. I wanted our walks to create and tell new stories about the repressed histories of the trails, in the process bringing back to public awareness the narratives of ceremony, clearance, and resistance that too often have been forgotten. I hope

---

53 As I wrote this, I was contacted by two young people (one Métis) interested in retracing our steps along the Battleford Trail after reading about the walk in a blog post.

54 A wooden frame used by several Plains Indigenous groups to drag loads across land, pulled by dogs or horses. Henderson, *Rediscovering the Prairies*, 22, describes building a travois for his prairie pilgrimages, using only traditional tools.

that this telling might be one small step in living out our Treaty 4
and Treaty 6 obligations—our relations—in a good way.

For Further Reading

A FORM OF plains pilgrimage, although not by that name, was
lived out in 2021 and 2022 by Indigenous scholar Tasha Beeds and
a group of primarily Indigenous women and Two-Spirit Water
Walkers. The group traced the North Saskatchewan River and on
to Lake Winnipeg, walking well over a thousand kilometres. Their
walk embodied the consistent overlap that exists among Indigenous
sovereignty, ecological concerns, and protest walks. An interview
with Beeds can be accessed in the podcast "What about Water?" at
https://www.whataboutwater.org/s03e09/. See also Ryan Kessler,
"Saskatchewan River Walkers Offer Prayer for Water during Journey
across Prairies," Global News, August 13, 2021, https://globalnews
.ca/news/8110771/saskatchewan-river-walkers-offer-prayer-
water-prairies/.

A brief but excellent introduction to the importance of journey
from a nêhiyawak perspective is Dwayne Donald, "We Need a New
Story: Walking and the wâhkôtowin Imagination," *Journal of the
Canadian Association for Curriculum Studies (JCACS)* 18, no. 2 (2021):
53–63. Donald also leads wâhkôtowin walks. From a Canadian perspective, see Ken Wilson and Matthew R. Anderson, "The Promise
and Peril of Walking Indigenous Territorial Recognitions Carried out
by Settlers," *International Journal of Religious Tourism and Pilgrimage*
9, no. 2 (2021): 46–54; and Ken Wilson, "Indigenous Practices and
Performances of Mobility as Resistance and Resurgence," *Studies in
Canadian Literature* 46, no. 2 (2022): 47–63.

For Canadians seeking to learn more about our history from an
Indigenous perspective, a brief but compellingly clear place to start is
Bob Joseph, *21 Things You May not Know about the Indian Act: Helping
Canadians Make Reconciliation with Indigenous Peoples a Reality* (Port
Coquitlam, BC: Indigenous Relations Press, 2018). Another is the
now classic from Thomas King, *The Inconvenient Indian: A Curious
Account of Native People in North America* (Toronto: Anchor, 2013).

Another helpful resource is Harold Johnson, *Two Families: Treaties and Government* (Saskatoon: Purich, 2007). Additionally, there are many helpful resources online, including the MOOC (or massive online open course) Indigenous Canada, offered for free by the University of Alberta.

There are many helpful introductions by Indigenous authors on Indigenous learning and pedagogical approaches. An early, and still good, treatment is Margaret Kovach, *Indigenous Methodologies: Characteristics, Conversations, and Contexts* (Toronto: University of Toronto Press, 2009). See also Linda Tuhiwai Smith, *Decolonizing Methodologies: Research and Indigenous Peoples* (2009; reprinted, London: Zed Books, 2012); Kathleen E. Absolon (Minogiizhigokwe), *Kaandossiwin: How We Come to Know* (Winnipeg: Fernwood, 2011); Shawn Wilson, *Research Is Ceremony: Indigenous Research Methods* (Winnipeg: Fernwood, 2008); and Leanne Betasamosake Simpson, *Dancing on Our Turtle's Back: Stories of Nishnaabeg Re-Creation, Resurgence and a New Emergence* (Winnipeg: Arbeiter Ring, 2011). See also Aubrey Jean Hanson, *Literatures, Communities, and Learning: Conversations with Indigenous Writers* (Waterloo: Wilfrid Laurier University Press, 2020).

For some important Indigenous perspectives on maps and mapping, see Mishuana Goeman, *Mark My Words: Native Women Mapping Our Nations* (Minneapolis: University of Minnesota Press, 2013), 3; Simpson, *Dancing on Our Turtle's Back*, 96–97; and Tuhiwai Smith, *Decolonizing Methodologies*, 55. On the relationship between race and mapping, see Sherene H. Razack, "When Place Becomes Race," in *Race, Space, and the Law: Unmapping a White Settler Society*, ed. Sherene H. Razack (Toronto: Between the Lines, 2002), 1–20; and Gwilyma Lucas Eades, *Maps and Memes: Redrawing Culture, Place, and Identity in Indigenous Communities* (Montreal and Kingston: McGill-Queen's University Press, 2015). On mapping and another early European explorer of northern North America, Samuel de Champlain, see Razack, "When Place Becomes Race," 12.

Starting in the 1990s and continuing into this century, a wave of research and writing has helped to reposition what it means to be

Canadian, including a re-evaluation of western Canadian history. Works by Indigenous and non-Indigenous authors include—to mention only a few—James Daschuk, *Clearing the Plains: Disease, Politics of Starvation, and the Loss of Aboriginal Life* (Regina: University of Regina Press, 2013); Eva Mackey, *Unsettled Expectations: Uncertainty, Land and Settler Decolonization* (Winnipeg: Fernwood, 2016); Roger Epp, *We Are All Treaty People: Prairie Essays* (Edmonton: University of Alberta Press, 2008); Charlie Angus, *Children of the Broken Treaty: Canada's Lost Promise and One Girl's Dream* (Regina: University of Regina Press, 2017); E. Brian Titley, *The Frontier World of Edgar Dewdney* (Vancouver: UBC Press, 1999); Bill Waiser, *A World We Have Lost: Saskatchewan before 1905* (Calgary: Fifth House, 2016); Garrett Wilson, *Frontier Farewell: The 1870s and the End of the Old West* (2007; reprinted, Regina: University of Regina Press, 2014); Gina Starblanket and Dallas Hunt, *Storying Violence: Unravelling Colonial Narratives in the Stanley Trial* (Winnipeg: ARP Books, 2020); Candace Savage, *A Geography of Blood: Unearthing Memory from a Prairie Landscape* (Vancouver: Greystone Books, 2012); Michel Hogue, *Metis and the Medicine Line: Creating a Border and Dividing a People* (Regina: University of Regina Press, 2015); Jennifer Reid, *Louis Riel and the Creation of Modern Canada: Mythic Discourse and the Postcolonial State* (Albuquerque: University of New Mexico Press, 2008); Sheldon Krasowski, *No Surrender: The Land Remains Indigenous* (Regina: University of Regina Press, 2019); and Trevor Herriot, *Towards a Prairie Atonement* (Regina: University of Regina Press, 2016). See also Mollie C. McGuire and Jeffrey S. Denis, "Unsettling Pathways: How Some Settlers Come to Seek Reconciliation with Indigenous Peoples," *Settler Colonial Studies* 9, no. 4 (2019): 505–24.

There are just not that many walking books written by settler descendants dedicated to the northern Great Plains. But those that exist are worth the read. Trevor Herriot's book *The Road Is How: A Prairie Pilgrimage through Nature, Desire, and Soul* (New York: Harper Perennial, 2014) is remarkable for the author's depth of understanding of the prairie environment and for how it weaves spirituality into plains walking. Norman Henderson's *Rediscovering the Prairies: Journeys by Dog, Horse and Canoe* (Victoria: TouchWood Editions, 2010) is alternately funny and poignant and remarkable for being so well written and thoughtful.

OLD MONTREAL TO KAHNAWÀ:KE

BACK IN MONTREAL, Sara Terreault and I settled on the idea of trying to walk with our students from Concordia to Kahnawà:ke Kanien'kéha (Mohawk) territory. To our knowledge, it had never been done by a group from a Montreal university. The way forward for our project was not clear. In fact, our first attempt to identify a footpath to Kahnawà:ke was almost shut down in the last few kilometres.

As the crow flies, Kahnawà:ke is not that far from Montreal. If you could walk across the St. Lawrence River on the Mercier Bridge from Lasalle (as was once possible), then it would take at most a couple of hours. These days the Mercier is definitely not walker friendly. We looked for another route, eventually settling on a way that I knew from cycling, the so-called Estacade (Ice-Guard Bridge) that crosses to Montreal's south shore from Verdun. We realized that we could cross the St. Lawrence River at Nun's Island to the northeastern bank of the St. Lawrence Seaway and then walk along the seaway the dozen or so kilometres to the lock at Ste-Catherine, Quebec. There, finally, we could cross to the mainland near Kahnawà:ke.

By any measure, this is the long way around. Pedagogically, however, it didn't seem to be such a bad idea for a pilgrimage. The seaway would give our students the experience of a long, tiring foot journey on a path that, in contrast to the concrete of Old Montreal, would give them hours of contact with trees, water, groundhogs, many different types of birds, and the occasional garter snake. By taking the edge of the seaway after walking through urban Montreal, we would expose our students to every possible ecological and historical niche. What we didn't realize, however, was that taking the seaway would also teach us about one of the most devastating moments in the long history of Canadian misdealings with the Kanien'kéha:ka. The seaway was one of the many betrayals by the Canadian government that led, indirectly, to the resistance at Oka a decade later and to the renaissance of Kahnawà:ke as the proud, independent nation that it is today.[55]

Sara and I found an old paper map of Montreal and the greater Montreal region including communities along the south shore. It contained the details that one would expect: black lines outlining the major thoroughfares, street names in regular print and neighbourhoods in boldface, and through the middle of it all Lac St-Louis. There was also an indication of the Lachine Rapids, so named because the first European fur traders hoped that, once they were traversed, the route to China might finally be open. Montreal's neighbourhoods were all there. But in the lower left corner of the map was a patch that stood out for having no detail whatsoever—just a grey area with the word *Kahnawake*.

Maps tell us not only about physical environments but also about our political and cultural mindsets.[56] This map hinted that the Kanien'kehá:ka community was alien territory—or even more tellingly that (as Tuhiwai Smith says of Indigenous Australians) "to be in an 'empty space' [is] to 'not exist.'"[57] We were surprised that the process of mapping Indigenous communities out of existence still exists in many Montreal and region representations.

Our plan was to walk first to Notre-Dame-de-Bons-Secours Church in Old Montreal. Bons-Secours is a lovely stone building built over a wooden church dating to 1655 (you might know it from

---

55 For more on the St. Lawrence Seaway, see Gerald R. (Taiaiake) Alfred, *Heeding the Voices of Our Ancestors: Kahnawake Mohawk Politics and the Rise of Native Nationalism* (Toronto: Oxford University Press, 1995), 158–61.

56 On the relationship between race and mapping, see Razack, "When Place Becomes Race," 5–7; and Gwilyma Lucas Eades, *Maps and Memes: Redrawing Culture, Place, and Identity in Indigenous Communities* (Montreal and Kingston: McGill-Queen's University Press, 2015).

57 Tuhiwai Smith, *Decolonizing Methodologies*, 55. On maps being more about ownership than about location, see Nadeau, *Unsettling Spirit*, 129.

the reference to it in Leonard Cohen's song "Suzanne"). At the church, in the underground museum, one can see the original seventeenth-century foundation. The church was the dream of Margaret Bourgeoys, canonized as a saint in 1982, a nun renowned for her work with the first colonists from France. In the days of Bourgeoys, her church was a pilgrim destination for the original habitants.[58]

From there, we would walk with our students through historic Griffintown and Pointe-St-Charles. Then we would skirt the neighbourhood of Verdun, crossing Île-des-Soeurs and taking the Estacade to the seaway. A long linear path on the seaway would lead to the second lock in the system, at Ste-Catherine, and a stay overnight. The following day we would walk into Kahnawà:ke. It seemed to be doable.

However, we had no idea whether there was a path from Ste-Catherine, a bedroom community of new houses on Montreal's south shore, across contested Indigenous land, to our final destination at Kahnawà:ke. We drove to Ste-Catherine, sure that since we had nine-tenths of the route planned out the last bit should be no trouble.

THE OFFICIAL AT the Ste-Catherine Town Hall was polite right up to the moment that we told her where we wanted to go. Suddenly, her face took on a pinched expression, the look of a bureaucrat hearing news that causes unexpected work. "Ah, non," she said, half turning away. "On ne peut pas. You can't walk from here to Kahnawà:ke. Impossible."

We were confused. On the counter, we had spread out the town's map that we had just taken from the pamphlet rack, with its "welcome to *notre ville* [our city], a wonderful-place-to-live, etc." We pointed to the grid layout of suburban streets, then to the dark shape at the edge of the paper that showed Kanien'kehá:ka territory.

---

58   Patricia Simpson, *Marguerite Bourgeoys and the Congregation of Notre Dame, 1665–1700* (Montreal and Kingston: McGill-Queen's University Press, 2005), 23.

"But there must be a path somewhere. Kahnawà:ke is along the river. You are right along the river. You're neighbours. There must be some way through?"

"Impossible by foot," the official repeated. She turned her face to the map that we had spread on the counter. It was one of those perfunctory scans in which eyes do not actually make contact with document. "There is no path." Hands on her hips. "Non."

"No way to walk from here to there?"

She shook her head. "You would have to go on the highway. I can tell you. I've lived here thirty years. I know. We have to stop traffic. You'd have to have a permit from the police. I'll contact *them*." She turned to the telephone. "This is a problem for them."

Sara and I exchanged glances. Could the police actually forbid a group of students and professors from walking from Ste-Catherine to Kanien'kehá:ka territory? Given the checkered history of the relationship between the various police forces and the First Nation, bringing in the local settler constabulary did not sound promising.

"Oh, no! No need to call them," I said quickly. "I guess it was a bad idea. Thanks anyway." We backed away. "Sorry to bother you! If you say there's no way to walk through, you must be right." "Thanks so much for your help!" we shouted over our shoulders as we exited through the door of the municipal office and back into the tidy, empty streets of a suburban city planted on the edge (in the *middle*, Kahnawà:ke residents would say) of a First Nation's territory.

A few minutes later, with the help of Google Maps, we easily found the little dirt road along the river that links the two communities. Clearly, the problem wasn't impassible terrain but impassible assumptions. When we asked around at the coffee shop in Kahnawà:ke, it was clear that most folks there knew the route. The fact that the non-Indigenous people who are their neighbours don't know—or don't seem to care to learn—a connection between the two urban environments is part of the story of this area.

Kahnawà:ke is a community that has had its land appropriated, moved, segregated, split, and outright stolen, again and again.[59]

These two communities, one overwhelmingly white and French speaking, the other Kanien'kehá:ka, represent two very different cultural and human geographies. There are stark differences of identity that have grown in the space between them. There is a kind of liminal territory between the suburban streets of Ste-Catherine and the town of Kahnawà:ke, a zone of scrub brush and industrial park where for years, until Kanien'kehá:ka Peacekeepers increased patrols, non-Indigenous residents of Montreal's south shore would drive to dump their garbage onto the First Nation's riverbank.

Sara and I had found our route. However, now that we had a walking path sketched between Old Montreal and Kahnawà:ke, we realized that we had another problem: it was not enough just to walk to Kahnawà:ke. We needed to know what, if anything, we and our students could do once there. Our problem was the usual issue of Canadians with regard to Indigenous Nations: we had gone at it backward. We had good intentions, but we realized that we did not know many Kahnawa'kehró:non.

The simple fact was that the walk had been our idea. We had not yet engaged in building relationships. Nor had we been invited. Who were we to decide to go on a pilgrimage from Old Montreal to Kahnawà:ke? Belatedly, we realized that the idea itself was a bit backward. We sent several emails to the Kanien'kehá:ka Onkwawén:na Raotitióhkwa Language and Cultural Centre. The emails were politely answered and then, when we followed up, quietly ignored. Eventually, we decided to drive to the community. Sara suggested that we check out the Riverside Inn Bed and Breakfast for our students, a house for rent in the heart of the town. Her suggestion made all the difference.

---

59 On Kahnawà:ke in the nineteenth century and early twentieth century, especially the recovery of the Traditional Longhouse, see Gerald F. Reid, *Factionalism, Traditionalism, and Nationalism in a Mohawk Community* (Lincoln: University of Nebraska Press, 2004). For more recent history, see Leanne Simpson and Kiera L. Ladner, *This Is an Honour Song: Twenty Years since the Blockades* (Winnipeg: Arbeiter Ring, 2010); and Alfred, *Heeding the Voices of Our Ancestors*.

The Riverside Inn B&B is an unpretentious, two-storey, historic stone home right up against the St. Lawrence Seaway. It wasn't always so close to the water. However, the Canadian government expropriated terrain all along the river's edge in Kahnawà:ke when the seaway was built, with police in some cases removing elderly inhabitants by force from their homes just before they were bulldozed.[60] The seaway is one of the more obvious examples of how our governments say that they are working with Indigenous Peoples, but then don't, especially when economic interests are involved. It is more than unnerving to look out the kitchen window of the Riverside Inn as a Great Lakes freighter passes, and a three-storey wall of steel slides by mere metres away, colonialism in action.

By dispossessing families and expropriating their homes to build the seaway, the Canadian government separated the Kanien'kehá:ka community from the water with which they had long had a relationship. It not only broke treaty agreements but also showed an ignorance of the link between water and life. It typified how our societies usually prioritize economic development over respect, acting against Indigenous understandings of the human relationship with the natural world whenever money is at stake.

Sara had made arrangements with the owner of the Riverside Inn, Kenneth Atsenhaiaton Deer, to meet and discuss renting the house for our students. I knew that he had been the publisher of the Kahnawà:ke newspaper, *The Eastern Door* (the Kanien'kehá:ka are the easternmost nation, traditionally considered the "eastern door," of the six-nation Haudenosaunee Confederacy). I knew little else about him.

Kenneth is a quiet, soft-spoken man. As we talked over details of our pilgrimage, he checked his phone calendar. "I can't be here on that day," he said. "I have to be in New York." We learned that Kenneth was a member of the working group then developing the

---

60   Despite its antiquated and now offensive language, see Omar Z. Ghobashy, *The Caughnawaga Indians and the St. Lawrence Seaway* (New York: Devin-Adair, 1961), especially 124ff.

United Nations Declaration on the Rights of Indigenous Peoples. The conversation gradually shifted from available bed space to his trips back and forth to New York City using a Kanien'kehá:ka passport. He chided us Canadians for how the Harper government was refusing to sign on to the UN declaration. He told us about the steps that he and other Indigenous leaders were taking to pressure the government.

We had gone to Kahnawà:ke simply to look for accommodation. By complete chance, we had met one of the community's traditional leaders. By the end of our kitchen visit, Kenneth had invited us to go with him to the Language and Cultural Centre. Before we knew it, we were seated with staff asking us how we could work together to make our department's student journey a success.

Over the years, Sara and I took students in our pilgrimage class on the walk from Old Montreal to Kahnawà:ke a number of times. We met other Kanien'kehá:ka educators, including Tommy Deer and Marion Delaronde. Orenda Konwowennotion Boucher guided us in thinking of Saint Kateri (buried in Kahnawà:ke) and of Indigenous relationships with the Catholic Church. Sara and I accompanied a group of Concordia's senior academic cabinet for meetings in the community. Once I led a "walking territorial acknowledgement" from Kahnawà:ke to Montreal in preparation for one of our conferences.[61]

Our department at Concordia University has an ongoing, healthy relationship with Kahnawà:ke, all because of Kenneth Atsenhaiaton Deer, Thomas Teiowí:sonte Deer, and other Kahnawa'kehró:non and because of Sara Terreault's suggestion of the Riverside Inn B&B. Together with our students, we have been privileged to learn about the Kahnawà:ke community, to visit the Traditional Longhouse, and to hear the Ohén:ton Karihwatéhkwen, "The Words that Come before All Else."

61　Kenneth Wilson and Matthew R. Anderson, "The Promise and Peril of Walking Indigenous Territorial Recognitions Carried out by Settlers," *International Journal of Religious Tourism and Pilgrimage* 9, no. 2 (2021): 46–54.

Kenneth Atsenhaiaton Deer, 2016. *Photo by the author.*

Kenneth Deer is a community organizer, a diplomat, a militant, an activist, an educator, and a follower of the traditional ways. His official position is secretary of the Traditional Longhouse, a title that covers much more. He and the longhouse were active in the resistance at Oka and in supporting the Wet'suwet'en starting in 2019. He was deeply involved in setting up the Kahnawà:ke Survival School, wrestling back community control of education for Kahnawà:ke's youth, who previously had to travel by bus to different suburban non-Indigenous communities.

Kenneth is not a Canadian, or a Quebecer, but a Kahnawa'kehró:non who has faced opposition from Quebecers and Canadians many times. Despite this resistance, again and again he has been willing to speak to non-Indigenous community, university, and church groups about right relations. Kenneth is a kind man who, with patience and good humour, educates those of us who are non-Indigenous. He became a friend both to Sara and to me, two sessional lecturers with our partly formed ideas. We had dreamt of a pilgrimage between Old Montreal and Kahnawà:ke as one way of learning to support Indigenous Peoples, only to discover individuals, such as Kenneth, who were in fact far more important allies to us. I'm extremely grateful for that first chance meeting and for his aid ever since with our initiatives. In 2015, Concordia University awarded Kenneth Atsenhaiaton Deer an honorary doctorate. To my mind, there are few more deserving persons.

For Further Reading
THERE ARE SEVERAL good resources for learning more about pilgrimage and its ambiguous links to peace and to peacemaking. See Matthew R. Anderson, "'Settler-Aware' Pilgrimage and Reconciliation: The Treaty Four Canadian Context," in *Peace Journeys: A New Direction in Religious Tourism and Pilgrimage Research*, ed. Ian S. McIntosh, Nour Farra Haddad, and Dane Munro (Newcastle upon Tyne, UK: Cambridge Scholars, 2020), 98–120; and Michael A. Di Giovine, "A Higher Purpose: Sacred Journeys as Spaces for Peace in Christianity," in *Pilgrims and Pilgrimages as Peacemakers in Christianity, Judaism and Islam*, ed. Antón M. Pazos (Farnham, UK: Routledge, 2013), 9–38.

On being settler-descended and living in treaty, see Greg Poelzer and Ken S. Coates, *From Treaty Peoples to Treaty Nation: A Road Map for All Canadians* (Vancouver: UBC Press, 2015); and Roger Epp, *We Are All Treaty People: Prairie Essays* (Edmonton: University of Alberta Press, 2008). From a more narrative and very readable angle, see Andrew Stobo Sniderman and Douglas Sanderson (Amo Binashii), *Valley of the Birdtail: An Indian Reserve, a White Town, and the Road to Reconciliation* (Toronto: HarperCollins, 2022).

FIBBERS AND FABULISTS

Colonialism, we have learned too late, is an utterly unreliable narrator.

—TREVOR HERRIOT[62]

62   Herriot, *Towards a Prairie Atonement*, 13.

HENRY KELSEY WASN'T just the first European to walk the Great Plains. He was the first to write about them. Although his style is unusual—Kelsey used rhyming couplets—what he said is not. In describing his experiences from 1690 to 1692, the young Hudson's Bay Company (HBC) clerk drew from stereotypes that would guide Euro-Canadian stories of the "frontier" for centuries.[63] The erasure of Indigenous narratives and Peoples that Starblanket and Hunt identify as foundational to the violent ways that Indigenous Peoples have been treated goes back to the beginning.[64]

The truth is that Kelsey was "a passenger, not a pathfinder."[65] Yet, despite the essential role of his Indigenous trading partners in guiding him west and south from Hudson Bay, to read his account you'd think that he travelled as a solitary hero. The unusual poetry reads as if he alone were braving the wilds. In lines heavy with the words *I*, *me*, and *my*,[66] Kelsey details the rigours of the journey and the unfaithfulness of the locals. Whenever he can, he makes not-so-subtle allusions to his personal heroism. He reports everything with an eye to staking out territory, in the interests of personal and corporate gain.

Kelsey's report relies heavily on elements that we see again and again in later writing. He states that the land is "wealthy" but that Europeans must protect themselves from its "wildness." This can only be accomplished, he implies, through intense masculine bravery. It is exactly the toxic blend featured in colonialist narratives up to our own day.[67] Kelsey undoubtedly had an affinity for travel and adventure, a readiness to engage the locals, and a talent for languages. He eventually wrote a dictionary of Cree (*Dictionary of*

---

63   Greenfield, "'Now Reader Read,'" 49.

64   Gina Starblanket and Dallas Hunt, *Storying Violence: Unravelling Colonial Narratives in the Stanley Trial* (Winnipeg: ARP Books, 2020), 120.

65   Bill Waiser coined this memorable description in "Say It Ain't So: Henry Kelsey Was a Passenger, not a Pathfinder," *StarPhoenix* [Saskatoon], April 7, 2020.

66   D.M.R. Bentley, "'Set Forth as Plainly May Appear': The Verse Journal of Henry Kelsey," ARIEL: *A Review of International English Literature* 21, no. 4 (1990): 15.

67   Starblanket and Hunt, *Storying Violence*, 37.

the Hudson's Bay Indian Language, 1720) and was put in charge of teaching it to other HBC employees.[68] Whatever his on-the-ground relationships with local Indigenous Peoples might have been,[69] Kelsey followed the usual pattern of being thoroughly colonial and greatly ambitious.

By the late nineteenth century, the cliché of Kelsey's Scottish-born HBC explorer had evolved into popular images featuring figures such as North West Mounted Policemen, American frontiersmen, and settler farmers. In newspapers and novels, both policeman and farmer were often pictured in a defensive posture vis-à-vis the land and its people. Starblanket and Hunt point out that the "white settler masculine ethos"[70] relies on a mastery of the land and needs to identify or invent a perceived threat to that mastery.

When Daniel Coleman analyzes the literature of the period, he notes the usefulness of the image of the "muscular Christian" (and its counterpoint, "maternal feminism") to the colonial enterprise: "With his untiring and virile physical body balanced by his spiritually sensitive heart, [the muscular Christian settler] made a perfect representation of the ideal Canadian who would carry out the hard physical work of territorial expansion, as well as the equally important work of building a new civil society."[71] From our twenty-first-century vantage, such stereotypes seem to be quaint and Victorian. However, their ongoing effects on everything from No Trespassing signs to public discourse on immigration mean that such ideas continue to have dangerous repercussions in the lives of real people.

While highlighting the heroism of the male protagonist and none-too-subtly teaching a patriarchal and racist image of Cana-

---

68   See Greenfield, " 'Now Reader Read,'" 33.

69   HBC traders were officially discouraged from having Indigenous partners, but this did not stop Kelsey or many after him. See Waiser, *A World We Have Lost*, 181–83.

70   Starblanket and Hunt, *Storying Violence*, 25.

71   Daniel Coleman, *White Civility: The Literary Project of English Canada* (Toronto: University of Toronto Press, 2006), 129. On Kelsey, see Coleman's chapter on "The Scottish Orphan" trope of English Canadian literature.

dian society, the heroic narratives reinforced a view of Indigenous Peoples as "other." Sometimes that other was threatening and sometimes romantically tragic. Either approach avoided having to deal with real Indigenous individuals, groups, and bodies and real Indigenous issues such as sovereignty, food supply, environmental damage, and treaty obligations.

On the stage of public opinion, Indigenous peoples were often painted with a single brush as one thing and one group. Even the way that Gabriel Dumont was portrayed following the North-West Resistance in 1885 (in 1886, he was featured in "Buffalo Bill" Cody's Wild West Show in the United States) succeeded in isolating one individual from the claims of the Métis for community rights by making him somehow "unique."[72] For Canadian voters, newspaper readers, and military personnel, "Indians" (including Métis) were most often "other": that is, unless like Dumont or Sitting Bull, they were somehow "exceptional."

From *Daniel Boone* to *Unforgiven*, frontier stories usually tell us more about our own place and time (and about us as the audience) than they do about any real people or places. Stories of the prairie as Canada's last frontier are among the most enduring myths of the nineteenth century.[73] In places such as Swift Current and Regina, frontier symbolism lasted well into the twentieth century. Words such as *frontier*, *settler*, and *pioneer* helped to define what it meant to be western Canadian. Unfortunately, the stories so useful in building group identity in small towns and cities such as Swift Current also justified and continue to justify a kind of rough individualism that turns out to be toxic to settler descendants and Indigenous people alike (although more lethal to the latter).

---

72   Matthew Barrett, "'Hero of the Half-Breed Rebellion': Gabriel Dumont and Late Victorian Military Masculinity," *Journal of Canadian Studies* 48, no. 3 (2014): 81.

73   E. Brian Titley, *The Frontier World of Edgar Dewdney* (Vancouver: UBC Press, 1999), 140.

Henry Kelsey Sees the Buffalo, by Charles William Jefferys (1869–1951). *Courtesy of Library and Archives Canada (C-024390).*

Canadian identity was built in opposition not only to the Indigenous Peoples but also to the American competitor to the south and the English, or Scottish, antecedent.[74] As Dwayne Trevor Donald puts it, "official versions of history, which begin as cultural interpretations of events, morph into hegemonic expressions of existing value structures."[75] That is, our stories not only *reflect* but also *create* reality. Good, cooperative stories build healthy communities. Toxic, competitive, or dismissive stories build toxic realities.

In Grade 3, for my delighted teachers at Ashley Park School in Swift Current, I reproduced a version of the painting *Henry Kelsey Sees the Buffalo* by Charles Jefferys. The painting is remarkable in several ways. Kelsey is in the centre of the painting, experiencing his first view of the Great Plains. He looks imperial, detached, and commanding. Around him, the Nakota and nêhiyaw guides are pictured falling to their knees or otherwise taking subordinate positions.

Over time, there were different iterations of the artwork. In later, coloured versions, Kelsey is increasingly painted in the fringed

---

74   Coleman, *White Civility*, 130.
75   Dwayne Trevor Donald, "Forts, Curriculum, and Indigenous *Métissage*: Imagining Decolonization of Aboriginal-Canadian Relations in Educational Contexts," *First Nations Perspectives* 2, no. 1 (2009): 3.

jacket and buckskin pants of an American plainsman rather than the breeches of a seventeenth-century Scotsman. In the later versions, the limited Indigenous equality of place of the earlier versions is dropped: the closest "Indian guide" to Kelsey disappears entirely. I no longer remember which version I sketched. Whichever it was, I won a ribbon for it at Swift Current's Frontier Days Exhibition.

The "disappearance of the Indian" was more than an artistic hope. The subjugation of the Canadian west and the forcible removal of its surviving Indigenous Peoples onto reserves were justified (when justification was attempted at all) by an appeal to the social Darwinism sweeping Europe and the Americas in the late nineteenth century.[76] Social Darwinism was the belief, based upon pseudo-science, that whites were the most highly evolved human beings. European and settler societies thus represented the apex of human achievement.[77]

In North America, this racism took a particular form: namely, the era of the "red man" on the prairie was past. According to the theory, it was only natural that Indigenous populations, or at least their political systems and their sovereignty, were to be replaced.[78] Social Darwinism borrowed from Darwin's scientific theory the concept of inevitability, an idea that handily excused Canadian lawmakers from responsibility for their draconian measures against Indigenous Peoples. After all, the sloppy thinking went, who could be blamed for contributing to a sad fate that no one, white or Indigenous, could escape?

Yet, after only a few decades, it became clear to the Canadian government and its Department of Indian Affairs that Indigenous Peoples were not going to disappear. At that point, a more subtle but still ultimately eugenic tactic was used: "Indians" must "better themselves."[79] This tactic had the same practical result since, according

76   Wilson, *Frontier Farewell*, 430.

77   Starblanket and Hunt, *Storying Violence*, 44–45.

78   Titley, *Edgar Dewdney*, 141.

79   C. Drew Bednasek and Anne M.C. Godlewska, "The Influence of Betterment Discourses on Canadian Aboriginal Peoples in the Late Nineteenth and Early

to this strategy, Indigenous Peoples were to become invisible by becoming indistinguishable from Canadians of European backgrounds, absorbed into the larger society.[80] This position was promoted right up to the 1970s and Pierre Trudeau's now-infamous "White Paper." Harold Cardinal, perhaps the foremost critic of the policy, critiqued it by saying that it had replaced the historic American slogan "The only good Indian is a dead Indian" with a Canadian version: "The only good Indian is a non-Indian."[81]

However, Canadian governments might have *said* that they wanted assimilation, but their actual policies contradicted it. Through restrictions on agricultural trade,[82] and virtual imprisonment on reserves through the "permit to pass" system,[83] the *Indian Act* created barriers yet demanded that Indigenous groups assimilate. Dan Kennedy (Ochankugahe) remembers how the pass system kept anyone from leaving for business or social reasons without permission from the Indian Agent, who could refuse to grant it for any or no reason.[84] Of course, such restrictions were totally in violation of the treaties. They prevented Ochankugahe's and other reserves from being promised homelands and turned them into de facto "concentration camp[s]."[85]

Twentieth Centuries," *Canadian Geographer* 53, no. 4 (2009): 444–61.

80   In 1931, Duncan Campbell Scott, the deputy superintendent general of Indian Affairs, stated that "it is the opinion of the writer that … the Government will in time reach the end of its responsibility as the Indians progress into civilization and finally disappear as a separate and distinct people, not by race extinction but by gradual assimilation with their fellow-citizens." Quoted in Joseph, *21 Things*, 77.

81   Harold Cardinal, *The Unjust Society* (Toronto: Douglas and McIntyre, 1999), 1.

82   Joseph, *21 Things*, 37.

83   Joseph, *21 Things*, 51. Joseph notes that the permit regulations were applied most stringently on the Prairies. See also Walter Hildebrandt, *Views from Fort Battleford: Constructed Visions of an Anglo-Canadian West* (Regina: Canadian Plains Research Center, 1994), 83.

84   Kennedy, *Recollections*, 87.

85   Kennedy, *Recollections*, 87. See also F. Laurie Barron, *Walking in Indian Moccasins: The Native Policies of Tommy Douglas and the CCF* (Vancouver: UBC Press, 1997), 5.

The power that officials exercised over Indigenous daily life also led to terrible social and sexual abuse.[86]

It was not by chance that I grew up in southwestern Saskatchewan without having ever knowingly met a Nakota, Niisitapi, or nêhiyaw person. It was because, a century earlier, in the 1860s and 1870s, Canadian government officials and police separated those groups from their lands as explicit government policy, removing them hundreds of kilometres from their ancestral home territories to the Qu'Appelle and Battleford regions and taking the southern belt of Saskatchewan over for Canadian economic exploitation.[87]

This is what Métis writer of that time Peter Erasmus called, with measured irony, "the entrance of so-called civilized living into these parts."[88] Such "civilized living" meant the eradication and removal of the original inhabitants. It would be a mistake to think that the numbered treaties were the last takeovers. Whether in the 1870s, the 1950s, the 1990s,[89] or the 2020s, and whether in Cypress Hills, Wet'suwet'en territory, or the St. Lawrence Seaway, "the issue has always been land."[90] Inevitably, the point of government policies was the practical eradication of Indigenous "uncertainty" (usually meaning people and always meaning ownership) from the Canadian political, geographical, economic, and cultural landscape.

It helped, and still helps, to justify such actions by governments and corporations if colonialists can portray themselves as being in danger. This provides an excuse for exercising the brutal removal of oppressed populations that, in reality, were and are little threat. Not many years ago we again saw video of heavily armed tactical police

---

86   Titley, *Edgar Dewdney*, 50.

87   Daschuk, *Clearing the Plains*, 94.

88   Peter Erasmus, *Buffalo Days and Nights*, ed. Henry Thompson (Calgary: Fifth House, 1999), 301.

89   On some of the Kanien'kehá:ka struggles to hold on to their land, see Thomas King, *The Inconvenient Indian: A Curious Account of Native People in North America* (Toronto: Anchor, 2013), 232–36.

90   King, *The Inconvenient Indian*, 217, 227–28.

Captive Scout, 1881, by Henry Sandham.
Photo taken by the author at the Montreal Museum of Fine Arts, special exhibit.
Public domain.

breaking down doors of cabins filled with Elders and female Land defenders whom the police insisted were somehow "threatening."[91]

A glance at the 1881 painting *Captive Scout*, by Montrealer Henry Sandham, shows how this worked in the nineteenth century. As in Kelsey's writing, and in Jefferys' painting, whiteness is in the foreground of Sandham's work. To be white is to be in the light, the centre of attention. The darker-skinned warriors in Sandham's work are sinister, indistinct figures who lurk in the shadows, their "plotting" unclear. In the final years of the last free Indigenous populations, Sandham, who often painted for *Century Magazine*, gave central

---

91   Matt Simmons, "RCMP Were Planning Raids while in Talks with Wet'su-
     wet'en Hereditary Chiefs about Meeting," *The Narwhal*, May 12, 2022, https:
     //thenarwhal.ca/rcmp-wetsuweten-meeting/.

Canadian audiences an image of their wildest fears.[92] In the painting, we see a blond-haired, white male scout, his muscles and lack of a shirt symbolizing Euro-Canadian masculinity, tied to the ground in a semi-sexualized position, awaiting the tortures of a group of "Indians," portrayed as dark figures in the distance.

The painting is chillingly ironic. In 1881, the reality on the plains was the opposite. At that time, it was the nêhiyawak, Niisitapi, and Nakota who were suffering terribly, starving and in rags, desperately trying to negotiate for enough food and shelter to survive.[93] Meanwhile, despite the emergency appeals of some local government officials, missionaries, and ranchers, government officials in Regina and Ottawa debated. Their tight-fistedness guaranteed further suffering and death.[94] Paintings like Sandham's, published in popular magazines, helped to harden voters to the loss of lives caused by government inaction during a time of mass starvation.

By 1881, more than three thousand Indigenous men, women, and children were camped in or near the Cypress Hills since they did not want to face another winter of famine farther north.[95] They endured a Saskatchewan winter in rags, with little to no food or shelter, and many died.[96] The year that Sandham painted *Captive Scout* was the year that, at Fort Walsh, Indian Agent Edwin Allen was fired for "mismanaging" deliveries of rations to the Indigenous groups there. He had been billing for nearly twice the quantity of beef distributed, effectively cutting the much-needed relief in half.[97]

---

92   For a comparison of mostly later "frontier" artwork in both the United States and Canada, see Brian W. Dippie, "One West, One Myth: Transborder Continuity in Western Art," *American Review of Canadian Studies* 33, no. 4 (2003): 509–41.

93   Erasmus, *Buffalo Days*, 250.

94   Daschuk, *Clearing the Plains*, 136.

95   Waiser, *A World We Have Lost*, 507.

96   Candace Savage, *A Geography of Blood: Unearthing Memory from a Prairie Landscape* (Vancouver: Greystone Books, 2012), 145–46.

97   Daschuk, *Clearing the Plains*, 140.

Such deadly corruption extended from the bottom to the very top of the colonialist structure.[98] Edgar Dewdney, appointed the first Indian Commissioner of the North-West Territories in 1879 and later the lieutenant governor, was well known for mixing public office with private and profitable enterprise. That the present-day capital of Saskatchewan is on property that Dewdney had bought for speculation is only the best-known example of what biographer Brian Titley calls his "self-serving opportunism."[99] In addition, Dewdney bought or had been given shares in a Benton, Montana, bank that then benefited from Canadian government contracts, including for food distribution to the Indigenous population.[100]

Dewdney might have been noteworthy for being such a high-profile man on the make, but he was hardly alone. The ecological, economic, and social convulsions that characterized especially the 1870s and 1880s on the northern Great Plains made reputations and fortunes . . . for settlers. Cases of sexual predation by newly empowered Indian Affairs officials against Indigenous women and girls were also common.[101]

The combination of so many colonial officials ready and willing to overlook human hardship and death in order to enrich or satisfy themselves, an official Canadian government policy that used starvation as a calculated tactic to move reluctant hunting societies onto restricted reserves, and supposedly to "extinguish" their title to lands,[102] and a complete environmental collapse in the traditional food source of the prairies, which occurred even more quickly than imagined,[103] all led to a decade of terrible famine and tragedy. Paintings like Sandham's helped to ensure that, against a backdrop

---

98   D. Aidan McQuillan, "Creation of Indian Reserves on the Canadian Prairies 1870–1885," *Geographical Review* 70, no. 4 (1980): 387.

99   Titley, *Edgar Dewdney*, 143, 93.

100   Daschuk, *Clearing the Plains*, 138, 143.

101   Daschuk, *Clearing the Plains*, 153; Titley, *Edgar Dewdney*, 50.

102   On this, see Krasowski, *No Surrender*.

103   Waiser, *A World We Have Lost*, 500–01.

of morally corrupt frontier capitalism, there were only sporadic expressions of sympathy for the prairie inhabitants.[104]

The effect of images that portrayed Indigenous warriors as an ongoing—if vague and indistinct—threat was to villainize the victim. In their constituencies, central Canadian politicians increasingly found it advantageous to turn their backs on the distant Indigenous groups.[105] "The government was well aware of the delicate balance between its policy of starving holdouts into submission and onto reserves and the risk of scandal from widespread death from hunger."[106] It was a cynical strategy, and a calculated policy that valued money above life, keeping food relief low to save cash even while people starved.

Whether or not Sandham himself realized it, for his painting to represent a blond, white man as a western "scout" was not only an injustice to the nêhiyawak, Nakota, Niisitapi, and others just then at the mercy of Ottawa. To portray the scout as white also erased the truth about another western group in delicate negotiations with the government of Canada at that time. The fact was that the best scouts, interpreters,[107] freighters, and even diplomatic representatives[108]

104　John Wilson Bengough's satirical portrayals in Toronto's *Grip* magazine of Macdonald's Indian policies draw attention both to Indigenous suffering and to corruption among those tasked with relief aid. Bengough's work and writing are not without problems, however. See Carman Cumming, *Sketches from a Young Country: The Images of* Grip *Magazine* (Toronto: University of Toronto Press, 1997).

105　Waiser, *A World We Have Lost*, 505. In terms of art and Indigeneity, Canadian painters such as the Group of Seven were soon painting landscapes without any Indigenous presence whatsoever. See Eva Mackey, "'Death by Landscape': Race, Nature, and Gender in Canadian Nationalist Mythology," *Canadian Women Studies/Les cahiers de la femme* 20, no. 2 (2000): 127.

106　Daschuk, *Clearing the Plains*, 136.

107　See Erasmus, *Buffalo Days*, especially chapter 14, concerning the Treaty 6 negotiations.

108　Allyson Stevenson, "'Men of Their Own Blood': Metis Intermediaries and the Numbered Treaties," *Native Studies Review* 18, no. 1 (2009): 67–90.

for the Canadians had always been the Métis.[109] In *Metis and the Medicine Line*, Michel Hogue points out that "Metis language skills, knowledge of Indigenous diplomatic and cultural protocols, and varied connections to different Indigenous people—whether familial, commercial, or otherwise—proved indispensable in the exchange of government directives, on the one hand, and Indigenous peoples' demands and the attendant securing of treaty agreements, on the other."[110] For decades, Canadian government officials, police, and settlers had depended on the Métis as guides, interpreters, provisioners, hunters, traders, border guards, and diplomats. As we witnessed many times on our prairie treks, often settlers created communities or the North West Mounted Police set up posts precisely where the Métis had already established themselves.

The reminiscences of Peter Erasmus in *Buffalo Days and Nights*[111] back up Hogue. The account by Erasmus is one of the few surviving Indigenous writings from this period. Others include the voice of Norbert Welsh in Mary Weekes's *The Last Buffalo Hunter*, Edward Ahenakew's *Voices of the Plains Cree*, and Dan Kennedy (Ochankugahe's) *Recollections of an Assiniboine Chief*.[112] Unlike the stories from settler traders such as Isaac Cowie, William Bleasdell Cameron, and others; from retired NWMP officers such as Cecil Denny or Sam Steele; or from missionaries such as John McDougall, *Buffalo Days and Nights* was written by a person whose kinship relations, family history, and Indigenous languages made him uniquely able to document the period from an insider's view. Written and remembered in English, the account by Erasmus was originally lived out in Cree.

---

109   See Michel Hogue, *Metis and the Medicine Line: Creating a Border and Dividing a People* (Regina: University of Regina Press, 2015); Brenda Macdougall, "Speaking of Metis: Reading Family Life into Colonial Records," *Ethnohistory* 61, no. 1 (2014): 27–56; and Chris Andersen, *"Métis": Race, Recognition and the Struggle for Indigenous Peoplehood* (Vancouver: UBC Press, 2014).

110   Hogue, *Metis and the Medicine Line*, 95.

111   Erasmus, *Buffalo Days*.

112   Kennedy, *Recollections*.

We tend to forget how rarely English was heard on the prairie during this period. Erasmus was an interpreter, guide, hunter, and diplomat. He was hired by Chiefs Mistawasis (Big Child) and Ahtahkakoop (Star Blanket), signatories to Treaty 6, as their "in-house" interpreter, a decision whose wisdom was evident in the opening meeting, as reported by Erasmus:

> "It was quite unnecessary to send for the man [Erasmus]," said the Governor [Morris, at the Treaty 6 negotiations at Fort Carlton]. "We have two interpreters hired by the government and it is up to the government to provide the means of communication."
>
> I had quietly interpreted these side conversations to the chief and he was prepared for an answer.
>
> "Very good," said Mista-wa-sis, "you keep your interpreters and we will keep ours. We will pay our own man, and I already see that it will be well for us to do so."[113]

Erasmus was remarkable in many ways: he was a Michif and Cree speaker and fluent in English, and he could read ancient Greek in addition to speaking a number of languages used in the North-West Territories. He was present as an interpreter from the nêhiyawak side at the Treaty 6 signing, and he was one of the members of the Palliser Expedition in 1857–60.[114] His autobiographical reminiscences make spellbinding reading.

Sandham's painting erased from the consciousness of central Canadians an entire group of people like Erasmus. The Métis were not only crucial to the establishment of the country, via their roles as interpreters, guides, and brokers for the numbered treaties but also, at that time, engaged in a political fight for the future of their nation, which they saw and demanded that others see as a political

---

113   Erasmus, *Buffalo Days*, 238.
114   Erasmus, *Buffalo Days*, 56–72.

Jerry Potts and Friends (left to right: Adams, D.B.R., Potts, Kidd),
November 21, 1875. Watercolour by R.B. Nevitt, NWMP surgeon in the 1870s.
Public domain.

entity.[115] Particularly as the resistance under Louis Riel and Gabriel
Dumont percolated, it is ironic that a painting such as Sandham's
should have been created.[116]

A more accurate picture is the watercolour *Jerry Potts and Friends*.
It was painted by NWMP surgeon R.B. Nevitt, much closer to the
prairie, in 1875. It shows famous scout, guide, and translator Jerry
Potts.[117] There is no "white scout" foregrounded and no false but
politically advantageous danger highlighted. Although his letters
home reveal the typical racism of the day, Nevitt's art lacks the romanticism and the propaganda of Sandham's painting. The contrast of

---

115 Andersen, *"Métis"*, 26, focuses on precisely that word, *nation*, as important as
opposed to the more traditional "mixedness" lens through which *Métissage* is
represented by colonial powers.

116 On how the Métis were engaged as scouts and border guards by the Canadian
government even during the resistance, see Hogue, *Metis and the Medicine
Line*, 179.

117 R.B. Nevitt, *A Winter at Fort McLeod*, ed. Hugh A. Dempsey (Calgary: Glenbow-
Alberta Institute, 1974).

Nevitt's on-the-scene watercolour with Sandham's central-Canadian, romanticized, and highly ideological painting could not be starker.

For Further Reading

ON MÉTIS HISTORY in the west and specifically in the areas covered by our walks, see Michel Hogue, *Metis and the Medicine Line: Creating a Border and Dividing a People* (Regina: University of Regina Press, 2015); Brenda Macdougall, "Speaking of Metis: Reading Family Life into Colonial Records," *Ethnohistory* 61, no. 1 (2014): 27–56; and Chris Andersen, *"Métis": Race, Recognition and the Struggle for Indigenous Peoplehood* (Vancouver: UBC Press, 2014).

On Kelsey's travels by canoe and foot onto the Great Plains, see Bruce Greenfield, "'Now Reader Read': The Literary Ambitions of Henry Kelsey, Hudson's Bay Company Clerk," *Early American Literature* 47, no. 1 (2012): 31–58; and the relevant sections in Bill Waiser, *A World We Have Lost: Saskatchewan before 1905* (Calgary: Fifth House, 2016).

On paintings like the images shown, and for a comparison of mostly later "frontier" artwork in both the United States and Canada, see Brian W. Dippie, "One West, One Myth: Transborder Continuity in Western Art," *American Review of Canadian Studies* 33, no. 4 (2003): 509–41.

For an analysis of what could be called "frontier literature" in its Canadian form, and the portrayals of pioneers both male and female, see Daniel Coleman, *White Civility: The Literary Project of English Canada* (Toronto: University of Toronto Press, 2006), 146ff., on "Janey Canuck in the West." On the masculinity of the prairie farmer, often a bachelor, see Cecilia Danysk, "'A Bachelor's Paradise': Homesteaders, Hired Hands, and the Construction of Masculinity, 1880–1930," in *Making Western Canada: Essays on European Colonization and Settlement*, ed. Catherine Cavanaugh and Jeremy Mouat (Toronto: Garamond, 1996), 154–85.

Written Indigenous accounts from the mid-to-late-nineteenth-century prairie comprise a rare but extremely valuable primary source. They include Peter Erasmus, *Buffalo Days and Nights*, ed.

Henry Thompson (Calgary: Fifth House, 1999); Dan Kennedy (Ochankugahe), *Recollections of an Assiniboine Chief*, ed. James R. Stevens (Toronto: McClelland and Stewart, 1972); Edward Ahenakew, *Voices of the Plains Cree*, ed. Ruth M. Buck (Regina: Canadian Plains Research Center, 1995); and (via a settler writer) Mary Weekes, *The Last Buffalo Hunter: As Told to Her by Norbert Welsh* (1939; reprinted, Saskatoon: Fifth House, 1994). Although not the same genre, see also Laura Smyth Groening, *Listening to Old Woman Speak: Natives and AlterNatives in Canadian Literature* (Montreal and Kingston: McGill-Queen's University Press, 2004).

It's important to hear Indigenous oral histories and to read those contemporaneous Indigenous written accounts that have survived against the following "prairie frontier memoirs": William Bleasdell Cameron, *Blood Red the Sun* (1927; reprinted, Calgary: Kenway Publishing, 1970); Isaac Cowie, *The Company of Adventurers: A Narrative of Seven Years in the Service of the Hudson's Bay Company during 1867–1874* (1913; reprinted, Lincoln: University of Nebraska Press, 1993); Cecil E. Denny, *The Law Marches West* (1939; reprinted, Toronto: J.M. Dent and Sons, 1972); Richard Berrington Nevitt, *A Winter at Fort McLeod*, ed. Hugh A. Dempsey (Calgary: Glenbow-Alberta Institute, 1974); David Elliott, *Adventures in the West: Henry Ross Halpin, Fur Trader and Indian Agent* (Toronto: Natural Heritage Books, 2008); John McDougall, *Pathfinding on Plain and Prairie: Stirring Scenes of Life in the Canadian North-West* (Toronto: W. Briggs, 1898); John McDougall, *George Millward McDougall: The Pioneer, Patriot and Missionary* (Toronto: W. Briggs, 1888); and John McDougall, *On Western Trails in the Early Seventies: Frontier Life in the Canadian North-West* (Toronto: W. Briggs, 1911). See also W.H. New, *A History of Canadian Literature* (Montreal and Kingston: McGill-Queen's University Press, 2003); and Robert W. Hendriks, *William Bleasdell Cameron: A Life of Writing and Adventure* (Edmonton: Athabasca University Press, 2008).

Chapter 2

THE TRADERS' ROAD, TREATY 4

EVERETT BAKER AND HIS POSTS

I FIRST HEARD THE NAME HUGH HENRY WHEN I STOPPED by the Swift Current Museum in February 2014. Swift Current is a small city of just under twenty thousand people in southwestern Saskatchewan. Like so many southern prairie communities, it began as a late-nineteenth-century rail stop created by the CPR expansion westward. The May 26, 1883, *Saskatchewan Herald* quotes a visitor as observing that the village established a year earlier was already "quite lively, with two stores, two hotels, [and] a billiard saloon."[1]

The Swift Current Museum is housed in a former Credit Union building. It sits on a service road at the highest point of the city, by the newer "railway," the Trans-Canada Highway. The rumble of passing long-haul trucks forms a constant ostinato whenever the front door of the museum is opened. On a break from visiting my mother at a local nursing home, I was looking for free internet. The museum had an accessible network. It also had an information desk. I had pieced together a funding proposal for walking the North West

---

1   "To Swift Current: Return of the Exploring Party," *Saskatchewan Herald*, May 26, 1883, 4, quoting the diary of a Mr. Walter Salsbury.

Mounted Police Patrol Trail[2] (the proposal was ultimately refused) and asked whether the museum staff knew of anyone who could help me to find more information on it. The person at the desk gave me the name of Betty McDougall from the Saskatchewan History and Folklore Society. She, in turn, put me in touch with Hugh.

When we chatted by phone, I couldn't believe my luck. Not only did Hugh have in-depth knowledge of the trail, but he was the person responsible for keeping it up! I had yet to realize just how fortunate I was. I emailed Hugh my plans, inadvertently revealing that I barely knew which trail it was that I wanted to walk. Jim Daschuk, author of *Clearing the Plains*, had been kind enough to meet me that first trip as well. He had also set me straight. Until that point, I had been under the impression that the NWMP Patrol Trail (its earlier Métis name being the Traders' Road) was more or less the path taken by the first NWMP recruits on their march westward in 1874. In fact, the so-called Great Trek, sometimes known as the March West, traced a line that, for the most part, runs considerably north of the Traders' Road.[3] The March West had been a disastrous shamble across the open prairie. In contrast, the Traders' Road had long been an established Indigenous route, following well-worn paths along the glacial uplands farther south.[4]

Despite its legendary status, the March West typified the worst of colonialist projects. It was plagued from the beginning by political interference, arrogant leadership, and lack of consultation with locals. Commissioner George Arthur French didn't or couldn't listen to the Boundary Commission surveyors who, with Métis guidance,

---

2   The NWMP Patrol Trail should not be confused with the Red Coat Trail, a designated section of highway running from Carlyle to Eastend along Highway 13, generally farther north than the NWMP Patrol Trail.

3   I was not the only person to persist in this mistake. In an email in March 2019, Hugh remarked that a presentation that he had just given in Climax, Saskatchewan, had been useful for correcting just this misunderstanding there.

4   Mike Fedyk, "History, Memory, and the NWMP Trail," in *Fort Walsh to Wood Mountain: The North-West Mounted Police Trail*, ed. Mike Fedyk (Regina: Benchmark Press, 2010), 1. See the map in Bill Waiser, *A World We Have Lost: Saskatchewan before 1905* (Calgary: Fifth House, 2016), 450.

had recently crossed the same territory. Prime Minister Alexander Mackenzie (the previous government under John A. Macdonald having collapsed) instructed the new police force to march farther north than the border in order not to antagonize the Americans.[5] French hired almost no Métis guides even though the Boundary Commission workers had made sure, earlier, to be aided by an entire troop of Métis rangers. The police column used central Canadian horses unsuited for the plains—even the official NWMP historian later wrote that "it is an admitted fact that almost all Canadian or American horses fail during the first season they are fed on prairie grass, and therefore it is little to be wondered that those of the police should have failed."[6]

In 1876, two years after his bumbling trek across the plains, French was forced to resign by the Mackenzie government. He returned to the British military.[7] One of the original officers on that expedition, Cecil Denny, describes horses dying, men struggling to drag heavy wagons across unsuitable terrain, and little provision made for water in a country that had precious little.[8]

I didn't want to make my own versions of such mistakes if I ever managed to initiate a western walk. Through that late winter and spring, my emails with Hugh became more and more specific. We decided to visit a portion of the NWMPT near a place called Chimney Coulee since I had just finished reading Candace Savage's excellent book about that area.[9] Hugh sent me some scanned maps from 1914 and passed on contacts with Wood Mountain Lakota First Nation and with Wood Mountain poet and author Thelma Poirier. Plans started to firm up.

---

5   Waiser, *A World We Have Lost*, 465.

6   Ernest J. Chambers, *The North-West Mounted Police: A Corps History* (1906; reprinted, Toronto: Coles Books, 1972), 23.

7   William Beahen and Stan Horrall, *Red Coats on the Prairies: The North-West Mounted Police 1886–1900* (Regina: Centax Books, 1998), 5.

8   Cecil E. Denny, *The Law Marches West* (1939; reprinted, Toronto: J.M. Dent and Sons, 1972), 22–24.

9   Candace Savage, *A Geography of Blood: Unearthing Memory from a Prairie Landscape* (Vancouver: Greystone Books, 2012).

The next time I was out west, Hugh invited me to join him and other volunteers on a day trip to maintain the old concrete posts erected by Everett Baker in the 1960s. I had seen a post or two in my youth but didn't know the story behind them. I was later to discover that my own family was a part of their history.

In early May 2014, I was back in Saskatchewan visiting my parents, little knowing that, even though it was my father's illness that brought me out, I would be back one month later for my mother's funeral. On a bright, warm, May morning, Hugh picked me up, and we drove west from Swift Current, turning south at Gull Lake to pass over the high ridge separating the Swift Current plateau from the higher plateau farther south, a feature known locally as the Bench.[10]

Gull Lake has the feel of home: I remember driving with my family south of the village while my mother sang us children's songs or years later, when I helped out on the farm, going into town by truck with her brother, my uncle, to fetch his mail. One summer, while working on a Saskatchewan government telephone plow crew, I spent several sleepless nights in the motel by the train tracks, shaken awake every hour or two by the vibration of passing freight trains.

One of the interesting features of this part of the Swift Current Creek watershed is that the weather to the north of the Bench can be quite different from that to the south. Temperatures to the south tend to be milder, with occasional warm winter winds called chinooks. To the west and south of the Bench are the sources of the Swift Current Creek where, in the 1870s, Isaac Cowie set up his clerk's post for the Hudson's Bay Company.[11] Gull Lake is also not far from where my paternal grandfather set up shop as a blacksmith at the beginning of the twentieth century.

---

10   On the Swift Current plateau, see G.A. Padbury, Donald F. Acton, and Colette T. Stushnoff, *Ecoregions of Saskatchewan* (Regina: Canadian Plains Research Center, 1998), 168.

11   Isaac Cowie, *The Company of Adventurers: A Narrative of Seven Years in the Service of the Hudson's Bay Company during 1867–1874* (1913; reprinted, Lincoln: University of Nebraska Press, 1993), 479.

With the exception of one or two curves, the highway from Gull Lake to Shaunavon is painfully straight. Hugh and I drove south, cresting the Bench by a cluster of tall wind turbines that was definitely not among my childhood memories. From there, we passed through another valley and up past the Pioneer Hall gravel road that led westward to where my mother and father had grown up. I could remember—barely—falling asleep as a young child with my cousins on the edges of the Pioneer Hall's dance floor, coddled in warm winter parkas while the adults danced the night away.

From the junction near Pioneer Hall, the highway runs due south to Shaunavon. It is a town of about eighteen hundred people and happens to be where I was born. In 1937, Everett Baker, originally from Minnesota, took a job as a "field man" for the Saskatchewan Wheat Pool.[12] In his new position, he travelled the province, organizing co-ops and promoting the cooperative movement. Baker worked in that capacity out of Shaunavon, where he lived until his death in 1981. He was a talented amateur photographer with an eye for catching the essence of people and their locations. Armed with a Leica that he had purchased for a hundred dollars (a small fortune at the time), and intensely interested in the people and the history of the province, he took advantage of his travels to photograph fairs, rodeos, church events, and families far and wide.[13]

In Montreal, I'd ordered a copy of Bill Waiser's collection of Baker photographs, a handsome coffee-table book titled *Everett Baker's Saskatchewan: Portraits of an Era*.[14] Flipping through the photos, I came across a very stylish young couple whom I realized with a

---

12   Grand Coteau Heritage and Cultural Centre, "Everett Baker of Shaunavon," in *Fort Walsh to Wood Mountain: The North-West Mounted Police Trail*, ed. Mike Fedyk (Regina: Benchmark Press, 2010), 76–83.

13   Finn Andersen, "A Glimpse into the Past through the Eye of Everett Baker (1893–1981)," in *Plain Speaking: Essays on Aboriginal Peoples and the Prairie*, ed. Patrick Douaud and Bruce Dawson (Regina: Canadian Plains Research Center, 2002), 89–92.

14   Bill Waiser, *Everett Baker's Saskatchewan: Portraits of an Era* (Saskatoon: Fifth House, 2007).

shock were my father's brother and his wife, showing off for the camera with one of my cousins as a baby in arms. Baker had taken the photo years before I was born.

Through the 1950s and 1960s, Baker delighted in giving slide-shows in hamlets and villages across Saskatchewan. He showed people themselves and each other in rich colour photographs, somewhat rare at that time. The thousands of Kodachrome slides that Baker took from the 1940s to the 1960s are a testimony to his relationship with that generation.[15] He often caught people at their most candid: he elicited a remarkable beauty, frankness, and pride in his subjects. But his collection is also unique for the fact that, at a time when many settler descendants were actively trying to forget that Indigenous Peoples existed, Baker made sure to include Métis and First Nations individuals and families in his photos. The Saskatchewan History and Folklore Society has made many of his photographs available online, including a section on his photos of First Nations and Métis communities and individuals. The collection is currently hosted on the University of Saskatchewan's platform.[16]

Not coincidentally, this dynamic individual was also the founding president of the society. Baker was perhaps the only one with the interest, the connections, and the influence to do what he did for the province: from 1960 to 1962, he cajoled farmers and ranchers all through southwestern Saskatchewan to help him mould and erect 260 eight-foot concrete posts to mark the North West Mounted Police Patrol Trail/Traders' Road. He rushed to do this before the horse and wagon tracks disappeared forever.[17] Baker financed much of the work on his own and donated labour and material.[18] Unfortunately, by 2015, the posts had again been some-

---

15   Andersen, "A Glimpse into the Past," 89.

16   See "Everett Baker Photos—Saskatchewan History," https://www.skhistory
      .ca/everett-baker-photos.

17   Everett Baker, "There's a Long, Long Trail A-Winding," in *Fort Walsh to Wood
      Mountain: The North-West Mounted Police Trail*, ed. Mike Fedyk (Regina:
      Benchmark Press, 2010), 84.

18   Baker, "There's a Long, Long Trail A-Winding," 87.

what neglected. When Hugh and I first met, one of his concerns was to find, map, and repair the posts, bringing the trail into the new millennium. I hoped that our walk would help him in that task.

At Shaunavon, we turned right and headed west, passing a cousin's farm on the way to Eastend. There we met Ron Volden, an old-timer and a member of the SHFS. The three of us drove out of town a short distance up an undulating gravel road to the site of Cowie's HBC trading post at Chimney Coulee. In 1871–72, Chimney Coulee was what was called a "flying post," a mobile winter encampment. Such "pop-up stores" were a feature of the last days of the bison, intended to counter American posts south of the border.[19] The idea was to offer a place where hunters following the diminishing herds could trade more quickly and the Hudson's Bay Company could keep its share of profits from the slaughter of the bison.

Chimney Coulee is a pleasant and sheltered valley. It rises gently into hills full of cottonwoods clustered around a stream that eventually runs north and joins other tributaries into the Swift Current Creek. It's a refuge from the baking heat and fierce winds of prairie summers. It's also an important historic site that many people, prior to reading Candace Savage's book, didn't even know existed.

Cowie's early-twentieth-century autobiography, *The Company of Adventurers*, is a fine example of the problems of the "frontier hero" genre. It couldn't be more different from Savage's book. Cowie, who overwintered in Chimney Coulee in 1871–72, was a curious and observant young Shetland Islander who must not have lacked fortitude. He had arrived on the prairie four years earlier, in 1867, just in time to witness the convulsions altering the cultural, linguistic, political, economic, and ecological landscapes. Cowie must have felt some connection to the Nakota and nêhiyaw whom he met, for soon after his arrival, during a smallpox epidemic, he volunteered

---

19   Michael Hogue, *Metis and the Medicine Line: Creating a Border and Dividing a People* (Regina: University of Regina Press, 2015), 70.

to help vaccinate local populations in the Qu'Appelle Valley.[20] Nor was Cowie shy to critique settler society. In his book, he wryly notes how the First Nations already under HBC influence were less likely to have good leadership because of the company's tendency to "divide to govern."[21]

However, his later recollections lose something of his youthful humility. His memoirs followed the typical "European heroic adventurer" model, an approach little changed from the rhymes of Kelsey centuries earlier, with the we-they attitude toward Indigenous Peoples that the term "frontier" carries with it.

Cowie's conversion to fabulist writing might have been commercially driven. His journals were first published in serial form for the Saturday editions of the *Winnipeg Telegram* and the *Manitoba Free Press* at the turn of the twentieth century. Unfortunately, the serialization of frontier literature meant that writers and editors did everything that they could to get readers to return for the following week's adventures. Cowie's paragraphs burst with lurid descriptions of "fiery-tempered" military men and Métis traders, the "gay cavaliers of the prairies," folks "fond of dress, dancing and gambling."[22] Cowie describes "spirited" ponies and Indigenous people who alternately show the "kindness and hospitality for which the Cree Indians are remarkable"[23] or who, with "aquiline features, . . . stately gait and dignified manners, look . . . every inch" to be "daring . . . warriors."[24] Such descriptions tend to reflect white consumer demand and Buffalo Bill Cody–styled self-promotion, not the author's own experiences.

---

20   James Daschuk, *Clearing the Plains: Disease, Politics of Starvation, and the Loss of Aboriginal Life* (Regina: University of Regina Press, 2013), 85, notes the importance of Cowie's impromptu vaccination program (his father was a physician in Scotland) but also shows how the Indigenous visitors helped to spread the vaccine.

21   Cowie, *The Company of Adventurers*, 305.

22   Cowie, *The Company of Adventurers*, 352.

23   Cowie, *The Company of Adventurers*, 388.

24   A description of Nakota Chief Growing Thunder in Cowie, *The Company of Adventurers*, 241.

These days there is nothing grand about what remains of Cowie's Cypress Hills trading site. Cowie himself wrote that the company had made a mistake in trying to trade in the liminal area among American whiskey posts, Métis camps, and nêhiyaw, Nakota, and Niisitapi territories. The Niisitapi in particular unnerved Cowie.[25] Nor is there much left of the Métis *hivernant,* or "overwintering," settlement.[26] The reason for the name Chimney attached to the coulee comes from the Métis, who built long row-house dwellings with fireplaces for each family. (The chimneys were still visible years later, although there is no trace of them now.[27]) Even the NWMP post that followed both Cowie's brief stay and the more permanent Métis settlement is gone.

Now all that is left are a few depressions in the prairie grass and some spots where a briefly funded archaeological dig carefully pried up the earth in one-foot (a third of a metre) squares. Standing in the sun by the poplars, listening to meadowlarks, I found it hard to imagine that, even though Cowie—a minor trader at the time—eventually judged the place unsuccessful for trade, in the 1871–72 season he still shipped out over 750 prairie grizzly pelts[28] and fifteen hundred elk hides.[29] Ecological disaster and mercantilism went hand in hand then, as they so often do now.

Eight years after Cowie's brief stay at Chimney Coulee, the bison had almost completely been hunted out, even from this last refuge of the Great Plains animals.[30] In the March 24, 1879, issue of the

25   Cowie, *The Company of Adventurers,* 459.

26   On *hivernant* camps, see Waiser, *A World We Have Lost,* 411–12.

27   Savage, *A Geography of Blood,* 95.

28   Prairie grizzlies, like other prairie dwellers, two- and four-legged, subsisted on bison. For a story of an encounter between a prairie grizzly and a bison cow, see Edward Ahenakew, *Voices of the Plains Cree,* ed. Ruth M. Buck (Regina: Canadian Plains Research Center, 1995), 39.

29   Information taken from the historical sign at the site of Chimney Coulee, likely taken from Cowie, *The Company of Adventurers,* 436. Note that Cowie decried the slaughter of animals in the previously untouched Cypress Hills "after the neutrality of the Hills had ceased owing to our [white] invasion" (437).

30   Already "by the 1860s, two-thirds of the animals were gone." Waiser, *A World We Have Lost,* 417–18.

Detail of mural in Eastend, Saskatchewan, May 2014.
Photo by the author.

Saskatchewan Herald (a newspaper based in Battleford), the editors noted that there were reports of "great distress" among starving nêhiyaw near where we were standing because of the lack of food and a winter that held on late.[31] With the demise of the bison, other large food mammals—deer, elk, and moose—were quickly hunted to near extinction. As Savage notes, "the entire Great Plains, from western Canada to Texas, [became] a slaughterhouse. The foundation for agricultural settlement was being laid in wholesale carnage."[32]

There are no traces now of those starvation times. After visiting Chimney Coulee, Hugh, Ron, and I had lunch in Jack's Café in Eastend, a landmark Greek Canadian prairie eatery. In her book, Savage (who lives part time in Eastend) describes a mural that Angie

31   "News from the Plains" [based upon a letter from Fr. Jean-Marie Lestanc], *Saskatchewan Herald*, March 24, 1879, 2.
32   Savage, *A Geography of Blood*, 89.

Doolias painted that still encircles the inside walls of the café.[33] The mural tells a visual tale of prairie history. It begins at one wall with the primordial arrival of human beings, then shows the sweep of Indigenous history, and then depicts the arrival of the red-coated NWMP and of wagonloads of settlers. It ends its optimistic visual narrative on the other wall, with wheat fields, oil wells, and a prosperous city on the horizon.[34]

What was striking is that there are no Indigenous people depicted in the last panels of the mural. As we sat eating, it was hard not to compare the mural to the history that we had just been walking only a few kilometres out of town and the boom-and-bust cycles that have so affected prairie towns.

Savage relates an anecdote of how two local Nekaneet First Nation men reacted humorously to the mural on a visit to the café.[35] Although it would be wrong to assume that Doolias was conscious of any goal other than painting a lovely depiction of history as she knew it, her art nonetheless participated in a settler narrative that portrays the Indigenous Peoples of the Prairies as having disappeared, and settlement as now complete, two common but mistaken assumptions.[36]

The day that we were there, the server was a member of the family. I attempted, with little success, to thank her in Greek for the meal. Some of the coffee-row folks at a nearby table tried hard not to look like they were listening. As we ate hamburgers and spanakopita, we talked about the Harvest Eatery in Shaunavon, another addition to what has become a robust food culture throughout rural Saskatchewan.

After lunch, we headed to another prairie oasis—Pine Cree Park—a place where, as a child, I sometimes camped with my family and explored the cutbanks, or dirt cliffs, that ring the coulee. This little wooded valley with its twenty-seven non-serviced campsites

---

33   For more on the Doolias (or Doulias) family, see Savage, *A Geography of Blood*, 28.

34   For more on the mural, see Savage, *A Geography of Blood*, 28–30.

35   Savage, *A Geography of Blood*, 29.

36   Dallas Hunt, "Nikîkîwân: Contesting Settler Colonial Archives through Indigenous Oral History," *Canadian Literature* nos. 230–31 (2016): 35.

is another spot connected with Everett Baker. It was Baker who advocated for it to be named a park, and he spent countless hours landscaping, cleaning, and preparing it.[37] Tellingly, people often get the name of the place wrong. Commonly, it is called Pine *Creek* Park, with a *k*. Even local tourist literature sometimes misnames it.

THE FIRST PRAIRIE walk might have been my idea, but it would never have happened without Hugh Henry. Had he not signed on after that first set of emails, I'm sure that my planned trek would have ended with my wandering around southwestern Saskatchewan lost.[38] Hugh knew the terrain, the trail, and some of the farmers along the route. My contacts, such as they were, were friends and relatives in patches here and there. As our partnership progressed, I was able to step back from the logistics and concentrate on writing and walking. Hugh not only knew the Frenchman River valley of our first walk but also made it his business in following years to learn the Battleford Route (2017), the Frenchman's Trail (2018), the Fort Carlton Trail (2019), and the Fort Ellice to Fort Qu'Appelle Trail (2021), as well as leading another Traders' Road excursion in 2020.

In his dedicated but typically understated way, Hugh gave presentation after presentation, drove out along country roads countless times to check direction markers and routes, and during winter months invited new walkers to join. He made a constant practice of working to increase Indigenous representation and presence, inviting nêhiyaw and Métis walkers and speakers, and making respectful contact with First Nations along our routes.

Hugh is not a tall man. But he has the quiet authority of someone with years of experience on the land. He has the solid, spare muscularity of a prairie hockey player, which he is. Where the rest of us tended to

37   Grand Coteau Heritage and Cultural Centre, "Everett Baker of Shaunavon," 80–82.

38   There are certain forms of the *dérive* practised by psychogeographers in which getting oneself lost while walking is part of the plan. It wasn't part of mine.

wear Gore-Tex and fancy walking boots, Hugh prefers being outfitted by Canadian Tire. His tastes are simple—canned beans, little to no sugar, and Old Style Pilsner—but as a former museum curator and an ongoing installation artist his creative perspective is often surprising.[39]

Hugh has consistently been the organizer, leader, and guide of our prairie pilgrimages. My feelings about his role in our walks are best summed up by an incident that took place during the second of our treks. In August 2017, we were in some low hills, just west of Highway 4, southwest of Elrose, Saskatchewan. A local farmer met us to tell us about the history and geography of Otter's Station, where we were starting our day. After the introduction and a little speech, the farmer suddenly turned and set off across the hills, saying that he knew a shortcut to get us to the next road junction and back onto the trail. A few of our group automatically followed. I noticed that Hugh, normally the leader, was hanging back. "What's up?" I asked. "I'm going this way instead," he said quietly. He pointed. "I think the old trail may be over there." Without fuss or announcement, Hugh walked alone to the opposite side of the coulee and off into the distance. As I watched him go one way and the farmer another, three of the trailing members of our group asked me which direction they should head. "When in doubt, follow Hugh," I said.

That maxim has certainly worked well for me. At every twist and turn on the trails, when I was in doubt, Hugh knew which way was best. Some might call it instinct, and it is probably partly that. More importantly, in preparation for each of our journeys, Hugh was the one poring over maps, driving to meet landowners, and scouting possible obstacles, lunch stops, and overnight spots. That day on the unmarked open land, after some quick deliberations, I led a group that followed Hugh. We ended up where we were supposed to be a good forty-five minutes before the farmer, scratching his head in surprise, appeared with his tired charges.

---

39   For instance, with the help of Richard Kotowich, in 2021 Hugh built what he terms an "installation/reconciliation action," a sculpture, at Wiwa Hill, the spot where his great-grandparents first settled.

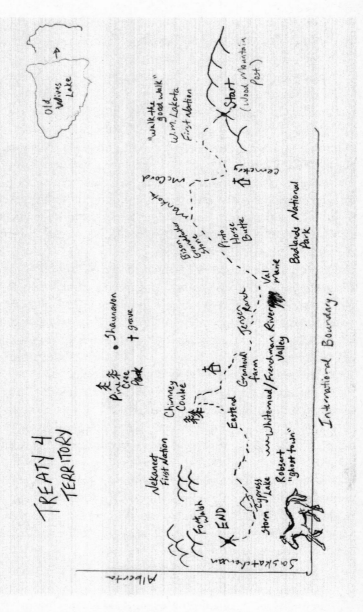

Sketch by the author of the Wood Mountain to Fort Walsh Trail.

THE NORTH WEST MOUNTED POLICE PATROL TRAIL/TRADERS' ROAD

*This story of the loss and regaining of identity is,
I think, the framework of all literature.*

—NORTHROP FRYE[40]

IN LATE JULY 2015, I flew from Montreal to Regina with a bin of camping gear. Thanks to a personal GoFundMe campaign and a grant from the Concordia University Part-Time Faculty Association, I was able to buy or borrow most of the other necessary items after landing. My brother and my sister-in-law loaned me their Toyota van, a single-burner camp stove, a sleeping pad, and several water carriers. The water containers turned out to be almost priceless. For my daily food needs, I was waiting on another contact, who had promised not only a tent but also some mystery provisions. I soon found out what was meant.

Hugh and I had planned our walk to take us from the prairie highland of Wood Mountain westward 216 miles to the other dramatic prairie highland of southern Saskatchewan/Treaty 4: the Cypress Hills. We were to follow surviving cart trails along a route that by the 1900s had already been used for generations but at that point had begun to appear as well on HBC maps, with descriptions of the terrain.[41] We hoped that we might still come across some of the nineteenth-century traders' and hunters' wagon ruts—and we did.

The tracks are better evidence than any literary document of the original purpose of the trail. Wood Mountain to Cypress Hills is now called the North West Mounted Police Patrol Trail, but it was first known as the Traders' Road, and the tracks prove that use. The trail was a continuation of a Métis merchant route that started farther east in Pembina and Saint Joseph and went west to Wood

---

40   Northrop Frye, *The Educated Imagination* (Toronto: Hunter Rose, 1963), 21.

41   Hogue, *Metis and the Medicine Line*, 30.

Mountain along a line of Métis trading posts and settlements.[42] West of Wood Mountain, the Traders' Road branched south at Stone Pile Crossing in the Frenchman River valley and, farther west yet again, at the Fort Benton branch near the Cypress Hills. Each branch led across the border.

Two years after the march west of the North West Mounted Police, an under-reported but crucial part of their work was collecting customs duties on trade that crossed the border at these points.[43] Creating a policing circuit on a trade route was no accident. Canadian police were formed to control trade and to suppress and ultimately remove the Indigenous populations that the government feared might compete or otherwise interfere with that trade.

South of where the hamlet of Wood Mountain now stands (it moved in the early twentieth century to be nearer the rail line) sit the ancient hills themselves. The provincial park and the historical site are nestled into those hills and their pretty wooded valleys. Wood Mountain is not so much a mountain as a set of highlands, one of the two high plateaus left standing in southern Saskatchewan/Treaty 4 after the last ice age. In sections, it rises nearly a thousand metres above the prairie,[44] its flanks dark with the poplar, aspen, ash, and Manitoba maple that caused the Métis arriving from Red River in the late 1860s first to overwinter and then to settle there more permanently, naming their new home *montagne de bois*.[45] From at least the 1860s, Wood Mountain had been a *hivernant* camp for Métis following the disappearing bison herds farther and farther west as well as for Métis families coming north from Milk River or south from Hudson Bay.[46] In 1871, there was a

---

42   David G. McCrady, *Living with Strangers: The Nineteenth Century Sioux and the Canadian-American Borderlands* (Lincoln: University of Nebraska Press, 2006), 3.

43   Chambers, *The North-West Mounted Police*, 40.

44   Padbury, Acton, and Stushnoff, *Ecoregions of Saskatchewan*, 170.

45   Hogue, *Metis and the Medicine Line*, 70.

46   Brenda Macdougall and Nicole St-Onge, in "Rooted in Mobility: Metis Buffalo-Hunting Brigades," *Manitoba History* 71 (2013): 30, note that not all Métis in the Wood Mountain–Cypress Hills region were Red River in origin.

settlement of about a hundred families living, hunting, and trading in the ravines along the north slopes.[47] Those families didn't disappear. Many of them still live, ranch, and farm there. Now they are increasingly speaking out about the long and uninterrupted Métis history in the area.

My original plan was to rent a small motor home in Regina as a sort of emergency shelter and supply vehicle for our walk. I thought of the nasty storms that can blow up on the prairie, sometimes in minutes.[48] Tenting would be fine normally, but the weather in August in Saskatchewan is nothing if not unpredictable, and there is very little shelter along the route that we planned to walk. What if we encountered a tornado, or a shear-wind storm, or golf-ball-sized hail, or—God forbid—snow? For weeks, I fell asleep at night imagining biblical-sized plagues.

I never managed to gather enough funds for the motor home. But I did raise sufficient money to hire a master's student from Concordia, Hayden Thomassin, a cheerful, rough-and-ready rugby player willing for a week to carry camera gear, drive supply vehicles, and do whatever odd jobs our little expedition required. Hayden was looking forward to seeing a part of the country that he had never visited.

Just before my flight, I made a quick trip to Kahnawà:ke to purchase sweetgrass and tobacco as gifts for presentation at the Wood Mountain Lakota First Nation. Another hope that I had for the trip almost didn't come to pass. Just days before my departure, an envelope arrived at my Montreal apartment from Brockville, Ontario. I had asked a colleague, Rev. Bruce Thompson, whether he could track down the grave of James Morrow Walsh for me. Walsh had led the NWMP force that built the fort named after him in the

---

47   Hogue, *Metis and the Medicine Line*, 79.

48   I had enough experience of shear winds and other prairie windstorms while growing up, but it was also interesting to read of others' first encounters. See Denny, *The Law Marches West*, 25; and "Excerpt of an Unnamed Officer Who Was with Otter," April 14–16, 1885, Canadian War Museum Archives, 58A 1 101.38.

Cypress Hills.[49] He had worked closely with Sitting Bull (Tatanka Iyotake).[50] He may have ridden the trail that we were about to walk more intensively than perhaps anyone before or since (although Métis traders along the route might contest that claim).[51] Sitting Bull had even asked Walsh to intercede on his behalf in Washington, DC, a diplomatic mission that Walsh was never allowed to make but indicated the trust that the Lakota leader had in the superintendent.[52]

For all his positive attributes, and his solidarity with the Lakota, Walsh was another self-promoting colonial figure. Young and dashing, he was the NWMP poster boy for many years and a darling of the American newspapers.[53] If anything, that lustre grew following his death.[54] He is still remembered as the stereotypical calm, cool, and often solitary mounted policeman who befriended Indigenous leaders.

Without taking away from Walsh's personal bravery, the self-congratulatory mythology of Canadians concerning the North

---

49 A portrait of "the dashing young officer [Walsh] who is likely to prove another Custar [sic]" is fairly typical of American treatments of the NWMP superintendent. See "Major J.M. Walsh," *Daily Journal* [Ogdensburg, NY], October 31, 1877; the article can be found in the James Morrow Walsh archives, Glenbow Archives, CA ACU GBA F1869-S0001-FL0001 (M 8065, file 01.11b), 44, and online at http://nyshistoricnewspapers.org/lccn/sn85054113/1877-10-31/ed-1 /seq-3.pdf.

50 Garrett Wilson, *Frontier Farewell: The 1870s and the End of the Old West* (2007; reprinted, Regina: University of Regina Press, 2014), 347.

51 Brian Porter, "James Walsh of the North-West Mounted Police," in *Fort Walsh to Wood Mountain: The North-West Mounted Police Trail*, ed. Mike Fedyk (Regina: Benchmark Press, 2010). See also the more journalistic treatment of Walsh by Ian Anderson, *Sitting Bull's Boss: Above the Medicine Line with James Morrow Walsh* (Surrey, BC: Heritage House, 2000).

52 Wilson, *Frontier Farewell*, 391–93.

53 "Sitting-Bull: The Veteran Hair-Lifter and One Hundred of His Braves 'Stood Off' by Maj. Walsh and Sixteen Mounted Police," *Chicago Tribune*, June 21, 1880, 8; available in the James Morrow Walsh archives, Glenbow Archives, CA ACU GBA F1869-S0001-FL0001 (M 8065, file 01.11b), 46–47.

54 See Anderson, *Sitting Bull's Boss*.

West Mounted Police is notable for its lack of historical nuance.[55] The fact is that the successes experienced by Walsh and other early NWMP officers were due far less to them and far more to the discipline and restraint of the Indigenous groups and leaders with whom they dealt, who were under such great pressure at the time. Desmond Morton points out that, although there were excellent NWMP officers and men, many of the officers owed their posts not to competence but to political connections.[56] That there was alcohol abuse both among officers and in the ranks is clear simply from the number of empty whiskey bottles found in archaeological digs and still on display at Fort Walsh.[57]

I had asked Bruce to send me dirt from Walsh's grave, a favour that turned out to be more complicated than I had thought. It seems that Walsh's grave is not easy to find. I'd had the notion that I would carry some earth from the grave with me on the trail and take it to the fort named after Walsh. Oddly, Walsh's central Canadian resting place is nearly forgotten even while the fort with his name on it receives increasing numbers of tourists. But perhaps that was to be expected. Already in his forced retirement to central Canada, Walsh felt that he was sidelined. He missed the west—at least the west that he'd known. Garrett Wilson reports that "Walsh built a fine home in Brockville that he named Indian Cliff, after a prominent feature of the Wood Mountain Uplands, the landmark that he searched for on bitter winter patrols from Fort Walsh. There he died on July 25, 1905, at the age of 65."[58]

Walsh's death points out a fact concerning place: physical features such as the trail are attached to narratives that jostle for attention and adherence. As I was beginning to learn from my Indigenous colleagues, a place is defined in some way by materiality, by ceremony, and by story. For those reasons, I hoped that the personal

---

55   Desmond Morton, "Cavalry or Police: Keeping the Peace on Two Adjacent Frontiers," *Journal of Canadian Studies* 12 (1977): 32.

56   Morton, "Cavalry or Police," 31.

57   Waiser, *A World We Have Lost*, 466–67.

58   Wilson, *Frontier Farewell*, 439.

ceremony of delivering some of Walsh's grave earth to the fort might be meaningful in some small way. The act seemed to be worth the time and trouble and fitting to the territory. I was glad that the parcel reached me in time.

On my arrival in Saskatchewan, I found another delivery waiting for me, this one a rather large box. Packed inside was a tent with a handwritten note bearing the cryptic message "Be VERY careful when opening." Beside the tent were my surprise provisions: a three-week supply of recently expired British Army rations. The rations with their little Union Jacks certainly saved me money, important to a part-time university lecturer self-funding his research. But seeing the provisions also made me laugh. It seemed to be so poetic. The first Brits to walk these territories were the surveyors. Instead of twenty-first-century rations, they had eaten what was the most sensible prairie food at the time—bison, the pemmican made from it, and sometimes bannock. I opened a box of rations. The silver-foiled packets turned out to be mostly Indian: beef madras, chicken tikka, and curried vegetables.

With my brother's van packed with gear, and more than a little apprehensive, I drove south and east from Swift Current to Wood Mountain. It had turned dry. In the long and hot summer evening, farmers were already harvesting. The asphalt became increasingly rough as I drove Highway 4 south, then turned east on Highway 13, finding my way south again until connecting with Highway 18, which once received the dubious honour of being voted the province's worst paved road.

Prairie villages skimmed by. These were places where I knew—or had once known—people: Val Marie, where my uncle Gustav, and his French-speaking bride, Hélène, had lived and posed for Everett Baker in the 1950s. It was in Val Marie where one night, as a road crew worker trying to sleep in my room above the bar, I'd looked out to see a bobcat chained to a post, sitting gloomily atop a terrarium that contained several rattlesnakes. I never got close enough to find out how many rattlesnakes or why they and the bobcat were there. I passed the hamlet of Aneroid, where the

Nostbakken family, whom I had known for years, had first settled and farmed. Not far from Aneroid is its larger neighbour Ponteix, where in university I'd worked briefly as a flagger for a survey crew preparing the roadbed for the same awful, disintegrating highway on which I was now driving.

Although I didn't know it when I was a teenaged rodman for the surveyors, that highway reconstruction had required an archaeological assessment. The assessment eventually led, in the 1980s, to an excavation. Near that same stretch of highway between Aneroid and Ponteix, archaeologists discovered the Nisga'a site, at 8,475 years before present (plus or minus 650 years) the oldest evidence of occupation recorded in Saskatchewan to date.[59] As I slowed on the highway, a herd of bison gazed placidly at me from across seven-stringed barbed wire. I was crossing territory that I hadn't seen for decades.

The violent near collapse of Indigenous prairie society in the late nineteenth century can be described simply, even if its effects were indescribably complex and horrific. From at least the 1850s, in large part because of the industrial use of bison hides, overhunting led to the extinction of herds that had once seemed to be endless. In turn, the loss of the herds spelled both environmental and human disaster. The northern and eastern ranges of bison migration were lost first. Northern Plains nêhiyaw were forced to move south, just as more and more Métis from the Red River area moved west, all in pursuit of the same animals.[60] American traders set up posts across the forty-ninth parallel. Meanwhile, American wolfers, rough and often violent hunters, many of them Civil War veterans who collected pelts by poisoning bison carcasses, joined Canadian wolfers on the territory. Their often violent tactics and disdain for Indigenous

---

59   David Meyer and Henri Liboiron, "A Paleoindian Drill from the Niska Site in Southern Saskatchewan," *Plains Anthropologist* 35, no. 129 (1990): 299–302.

60   Denny, *The Law Marches West*, 29, describes the Métis hunters returning from the Cypress Hills whom the North West Mounted Police met on their trek westward.

life climaxed in the 1873 Cypress Hills Massacre, the unprovoked slaughter of a group of peaceful Nakota families.[61]

In the early to mid-1870s, Wood Mountain and the Cypress Hills were among the last refuges of the few bison that still managed to move across the plains.[62] They were the sites of increasing competition and occasional conflict among Nakota, Lakota, and Métis in the Wood Mountain area and nêhiyaw/Anihšināpēk, Métis, and Niisitapi farther west. The mass killing of the bison disrupted the traditional role of the Cypress Hills, "sacred to the tribal groups of the northern plains" and "considered international territory."[63] Environmental refugees, and warfare resulting from environmental degradation,[64] are hardly new phenomena.

In short, from the 1860s through the mid-1880s, the Wood Mountain–Cypress Hills corridor was at the centre of violent political and environmental events that would mark the future of the continent. The Wood Mountain Post sits twenty-two miles—about thirty-five kilometres—north of Canada's border with the United States. In the 1860s and 1870s, Wood Mountain was at a crossroads between Nakota/Lakota and Métis movements both north and south and east and west.

In those years, Métis entrepreneur Jean Legaré established a trading post at Wood Mountain near another Métis businessman,

---

61   Much has been written about the Cypress Hills Massacre. For an account from one of the Wood Mountain Nakota who had been at the camp, see Dan Kennedy (Ochankugahe), *Recollections of an Assiniboine Chief*, ed. James R. Stevens (Toronto: McClelland and Stewart, 1972), 44–47.

62   For instance, it was to the Cypress Hills that Norbert Welsh travelled in 1878 on one of his last, and unsuccessful, attempts to hunt bison. See Mary Weekes, *The Last Buffalo Hunter: As Told to Her by Norbert Welsh* (1939; reprinted, Saskatoon: Fifth House, 1994), 99.

63   Ray Aldred, "A Shared Narrative," in *Strangers in This World: Multireligious Reflections on Immigration*, ed. Hussam S. Timani, Allen G. Jorgenson, and Alexander Y. Hwang (Minneapolis: Fortress Press, 2015), 202.

64   Welsh relates an unsuccessful attempt by Cree hunters to exact a "bison payment" from Métis hunters. Weekes, *The Last Buffalo Hunter*, 51–52. See also Savage, *A Geography of Blood*, 93.

Antoine Ouellette.[65] Isaac Cowie, who had been at Chimney Coulee, also set up trade nearby. These merchants were part of a larger trade war.[66] Cowie complained that Ouellette, briefly based on the American side of the border, was siphoning off hides to posts along the Missouri River (Americans, who paid more for bison robes, and often used alcohol as part of the trade, almost doubled the HBC traffic).[67] The extent to which the Canadian government's harsh negotiations with Métis, and the three-pronged Canadian nation-building effort of mounted police, treaties, and European settlement, all arose out of trade and border concerns cannot be overlooked. Two years after the march west of the North West Mounted Police, an under-reported but important part of their work was collecting customs duties on trade crossing the border.[68]

The simple fact of a border allowed the Canadian government to define Sitting Bull (Tatanka Iyotake) and the thousands arriving in this region after the Battle of Little Big Horn as refugees and therefore "American Indians." The categorization conveniently overlooked the fact that Lakota had moved into and out of the "Canadian" area for years; the goalposts, not the game, had recently moved.[69]

At the same time, the role that the Métis community, and Ouellette and Legaré in particular, played in the resolution (if one can call it that) of the crisis cannot be overestimated. During some of the worst of the famine faced by the Lakota, while the Canadian government turned its back, Legaré personally fed Tatanka Iyotake's warriors and their families. In his 1881 report, Commissioner A.G. Irvine

---

65   On the fascinating life and claims against the government of Ouellette, see Hogue, *Metis and the Medicine Line*, 183, 223–25.

66   Hogue, *Metis and the Medicine Line*, 79.

67   Hogue, *Metis and the Medicine Line*, 80. See also Cowie, *The Company of Adventurers*, 350.

68   In 1876, the NWMP comptroller reported revenues of nearly six thousand dollars in the Cypress Hills area for 1875, the first partial year of operation for Fort Walsh. See Chambers, *The North-West Mounted Police*, 40.

69   Claire Thomson, "Lakota Place Names in Southwestern Saskatchewan," *Folklore* 41, no. 3 (2020): 35–39.

noted that "Mr Legarrie [sic] must have been put to considerable personal expense, judging from the amount of food and other aid supplied by him."[70]

Later, when Tatanka Iyotake finally followed those who had drifted back south, it was Legaré who was tasked by Walsh with accompanying the Lakota Chief and reimbursed—only in part—by the American government. Legaré never fully recovered his expenses from either side of the border.[71] Yet, during the Riel Resistance, he again supported the Canadian government. Against the advice of others in his community, he aided Métis scouts in the Wood Mountain area to help the North West Mounted Police patrol the border. In what had already become a pattern, Legaré did so even while white settlers near Moose Jaw barricaded his wagons out of racist fear.[72]

When Hugh and I visited Wood Mountain together with Thelma Poirier in preparation for the walk, she pointed to dimples in the distant earth. "Do you know what those are?" she asked us. "No idea." "Métis pemmican depots," she said. Pemmican, made from bison tallow, berries, and dried meat,[73] could be stored in what were called parfleches and buried for later use or trading.[74]

I didn't know exactly what to expect on arrival in Wood Mountain. But I knew that Hugh would be there, probably already set up and mapping our route. There's a wide, shallow stream that runs through the campground at Wood Mountain. I was surprised to discover that the road leading to the tenting and camping sites crossed right through the creek. After some hesitation, I drove the van down through the water and back up the other bank, marvelling at the fact that there was no bridge. I remembered what I always told my students in my Theology in Film classes at Concordia University:

---

70   Chambers, *The North-West Mounted Police*, 55.

71   Wilson, *Frontier Farewell*, 443.

72   Hogue, *Metis and the Medicine Line*, 176–77.

73   Welsh describes the making and temporary storage of pemmican in Weekes, *The Last Buffalo Hunter*, 60.

74   Kennedy, *Recollections*, 92, 140, recalls the filling of parfleches and the times of starvation for the Assiniboine when they were emptied.

"When a filmmaker has a character go through water," I say to them, "it's often an allusion to some kind of baptism. Expect a life-changing experience."

At the campground, Hugh was waiting, as was Richard Kotowich, an educator from Regina whom I'd first approached about the project at the suggestion of my ex-wife. Richard is an angular man with a ready smile and a way of speaking about sweat lodges and eighteenth-century European philosophy in the same sentence. He and I had met and immediately bonded in Regina as I told him my dreams for the trek. Richard is Métis and had long worked with groups whose traditional Lands are in the Cypress Hills. When he heard the crazy idea of walking westward from Wood Mountain, he signed on immediately.

Tim Cresswell says that "places are sites where stories gather."[75] If so, then the two ends of the trail, the Wood Mountain Historical Site and Fort Walsh in the Cypress Hills, are both doing relatively well. Thanks to Thelma Poirier and Andrew Suknaski, Wood Mountain stories have been part of Canadian prairie literature for the past fifty years or so.[76] Dan Kennedy's *Recollections of an Assiniboine Chief* also recalls the Wood Mountain highlands. At the other end of the trail, Cypress Hills is the setting for a number of books from the early years of the twentieth century to the present.

It's the trail itself that regularly threatens to fall into obscurity.[77] Most visitors to Fort Walsh probably don't realize how connected it was to Wood Mountain or how crucial the path between the two places once was to both Indigenous Peoples and the history of Canada.

---

75 Tim Cresswell, *Maxwell Street: Writing and Thinking Place* (Chicago: University of Chicago Press, 2019), 181.

76 Thelma Poirier, *Rock Creek* (Regina: Coteau Books, 1998); Thelma Poirier, *Rock Creek Blues* (Regina: Coteau Books, 2011); Andrew Suknaski, *Wood Mountain Poems* (1976; reprinted, Regina: Hagios Press, 2006). Ken Wilson first brought my attention to Suknaski. See Ken Wilson, "Wood Mountain Walk: Afterthoughts on a Pilgrimage for Andrew Suknaski," *International Journal of Religious Tourism and Pilgrimage* 7, no. 1 (2019): 123–34.

77 Fedyk, "History, Memory, and the NWMP Trail," 9.

Official histories of the two posts tend to celebrate the North West Mounted Police and the final "triumph" of western Canadian settlement.[78] With some exceptions, they tell a settler version of prairie history.[79] Especially in narratives of the Cypress Hills, the period of time emphasized by tour guides and tourist literature is precisely that brief moment in the fort's history that preceded the significant influx of settlement.[80] This momentary prelude was when the police were seen by many Indigenous groups, and appear often to have seen themselves, as allies of the various Indigenous groups rather than their jailors.[81]

Focusing on this brief window in the history of the region valorizes the North West Mounted Police and ignores or romanticizes Indigenous Peoples—placing them firmly in the past and away from the contemporary demands, especially on issues of Indigenous sovereignty.[82] It ignores how anomalous this earliest period was in Canadian policing history. As Métis author and lawyer Bruce McIvor has written, "Canadian state-sanctioned violence against Indigenous people is not simply a matter of history and easy apologies. It is a modern-day reality. Think back over the last 20 years: Oka, Gustafsen Lake, Ipperwash, Burnt Church, Elsipogtog, Unist'ot'en."[83] Whether

---

78   See Beahen and Horrall, *Red Coats on the Prairies*, 27.

79   The purpose of heritage "is almost always that of fostering the definition of group . . . since heritage is by definition 'ours.'" Michael A. Di Giovine and J.-M. Garcia-Fuentes, "Sites of Pilgrimage, Sites of Heritage: An Exploratory Introduction," *International Journal of Tourism Anthropology* 5, nos. 1–2 (2016): 7.

80   Soren Fanning, "Forging a Frontier: Social Capital and Canada's Mounted Police, 1867–1914," *American Review of Canadian Studies* 42, no. 4 (2012): 515–29.

81   "Letter from Commissioner James F. Macleod to Secretary of State, R.W. Scott, May 30, 1877," in *Sessional Papers of Canada* 1878, vol. 4, 34–35.

82   Thomas King, *The Inconvenient Indian: A Curious Account of Native People in North America* (Toronto: Doubleday, 2012), 35. Perhaps the most damning example of this can be found in the writings, when combined with the bureaucratic work, of Duncan Campbell Scott. See Mark Abley, *Conversations with a Dead Man: The Legacy of Duncan Campbell Scott* (Madeira Park, BC: Douglas and McIntyre, 2013).

83   Bruce McIvor, *Standoff: Why Reconciliation Fails Indigenous People and How to Fix It* (Gibsons, BC: Nightwood Editions, 2021), 90.

consciously or unconsciously, the stories of early NWMP valour help to cover over the much longer Canadian policing narrative that we tend to ignore, stretching from the hangings in Battleford in 1885 to the "lethal overwatch" of the Royal Canadian Mounted Police during events in Wet'suwet'en territory.

Hugh raised his eyebrows while I unpacked all my gear. But he said nothing. We all had a good—if somewhat shocked—laugh when I pulled the pop-up tent that my sister had left for me out of its bag for the first time. It sprang out like something alive, a jack-in-the-box immediately ready to be staked down. I had never seen anything like it. The tent was convenient. But it wasn't big. Nor did it look like it could withstand even a moderate wind. I cooked up some of my expired rations, and we chatted about our plans for setting out.

Hugh suggested that we visit the grave of Jimmy Thomson, one of the first NWMP recruits, a man who had come west only five years after the March West and had married Iha Wastewin, one of the Lakota who had come north. Thomson's grave, together with Wastewin's, was near the historic remains of the post.[84] We trekked the hills, careful to avoid cacti. That evening we discovered that tough prairie spear grass had already worked its way into our socks, a sign of things to come.

Although it wasn't ideal, we decided that each day we would piggyback two vehicles. After breakfast, we would drive both to the end of the day's walk, leave our tents and gear, and then return one to the starting point to leave in a shady spot. At the end of the day's walk, we would reverse the process. This took over an hour away from our time to walk the trails, reducing the distance that we covered. It also meant that throughout the day we would have no emergency transport. But without dedicated vehicle support there

---

84   Garrett Wilson, "Jimmy Thomson," in *Fort Walsh to Wood Mountain: The North-West Mounted Police Trail*, ed. Mike Fedyk (Regina: Benchmark Press, 2010), 57. It is worth noting that, for the first few years, NWMP recruits were promised land grants upon the successful completion of their terms of service.

was no way around the problem. For the first of many nights that trip, I fell asleep to the yip and call of coyotes.

WOOD MOUNTAIN POST

THE WOOD MOUNTAIN hills and their larger sibling the Cypress Hills (called Manâtakâw by the nêhiyaw, Awai'skiimmiiko by the Niisitapi) are the highest points between the Rocky Mountains in the west and Labrador in the east. Allen Jorgenson says that the hills are "a beautiful aberration on the hauntingly intoxicating Great Plains, which was once the basin of an ancient inland sea."[85] As the Northern Plains became a sea of grass, the two highlands formed rocky outcrops along an unglaciated ridge that divides several continental watersheds. These prairie oases offer rare treed high country amid thousands of square kilometres of prairie. They have been refuges for moose, elk, deer, and (before the late nineteenth century) bison, wolves, bears, and cougars. Some of those creatures once "hunted out" are only now slowly returning to the area following the disruptions of settlement.

Bison were once plentiful. The decline of the herds in the 1860s and 1870s, everywhere precipitous, was even more pronounced around Wood Mountain with the pressure of the thousands of Lakota refugees hunting there to survive.[86] The drain on resources would be felt for years. Poirier remembers her grandmother writing letters to the local newspaper editor defending the deer that only then were beginning to recover their numbers after being nearly hunted out by the hungry Lakota.[87]

The morning of our inauguration into prairie walking was sunny and cool. Wisps of light fog hung on in the hollows and shady areas of the park. After breakfast, we were met by Judy Fitzpatrick, representing the Wood Mountain Post. Beside her stood two RCMP constables

85   Allen G. Jorgenson, *Indigenous and Christian Perspectives in Dialogue: Kairotic Place and Borders* (Lanham, MD: Lexington Books, 2021), 76.

86   Hogue, *Metis and the Medicine Line*, 103.

87   Poirier, *Rock Creek*, 127.

from the nearby Assiniboia detachment: Staff Sergeant Michael Shortland and Constable Caroline Robert. Hugh had arranged for a short ceremony in which he and I would be entrusted with "papers" to carry to Fort Walsh. Hugh thought that it would be interesting to mirror such commissions carried by NWMP riders such as Jimmy Thomson or Major Walsh during the heyday of their use of the trail.[88]

On December 21, 1876, after a three-and-a-half-day ride from Fort Walsh (our walk would take twenty-one days), Walsh visited White Eagle, a Chief of the Santee who had traditionally camped at Wood Mountain; Walsh then went on to meet with Lakota and other groups who had come north.[89] Not long after, on May 5, 1877, Sitting Bull arrived across the border near the Cypress Hills with a large group.[90] In one of the many sad ironies of this decade, the North West Mounted Police, who later forced them north and east, were first called on by the Nakota and nêhiyaw as allies to help safeguard their traditional hunting grounds against the southerners.[91]

Throughout 1877 and into early 1878, politicians in the House of Commons in Ottawa debated how expensive the presence of the Lakota refugees would be and how best to handle the situation.[92] In what was to become a Canadian tradition, the government's tools against the Lakota were a few mounted police and expedited starvation. Most of the Lakota were forced by hunger and lack of government relief back south of the border, where Tatanka Iyotake

---

88 For a description of the trail in the late 1870s in winter, see "Letter to Cora Walsh," 1890, Glenbow Museum Archives, CA ACU GBA F1869-S0002-FL0001 (M-3636), 2–3.

89 "Report of Insp. Walsh, Dec. 31, 1876," in *Sessional Papers of Canada* 1878, vol. 5, 4–28. Chambers, *The North-West Mounted Police*, 47–48, mistakenly places Sitting Bull among this earlier group.

90 "Letter from A.G. Ervine [sic], Asst. Commissioner NWMP, May 23 and May 25, 1877," in *Sessional Papers of Canada* 1878, vol. 5, 4–33.

91 Chambers, *The North-West Mounted Police*, 49. See also "Letter from Commissioner James F. Macleod to Secretary of State, R.W. Scott, May 30, 1877," in *Sessional Papers of Canada* 1878, vol. 4, 34–35.

92 Wilson, *Frontier Farewell*, 344.

was eventually murdered.[93] Only a small group of resisters stayed; they were finally and reluctantly "given" a reserve in 1910.[94]

I'd had a good breakfast: muesli and dried fruit from my British rations, along with a fried egg shared by Richard, who'd brought a full camp kitchen from Regina. In honour of previous pilgrimages, that first day I wore a Camino de Santiago T-shirt. Some folks arrived from Swift Current. Videographer Norris Currie was there, along with Harold Steppuhn, a retired government of Canada research hydrologist who would soon become a feature of our walks. Norma Hain, an amateur naturalist, spent the first morning walking with me and explaining various native plants.

The ceremony with the RCMP did not last long. I was anxious to get going and could feel others chafing as well. We received our "commission," stopped briefly for group photos at the first (or last depending on how you look at it) of Everett Baker's concrete posts, and set off into the trembling aspen and chokecherry bushes.

Hugh led us down a path hollowed through the trees, over a small bridge, and eventually out of the brush and onto open pasture. The route led downhill through gullied country, on to the northwestern flank of the hills, and eventually on to the Wood River plain that extends west to the village of Cadillac.[95] Apart from some alfalfa fields and a few places where the soft summerfallowed earth made walking difficult, we were in ranch country. The proof was in the fencing. By noon, we had already gone over, under, or through about a dozen barbed-wire fences and avoided several herds of cattle (although it was more difficult to avoid the increased numbers of flies). In a few places, the grass was mid-thigh, but most often it was around our ankles.

There's something jovial about the start of a great adventure. We were all feeling excited and a bit nervous. Richard carried an

93   Many histories of Sitting Bull's time in Canada exist. See Wilson, *Frontier Farewell*, 281–438.

94   Wilson, *Frontier Farewell*, 444; Thomson, "Lakota Place Names."

95   Padbury, Acton, and Stushnoff, *Ecoregions of Saskatchewan*, 168–70.

Armani bag that he and his wife, Pat, had picked up in Europe, the perfect size for his camera equipment but somewhat odd looking on the prairie. The irony of passing the Armani across barbed-wire fences in a desolate part of southern Saskatchewan at first occasioned laughs and photo-ops. Hayden found a set of deer antlers and, wide-eyed, tucked them in his pack. "You'll see more," we told him. He didn't believe us.

Perhaps because of the photos, and some video stops to describe the route, the walking was slower than we had planned. We arrived at Wood Mountain Lakota First Nation just as its members were breaking for lunch from their morning annual general meeting. The irony of settler descendants showing up in Indigenous territory just in time to eat did not escape us. If the Lakota were thinking the same, they were nonetheless gracious. Dave Ogle, the band councillor with whom we'd been in touch, informed us that we were welcome to join them. We lined up, filled our plates with pork chops, new potatoes, and fresh-baked buns, and joined the others at outdoor tables.

Most Wood Mountain Lakota no longer live on the tiny First Nation but return to it for general meetings, powwows, and other events. The couple seated beside me pointed to our packs and walking poles and politely asked me what we were doing. When I said that we were walking from Wood Mountain to the Cypress Hills, the man almost choked on his bun. "Can you believe that?" he grinned at his partner. He slapped me on the back. "You can walk across the prairie all you want, white man," he laughed. "Me, I'll take my Ford." After lunch, an Elder gathered us into a ceremonial circle at one of the outlying tents. He smudged us[96] and told us that we were going on a journey similar to what the Lakota had always done when "new discoveries await on the Land."[97] "Walk the good walk," said the Elder as he offered each of us in turn the smoke from the smudge bowl.

---

96   Smudging is a traditional ceremony among many Indigenous Peoples involving the blessing of being offered smoke from a small amount of sweetgrass or sage.

97   As did the nêhiyaw. See Ahenakew, *Voices of the Plains Cree*, 50.

Following the smudging, Harold and Norma left to walk back to Wood Mountain, Harold promising to rejoin our group later in the journey. We were reduced to four pilgrims. The walking—and the afternoon heat—stretched on. We passed through fence after fence across open prairie and along cropped fields. Finally, the afternoon ended with an interminably long march straight west on a gravel road, up a series of escalating hills, toward a Ukrainian Catholic church south of the hamlet of Glentworth. By 5 p.m., I had gone through all the water that I was carrying and still had several kilometres left to walk; water would be an issue for much of the trek. The little white church beckoned from its solitary perch at the top of the hill. Tired of slowing down for his elders, Hayden pushed ahead.

By this point, we had been walking for hours into a hot west wind. The gusts were strong enough that our approach scared up clouds of grasshoppers that would then be caught in the wind and ping off our bodies like flung gravel. It didn't hurt, but it was annoying as hell.[98] Every now and then a badger would pop out of a hiding place ahead, waddle indignantly along the road a few metres, and disappear again into the wild oats and yarrow lining the ditches.

If you have never walked mixed-grass prairie, the first thing to get out of your mind is that it is flat. Even the roads and the field edges were not flat. Prairie pastureland is often hilly. The Wood Mountain plateau and the Wood River plain consist of slopes with deeply cut ravines. At lower elevations, the prairie is dotted with glacial kettles, some with sloughs of brackish water, others with alkaline beds at their centres. Imagine open expanses of slightly undulating hills covered in tawny grass. The hills don't seem to be much at first. Yet they often stretch nine to fifteen metres from trough to crest and are covered with cacti, sage, milkweed, buckbrush, and various poking grasses. From a distance, the effect is like looking at the loose skin of a tawny-golden dog, or a big cat, rumpled in giant furrows.

---

98   Denny, *The Law Marches West*, 21, comments on the locusts during the NWMP trek westward in 1874.

Cowie mentions the Wood Mountain cart trail in his reports in 1867. We ran into the original tracks several times that day near Six-Mile Creek.[99] The creek gets its name from being about six miles (nine and a half kilometres) west of the Wood Mountain Post—it would have represented a final stop for riders and walkers. There is often an odd number of tracks, which seems to be unusual considering that drivers rode two- or four-wheeled carts. However, Poirier had traced the cart trails on paper for me. She explained how Red River drivers would set one wheel in the tracks of preceding carts so that there was always some overlap in the group, keeping the horses in line.

In general, the Traders' Road followed trails that Indigenous Peoples used for millennia to walk east and west along the continental divide. The divide's higher altitudes offered cooler temperatures, abundant wildlife, and treed shelter. Its uppermost geological formation, about a hundred metres thick, has the strange names of Ravenscrag in Canada and Fort Union in the United States. It forms a bedrock base for the long, sinuous ridge. In most places, the trail sits on up to a metre and a half of glacial till, with deeper deposits in end moraines. Prairie soil developed from the till, and, in the long course of geological time, grassland invaded that soil.[100]

No water courses cross the divide, making it a natural highway for humans and animals—and eventually for us. Harold, our group's hydrologist and geographer, told me later that the continental divide that we were walking was important because it splits continental surface waters into two of the four oceanic destinations: the Saskatchewan River basin via the Nelson River to the Atlantic and the Missouri River basin via the Mississippi River to the Gulf of Mexico.

BY THE END of that first day of walking, the only water that I was thinking of was that which none of us had any longer in our canteens.

---

99   Cowie, *The Company of Adventurers*, 342.

100   Harold Steppuhn, email to the author, March 5, 2019.

We reached the church, parched and exhausted, at 7 p.m. Our feet were sore. We were heat blasted. Maps note the name of the church as the Church of the Assumption of the Blessed Virgin Mary. The cemetery was established in 1914, and the present church was built in 1923. We peered inside at the altar area. With its cozy pine tongue-and-groove boards, it resembled the inside of a ship. There were two angels in mosaic tile on either side of the altar and an icon of the Virgin Mary on a little stand in front.

We hurried to put up our tents and the gazebo on the prairie grass yard beside the cemetery. Even though the sun sets late in July, after fetching the other vehicle from Wood Mountain for the next step of the journey, there was barely time to make a quick evening meal before nightfall. As darkness descended, an unexpected sight met our exhausted eyes: one by one, little lights popped on in the cemetery just below our tents. The graves, marked with solar-panelled light posts, suddenly became radiant in the increasing blackness of the country night.

I thought of prairie poet Tim Lilburn's lines:

> Earth, earth, earth, stone lobed, blue, earnest
> blundering Godward . . .
> the dead
> bunched as flowers in its arms, the stone-sung-to
> dead . . .
> . . . singing trampoline of winds.[101]

Lilburn certainly got the wind right: that night it never let up. The gusts increased, and our exposed position at the top of the hill meant that the tents and our camp gazebo shuddered and shook all night long. I crawled into my small pop-up, now thankful for its low profile. Reflections of the lonely lights danced and played on

---

101   Excerpt from Tim Lilburn, "I Bow to It," in *Desire Never Leaves: The Poetry of Tim Lilburn*, ed. Alison Calder (Waterloo: Wilfrid Laurier University Press, 2007), 13.

the nylon. I fell asleep listening to the wind rip at our little pieces of fabric. If there were coyotes, there was no way to hear them.

By morning, the gusts had abated. We set out for the hamlet of McCord, testing our day-two feet for blisters. That evening in McCord, Hugh and I were to give a presentation sponsored by the SHFS and the local museum. We had decided that Hugh would talk about the history of European settlement of the area and show slides from the Everett Baker collection, in some ways repeating Baker's own style of presentation from decades before. I would talk about how our walk fit world traditions of pilgrimage, especially in light of responsibilities to the Indigenous Peoples who first made the trails.

We walked less open pasture and more road than the first day, although a part of our walk took us along Wood River. In that area, the wide and gentle creek gathers water from the north and west slopes of the Wood Mountain plateau and meanders northward, eventually draining into Old Wives Lake.[102]

As we walked along the banks, our ears were full of the drone of insects and our noses the odour of sweetgrass, a strong and pleasant scent that I couldn't remember ever smelling before and had to ask Hugh to identify. I let the others go ahead. I walked alone for a while, singing as much as I could remember of Connie Kaldor's beautiful ballad to Wood River. When I caught up to them, Hugh told one of the stories that he had heard about Old Wives Lake. There are several versions of the tale. In one, the lake is haunted by the voices of murdered nêhiyaw and Nakota women who tended fires at night to cover the retreat eastward of their people just before a Piikuni raid. Dan Kennedy (Ochankugahe)'s book *Recollections of an Assiniboine Chief* tells a similar story, but his version reverses the action: in his account, the alkaline marsh, Old Wives, or Wah-Gan-Kana-Tee, was so named because it was haunted by the spirits of Piikuni women whose men were killed in a retaliatory raid by the Nakota in the early 1800s.[103]

---

102   Hugh later emailed me that in some early maps Wood River is referred to as Old Wives Creek. Hugh Henry, email to the author, June 27, 2023.

103   Kennedy, *Recollections*, 119–22.

Kilometres and hours later, when we walked into McCord, we were met by Audrey and Bill Wilson. Bill opened the community hall for us, and Audrey showed us the museum. After the surreal isolation of our hill-top camp by the cemetery, it was pleasant to set our tents among the trees in the shade of an old CPR station, built in 1928 and converted to a museum after its closure in 1970.[104]

Audrey, Bill, and other volunteers have kept the rooms of the train station as they might have looked in the early part of the previous century, complete with a telegraph desk. We had time for only the briefest of tours before heading over for a potluck meal. It must have been good food—I remember filling my plate twice—but the highlight for me was a real jellied salad. In recent years, jellied salads have become kind of a punchline to jokes about rural cuisine. However, this one was a masterpiece: nine levels of gelatine and fruit, its pleasing palate of colours matched by a lovely, variegated taste more reminiscent of tiramisu than anything from a can. I would go back to McCord just for that salad.

The 2006 Canadian census put McCord's official population at forty people. That night there were forty-nine in attendance at our talk. Thelma Poirier came to read her poetry and to check on our progress. People listened politely to my portion of the presentation. But during Hugh's showing of Everett Baker's slides of McCord from the 1950s and 1960s, the group came alive: people began to shout out the names of the old-timers on the screen. Several times polite disputes arose about who, exactly, was this or that young person shyly peeking out at Baker's camera. Several of the children in the old slides were now seniors in the audience. All in all, it was a wonderful event, and Hugh and I visited late with folks in a warm and clear prairie evening.

The next day, after a third long and hot day of mostly road walking, we arrived at the town of Mankota. Instead of tenting there, we checked into the hotel, where it felt luxurious to shower off some

---

104   Museums Association of Saskatchewan, "McCord and District Museum," http://www.southcentralmuseums.ca/mccord.html.

of the prairie dust. Along the highway, a cattle auction was on, and after cleaning up Hayden and I spent some time leaning over the boards listening to the cadence of the auctioneer. Hugh and I had our second presentation: this time about thirty people attended. The pattern of the night before was repeated: a politely interested but quiet response to my talk and clear delight at seeing Baker's old photos, many featuring locals as children. Hugh was kept busy taking notes from those who recognized themselves or others.

The following evening we were invited to camp overnight in the farmyard of Keith and Margaret Walker southwest of Mankota. Over the next few weeks, we were to discover that no two of these farm or ranch invitations were ever the same. Through no fault of our hosts, who were always gracious, we never quite knew what to expect when we arrived at a working farm or ranch. Much depended not only on our hosts but also on the cycles of harvesting, repairing breakdowns, hauling bales or cattle or grain, and doing all the other tasks that characterize life on a ranch or farm.

Our welcome at the Walkers was extraordinary: once our tents were up, they invited us into the house for teriyaki pork chops and potato salad and set out trays of cold beer and soft drinks. Margaret is one of those prairie women who can (and do) organize everything from school board meetings to cattle drives. She asked Hugh about our route. Within minutes, she was on the phone checking with other farmers and ranchers to confirm our arrival. As the evening wore on, neighbours and relatives came over. Dave and Esther Green from Swift Current showed up with their horse trailer, ready to join us on the next day's journey.

Soon it was a large gathering, everyone talking at once, cowboy hats and baseball caps spilling from the kitchen out through the patio onto the small lawn, the Walkers' granddaughter, Randie, going around with drinks and desserts. Margaret showed us a good-sized lodgepole pine. "That's from Cypress Hills," she proudly announced. "We brought it as a little seedling and put tires around it and protected it from the mule deer until it grew up." We told them about the coyote that we had scared up that day, a young one that must have been sleeping in the low prairie cedar. We had also come across our first "bison wallows": depressions in the earth, often around large boulders. A wallow was a place where bison could rub their backs in the dirt and up against the rock. As a result, the shanks of the boulders that we had encountered were rubbed so smooth by generation after generation of bison that they felt like skin.

The conversation never lagged. But after a while, I noticed Richard's and Hayden's heads starting to nod. Twenty or more kilometres a day on foot in the heat made us all tired. That day my water supply had run out after only fourteen kilometres, and I was so hot by the end of the walk that I had lost a clear sense of where I was headed and had to be herded along by the others.

Soon both Richard and Hayden excused themselves and headed for sleep. A while later I found my tent and rolled in; Hugh stayed visiting long after the rest of us had left. As I fell asleep, I could hear Dave and Esther's horses moving around in their trailer, the concussions like prairie thunder.

It took seven years
For Hannah to knit a violet sleeve

So long
It went twice around the rocker

And once
Around her neck.
It took seven years
Before an arm reached out that fit.

—THELMA POIRIER[105]

---

105   Thelma Poirier, Glentworth, Saskatchewan, a poem written into my walking diary.

THE NEXT MORNING Hugh dropped by as I tried to cram my little tent back into its bag, a bit of a puzzle with a pop-up tent, which is under constant tension and requires complex folding and compressing to pack.

"Two little tics this morning," he said.

"Oh, yeah?" I answered. "Do we have a vehicle problem?"

"No, no," he gestured impatiently. "*Tick* ticks. On my body. You may want to check yourself."

I immediately felt itchy.

That day our plan was to climb gradually up a promontory known locally as Pinto Horse Butte, where the North West Mounted Police had established a temporary post in 1877. Hugh had set up a long day of walking across open prairie, with few roads or fences to slow our progress. We soon realized that this was our favourite terrain, but it meant being far from roads and potential vehicles to help us.

The Walkers' granddaughter, Randie, trekked with us for about ten kilometres, until lunchbreak. Even though we had been on the trail only a few days, it was fun to see how her energy—running this way and that, looking at interesting sights—contrasted with the long-haul approach that the rest of us had already adopted. Not long after we started, a mule deer buck jumped a barbed-wire fence and waded into a field of canola. It was exhilarating to watch his tawny-golden antlers and head above a field of yellow in the early morning sunlight.

It was the fourth consecutive day of scorching heat. By this point, I was despairing of how to carry enough water to last the full route but not be completely hunched over by its weight. That day I needn't have worried: at the end of our morning of gradual climbing, we neared the crest of the butte, where we were surprised to see several half-ton trucks bivouacked. They were stopped right in the middle of the only road that we intersected that day. Their tailgates were down.

The Walkers had brought fresh, cold water. Fern and Howard Olson were also there. They had cut open several crisp, cool watermelons, which they placed on the tailgates along with freshly baked rhubarb cake. We rested a while in the shade of their vehicles. There was an older rancher there as well. As I sat in the lee of one of the vehicles, spitting watermelon seeds and watching a black cricket toil away under a feather of some kind, the rancher pointed over the prairie in the direction that we were going. He poked me in the shoulder. "Keep your eyes open," he advised. "Years ago I was out there looking for cattle, and I came across a rock with the name Jerry Potts carved into it."[106]

Even with my mouth full of watermelon, that caught my attention. Potts was the Métis scout who'd done more than anyone else to pull success from the disaster-ridden NWMP March West. He was and remains a legend of nineteenth-century prairie history.[107]

"Where?" I asked the rancher. "Can you show us?"

He shook his head. "Thought I'd remember but can't. I've gone back a few times to try to find it but never could. It's out there somewhere. Maybe you folks'll come across it."

Later I made the mistake of mentioning Pinto Horse Butte to Harold, our fellow walker and resident geologist/hydrologist. "Welllll," he began. If Harold disagrees with you, then he will duck his head slightly in a way that I came to recognize over the years, appearing to look away while still keeping his sharp blue eyes trained. "It's not a butte. Not really. It's a small uplands.[108] If you want to see a real butte, then look at Six-Mile Butte." Harold is a scientist but always, also, a teacher.

As we walked west after our surprise lunch, Seventy-Mile Butte, another uplands, sat distant and purple to the south. I was struck by

---

106   The literature on Potts is extensive, some of it scholarly and, as is typical for this subject, other pieces more popular. See Rodger D. Touchie, *Bear Child: The Life and Times of Jerry Potts* (Victoria: Heritage House, 2005).

107   Hugh A. Dempsey, "Jerry Potts: Plainsman," *Montana: The Magazine of Western History* 17, no. 4 (1967): 12–17. See also the recollections of Potts in Denny, *The Law Marches West*, 41.

108   Later, while researching the area, I would discover that Pinto Horse Butte (identified as such in the 1885 Geological Survey) is likely just a western ridge of the much larger Wood Mountain uplands, which was what Harold was trying to tell me. See the map in Padbury, Acton, and Stushnoff, *Ecoregions of Saskatchewan*, 161.

how the names of so many features of this area derive from the trail and from Wood Mountain as a destination. We had crossed Three-Mile Butte,[109] Six-Mile Creek, Eight-Mile Creek, and Ten-Mile Creek, all named after distances to the Métis settlement and to the post.

Tatanka Iyotake was camped at Pinto Horse Butte in the late summer of 1877 when he met Walsh again. (Walsh had first met the Lakota leader in the Cypress Hills in May that year when Sitting Bull led a large group across the newly marked border.) At Pinto Horse, Tatanka Iyotake repeated his intention to settle north of the border. Walsh was more receptive to the idea than officials in Ottawa would be. In a tactical act of magnanimity, he granted Jean Louis Legaré the right to sell the Lakota ammunition that they could have taken by force at any time if they had wished.[110]

The fact that Walsh was able to establish guidelines so effectively with the Lakota so soon after they had routed a greatly superior American military force at Little Big Horn has been written about at length. Even at the time, explanations were sought in the unusual character of NWMP constables such as Walsh[111] and Sam Steele. I prefer the explanation given by Peter Erasmus. He was there at the time and, as a Métis guide and diplomat, knew the workings of the prairie First Nations better than the reporters and readers from Chicago, New York, and Montreal who first idolized Walsh and then abandoned him.[112] Erasmus gave the credit for the early years

---

109   Thomson, "Lakota Place Names," 37, notes that the Lakota name for Three-Mile Butte, in translation, is Peppermint's Hill, after a Lakota man who had a fast and vision quest there.

110   Wallace Stegner, *Wolf Willow: A History, a Story, and a Memory of the Last Plains Frontier* (Lincoln: University of Nebraska Press, 1980), 116. See also "Letter from Commissioner James F. Macleod to Secretary of State, R.W. Scott, May 30, 1877," in *Sessional Papers of Canada* 1878, vol. 4, 34–35.

111   See the James Morrow Walsh archives, Glenbow Archives, CA ACU GBA F1869-S0001-FL0001 (M 8065, file 01.11b), 18.

112   See, for instance, "Sitting Bull and His Band," an article by a *New York Herald* correspondent, in the James Morrow Walsh archives, Glenbow Archives, CA ACU GBA F1869-S0001-FL0001 (M 8065, file 01.11b), 17. An attached letter to the editor is even more complimentary: "We are glad to hear of the safety of

of peaceful coexistence not to the North West Mounted Police but to the Nakota, Lakota, and nêhiyaw: "The chief and his councillors administered the [Indigenous] laws for their band and the tribe recognized the necessity for rules governing individuals who at times broke the rules set by their leaders, for the benefit of the majority. That, in my opinion, is what made possible the successful role that this small Force played."[113]

Desmond Morton, the dean of twentieth-century prairie historiography, agreed with Erasmus that it was the attitude not of the police but of the Indigenous groups that ensured early NWMP success.[114] This is a fact of our history that more Canadians should know. The cooperation that marked those first years of prairie contact, and on which we have often congratulated ourselves as being stereotypically "Canadian," arose in fact from the careful evaluation of Indigenous Peoples who had been weakened by epidemics and faced a future without the bison that had sustained them for living memory. The best of this region's character was forged less by settler Canadians and more by those who treatied with them.

During our cross-country trek that day, we found several cattle skeletons. Hugh discovered five of Everett Baker's concrete posts new to the SHFS database. Each time he sat in the sage and took the GPS location, assessing the state of the 1960s concrete for his notes. Spear grass was becoming a constant irritation. It worked its way through the leather of our boots and into our skin, where the little pronged heads broke off after digging into the sensitive tops of our feet. The laces of our boots were furry with it.

The afternoon stretched on in a bewildering mix of heat, dust, cactus, bleached bones, and grass. The wind had become omnipresent,

the brave and generous Major Walsh, whose name and deeds of course are know[n] throughout the whole of the great North-West."

113 Peter Erasmus, *Buffalo Days and Nights*, ed. Henry Thompson (Calgary: Fifth House, 1999), 240. See also Greg Poelzer and Ken S. Coates, *From Treaty Peoples to Treaty Nation: A Road Map for All Canadians* (Vancouver: UBC Press, 2015), xiii.

114 Morton, "Cavalry or Police," 27–37.

sighing at our faces out of the west, as we walked between hills and low alkali kettles, most with no water, some ringed by marsh grasses. Somehow our little group spread out across a few hundred metres of the heather. Although we were all going the same direction, we lost sight of each other in the endless undulations. At one point, I stumbled down and into a bison wallow. At its centre sat a magnificent solitary boulder, a rock the size of a small car. I called to the others, but no one was in earshot. Eventually, over the hill, I came across Hugh resting beside some tall sage, waiting for the group to catch up to him. I told him about the wallow. He went to take a look.

"That's not just a boulder," he said on his return. "Did you notice its form? It's shaped like a bison. A sleeping bison." As Hugh took photos, Richard caught up to us. His voice immediately hushed. "This is a grandfather," he told us. Richard put tobacco down among the scattered stones at the boulder's base and said prayers before we moved on.

Gradually, we made our way westward. Occasionally, we scared up more deer or Hungarian partridges that would wait until we were nearly overtop them and then explode underfoot. A small group of antelope zig-zagged away at our approach, their precise directional changes similar to those of a murmur of birds. Once some kind of lizard scurried down a hole, reminding me that we were now in rattlesnake country. Overhead, Swainson's hawks stretched their wings in the cloudless sky and cried their disapproval of our presence.

Finally, we dropped from the darkening hills toward our evening destination, a service farmyard only a few kilometres from the village of Val Marie. By the time we were done fetching vehicles, it was again late. Denis Duquette kindly let us put up our tents among the oil and gas tanks, sheds, parked vehicles, and hedges of the yard. The Greens fetched their trailers and loaded their horses. "The heat really got to the horses today," said Esther. "I don't know how you folks are doing it on foot." They drove off, and I fell asleep that night to dreams of milkshakes.

The next morning we had our first cool temperature and rain. The sky was overcast, indeterminate and silver. We had a short walk

The author (right) and David Green (on horse)
near Pinto Horse Butte, 2015. *Photo by Richard Kotowich.*

into Val Marie, half a day on asphalt. Val Marie, population 120, is just north of Grasslands National Park, which among other things is a "Dark Sky Preserve, and the quietest place in North America, according to acoustic ecologist Gordon Hempton."[115] It certainly was quiet that day. A light drizzle started. Our boots on the edges of the corn-crumbled pavement were the noisiest things that we could hear. Our conversations were subdued, in part because we were watching for vehicles. Hayden was done his week of walking; the next day he was headed back on a plane to Montreal. Richard also had to head back to Regina, although he left me his Australian driver's hat for the sun and promised to rejoin us later on the trek.

I had to drive to pick up supplies in Swift Current, and then Hugh and I had another community presentation, this time at Prairie Wind and Silver Sage, an artists' co-op in Val Marie. Robert

---

115   Madonna Hamel, "Pop 89: Deep Scribe Preserve," *Your West Central Voice,*
       https://www.yourwestcentral.com/articles/pop-89-deep-scribe-preserve.

and Mette Ducan, owners of The Convent Inn, a stately brick bed and breakfast in a former nuns' residence, had very kindly offered me accommodation. I wanted to interview them. I was also looking forward to meeting Saskatchewan writer, naturalist, and political activist Trevor Herriot, whom Hugh had invited to drive out from Regina to present with us.

For Further Reading

For a map of the Traders' Road/North West Mounted Police Patrol Trail, see Wilson, *Frontier Farewell*, 218–19. Another map that puts this trail in the context of multiple routes across the Prairies can be found in Waiser, *A World We Have Lost*, 450.

Although copies might be hard to find, an excellent introduction to the North West Mounted Police Patrol Trail/Traders' Road is a small book edited by Mike Fedyk, *Fort Walsh to Wood Mountain: The North-West Mounted Police Trail* (Regina: Benchmark Press, 2010). One of the treasures of this slim volume is a piece by Everett Baker, "There's a Long, Long Trail A-Winding," 84–89, about his work posting the trail in the 1950s and 1960s with the now iconic concrete markers. For more on James Walsh, see Brian Porter, "James Walsh of the North-West Mounted Police," in *Fort Walsh to Wood Mountain: The North-West Mounted Police Trail*, ed. Mike Fedyk (Regina: Benchmark Press, 2010), 26–36. There is also a more journalistic and somewhat adulatory treatment of Walsh by Ian Anderson titled *Sitting Bull's Boss: Above the Medicine Line with James Morrow Walsh* (Surrey, BC: Heritage House, 2000).

For a thoughtful academic critique of the North West Mounted Police and their role in colonization, see Soren Fanning, "Forging a Frontier: Social Capital and Canada's Mounted Police, 1867–1914," *American Review of Canadian Studies* 42, no. 4 (2012): 515–29. For a contemporaneous account, see "Letter from Commissioner James F. Macleod to Secretary of State, R.W. Scott, May 30, 1877," in *Sessional Papers of Canada* 1878, vol. 4, 34–35. For those who might doubt the colonialist status of the North West Mounted Police, early recruits were promised free land grants upon successful completion of their terms of service. See Garrett Wilson, "Jimmy Thomson," in *Fort Walsh to Wood Mountain: The North-West Mounted Police Trail*, ed. Mike Fedyk (Regina: Benchmark Press, 2010), 57. Thomson (and his descendants) show how complex and intertwined colonial history and Indigenous history were to become.

For a nineteenth-century account of nêhiyaw foot journeys on the same land that we were walking, see Edward Ahenakew, *Voices of the Plains Cree*, ed. Ruth M. Buck (Regina: Canadian Plains Research Center, 1995), 50.

VAL MARIE TO THE WHITEMUD RIVER VALLEY

THE NEXT EVENING three dozen people filled Prairie Wind and Silver Sage in Val Marie for our presentation. My cousin Helen (the baby in one of Baker's photos) and her partner had driven to Val Marie from Saskatoon, and friends from Outlook made the trip as well. Hugh, Trevor, and I were introduced. Having read two of Trevor's books and long admired his ecological advocacy, I was anxious to hear him speak. I was not disappointed. Trevor is a tall, lean naturalist who, to adapt the words of Paul Simon, wears his passion for the prairie like a thorny crown. Advocating for the land has become his life's work. Madonna Hamel was there as well. She is an author, journalist, artist, and musician who had moved to Val Marie to research family history and ended up staying there. Among her other artistic outputs, she was developing a one-woman show titled *My Sister's Apron*. She promised to walk with us on her days off. Nature photographer James R. Page, also a resident of Val Marie, was there to show his interest in the trail. He is the subject of the 2022 Cannes award-winning documentary *Wild Prairie Man*. Whenever I saw him, he was wearing one of those long-pocketed vests that photographers often use to keep filters and lenses handy. Another talented photographer, Branimir Gjetvaj, had come with Trevor from Regina to shoot some of the walk. Seeing Branimir the next day, heavy with camera gear, struggling to get photos with lanky and intense Trevor beside him, gesturing here and there and pointing out each aspect of the prairie ecosystem, was a picture in itself.

The next morning I said goodbye to Robert and Mette at the convent. Robert was fighting cancer and spoke passionately about his dreams for the village and for the B&B. I teased Mette, who is Danish, about Scandinavians not enjoying hugging, but we hugged anyway. Then Hugh and I made our way across the highway, through the ditch grasses, and into the community pasture.

At first, we were a dozen walkers, the largest group so far. I was pleased with the turnout—until I realized how glacial our pace was as a result. Between two professional photographers and a rapt audience there for Trevor's commentary on prairie habitats, we barely moved. I was fascinated by how deeply Trevor knows the prairie. He showed us an incredible array of life in a simple square metre of grass. Hunched down, he pointed out alfalfa, sweet clover, white clover, puff balls, blazing star, club moss, ground lichen, yellow cone flowers, sage, and tickle grass, all in a patch that up to that point I would have called "bald prairie." We saw a rare falcon. Trevor drew our attention above our heads to the descending spiral of birdsong that I'd been hearing for days but had no idea why. "That's a Sprague's pipit," he said. "They sing on the wing. They'll lock their wings at five hundred feet and sing all the way down."

Trevor pointed again to our feet, to dung beetles toiling away at a cowpie, and told us how certain pesticides ingested by cattle kill the life that tries to live in their manure. We came across a lodge ring, and Trevor showed us how the natural environment was both disturbed and revitalized around the historic remains. He talked of how a commons, shared among many ranchers, is essential to preserving the prairie ecosystems that industrial farming can so easily destroy. "These are two powerful but opposing ideas—the idea of the public good and the idea of private property," he writes, "but for centuries now they have been at loggerheads for want of a

third element to resolve them: the idea of the commonwealth."[116]
The combination of Trevor's politics, his ardent sense of justice in
ecology, and his clear love of the land was fascinating. But it took a
full day to walk the thirteen kilometres to Branimir's car.

After that, Hugh and I were the only two left, and we still had
eight kilometres to trek. We passed a local Hutterite colony[117] and
continued to an abandoned farmyard where we had dropped a
vehicle and our tents for overnight. Hugh's suppers and breakfasts
were minimal: often Hugh would simply open a can of beans. I had
my British army rations, but they tended to require heat and time.
That night I was too tired to eat. In any case, the prairie grass was so
dry that I wouldn't have dared light my camp stove.

Hugh and I had taken on more supplies on a quick trip up to Swift
Current during our day off. That night I fell asleep hungry. Listening
to the yapping of coyotes, I remembered hearing that during the 1870s
all the NWMP posts along the border were supplied by American
traders, many from Fort Benton. The irony was that the police were
there to stamp out American trade, especially the illegal trade in
whiskey, even while depending on Montana companies, some of
which had earlier smuggled and sold the same whiskey north.

At the time, the implications of the bison apocalypse and of
being forced into a money economy were not lost on the locals. The
Anihšināpēk, nêhiyaw, and Nakota leaders knew that the Hudson's
Bay Company had received three hundred thousand pounds stirling

---

116   Trevor Herriot, *Towards a Prairie Atonement* (Regina: University of Regina
Press, 2016), 94. Norman Henderson seems to be at odds with Herriot's (and
Savage's) positive evaluation of nineteenth-century bison in the ecosystem
of the Northern Plains. See Norman Henderson, *Rediscovering the Prairies:
Journeys by Dog, Horse and Canoe* (Victoria: TouchWood Editions, 2010), 159.

117   Hutterites are a communal-living branch of the larger Swiss-origin Mennonite-
Anabaptist Christian tradition. They live a somewhat separate life on their
"colonies" with varying degrees of interaction with and accommodation to secular
society depending on the colony and its tradition. On Hutterite settlement in
Saskatchewan, see Alan B. Anderson, *Settling Saskatchewan* (Regina: University
of Regina Press, 2013), 128–30.

for the sale of Rupert's Land. Quite properly, they objected that, since the land was theirs, the money should be as well. Pisqua is reported to have pointed to company representatives at Fort Qu'Appelle during the Treaty 4 signing and saying, in Cree, "You told me that you had sold your land for 300,000 pounds. We want that."[118] They never received any part of the dominion's payments despite a far more solid and legal claim to the payments than the company ever had.

To make up for our slow progress from Val Marie, the next morning Hugh and I started early and walked fast. The morning was cool and the light diffuse, very unlike the heat of the previous week. We quickly put in twenty-one kilometres, the first sixteen on roads heading west and north. Once again white-tailed and mule deer sprang away as we walked. For the first time, there were also ragged lines of ducks and geese high above. Still fresh from the previous day's tutorial with Trevor, I managed to identify some eastern kingbirds that flitted away from ditches as we approached and one yellow-headed blackbird that bravely stood its ground. On the open prairie, we came across scattered pieces of a dead sheep, its red-soaked hide bound into the gristle and bone. This was a strange sight in country where sheep are not a usual livestock animal. Perhaps to underline why, not long after, we spotted a lone coyote loping carefully sideways to us across the rumpled sedge, tongue lolling.

Mid-afternoon turned sunny and hot. Hugh led the way through a pastureland shortcut, and by a large bison wallow boulder, before we crested the south bank of the vast Frenchman River valley.[119] From there, we descended several coulees toward our stop that evening at the Terry Jensen ranch. There the trail diverges from the continental divide. Instead of following brown, slow rivers like Wood River that

---

118 Rudy Wiebe, *Big Bear* (2008; reprinted, Toronto: Penguin, 2011), 55. Also see Robert J. Talbot, *Negotiating the Numbered Treaties: An Intellectual and Political Biography of Alexander Morris* (Saskatoon: Purich, 2009).

119 Thomson, "Lakota Place Names," 37, points out that the Frenchman River, also known as the Whitemud River, was called Coyote River by the Lakota, a name "which may have come from Lakota people's own experiences or memories from that place."

Walking the community pasture west of Val Marie, Saskatchewan, August 2, 2015. *Photo by James R. Page.*

lead east and north to Old Wives Lake, the trail turns to follow the Missouri River's upstream Frenchman River.[120] As we approached the ranch, we startled another coyote that must have been hanging around the yard; we found out later that the Jensen's farm dog had been maimed in an attack not long before.

I set my tent under some overgrown aspen at a distance from the ranch, one eye on thunderclouds forming to the west. They were quickly overhead. It rained hard for a few minutes, followed by a magnificent sun shower, rain flashing golden against the dark

---

120   For the glacial history of this divide, see Eric Clausen, "Wood River–Frenchman River Drainage Divide Area Landform Origins, Southern Saskatchewan Canada," 2011, https://geomorphologyresearch.com/2011/12/01/wood-river-frenchman -river-drainage-divide-area-landform-origins-southern-saskatchewan-canada/.

horizon. Finally, a deep golden luminosity flooded straight across the valley under the cloud cover. The sun's last rays lit the farmyard and the pasture just to our east. Under a bright rainbow, a small herd of horses played and galloped, chasing each other across a grassy field pearled with water droplets. At least for that moment, I wished that one of the professional photographers was still with us.

A SPIRITUALITY OF UNSETTLING

> Voice dancer pawâkan, the Guardian of Dreams and Visions, prayer, brings to you this gift. . . . The walk began before I was a seed. My mother strung my umbilical cord in my moccasins.
>
> —SKY DANCER LOUISE BERNICE HALFE[121]

THE TRUTH AND Reconciliation Commission was unusual for how much space it gave to spirituality. Throughout the reports, there was a valuation of the spiritual aspect of life that must have seemed odd, at least to any Canadians who stopped to consider it. Partly, this is explained by the commission addressing the role that Canadian churches played in setting up and running Indian residential schools. But the commission goes further: its statements imply, or perhaps better *assume*, that spirituality is part and parcel of what it means to be human and especially Indigenous.

Part of the violence perpetrated by the residential school system was that such "schools" were designed to separate Indigenous children not only from their languages and cultures (and far too often from their very lives) but also from the traditional beliefs inextricably bound up with those languages and cultures.[122] These prohibitions

---

121   Sky Dancer Louise Bernice Halfe, *Blue Marrow* (Regina: Coteau Books, 2004), 1.

122   For a chilling overview, see Charlie Angus, *Children of the Broken Treaty: Canada's Lost Promise and One Girl's Dream* (Regina: University of Regina Press, 2017).

were also forced onto the First Nations in what should have been their sovereign territories. From 1880 to the removal of the relevant clauses in 1950 (and despite treaties that say nothing of the sort), the *Indian Act* forbade the practice of many ceremonies, including the Potlatch, the Shaking Tent, the Thirst Dance/Sun Dance,[123] the Giving Away Dance,[124] and the Vision Quest.[125]

Under the *Indian Act*, many of the sacred items associated with these ceremonies were confiscated.[126] Thousands of irreplaceable religious items were lost or often stolen under the guise of "anthropology."[127] The Victorian age was an age of collecting, and Indigenous "artifacts" were a bonanza. In the James Morrow Walsh archives is a newspaper clipping of a letter to the editor publicly thanking Walsh for "genuine relics of Sitting Bull, the far-famed warrior," the relics now hanging in a Presbyterian manse.[128] In 1891, Isaac Cowie, under the direction of anthropologist Franz Boas, sent nêhiyaw items to the World's Fair in Chicago for display.[129] They were likely never returned. The relationship between "frontier-men" such as Cowie and the developing field of anthropology under individuals such

---

123   The 1906 official NWMP history calls the Sun Dance a "debasing and cruel" practice and does not mention the legal prohibition. See Chambers, *The North-West Mounted Police*, 42. But see also Ahenakew, *Voices of the Plains Cree*, 46–47.

124   See the description in Weekes, *The Last Buffalo Hunter*, 47–50.

125   Blair Stonechild, *The Knowledge Seeker: Embracing Indigenous Spirituality* (Regina: University of Regina Press, 2016), 109.

126   See Ahenakew, *Voices of the Plains Cree*, 94–95.

127   Bob Joseph, *21 Things You May not Know about the Indian Act: Helping Canadians Make Reconciliation with Indigenous Peoples a Reality* (Port Coquitlam, BC: Indigenous Relations, 2018), 49.

128   "Letter to the Editor," *Brockville Recorder*, clipping in the James Morrow Walsh archives, Glenbow Archives, CA ACU GBA F1869-S0001-FL0001 (M 8065, file 01.11b), 17.

129   Cowie, *The Company of Adventurers*, 295. Cowie also says that he was asked by the pioneering American anthropologist to "take measurements" of the North Saskatchewan River Peoples. He tells the story of meeting a man whom he had first run into twenty years earlier along the Swift Current Creek.

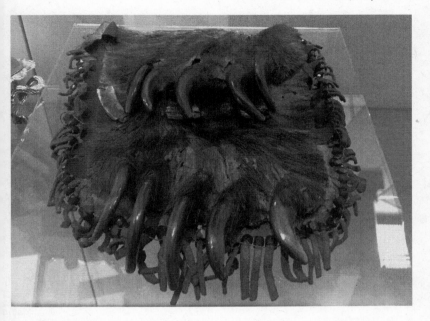

Plains "Indian" (nêhiyaw?) medicine pouch. After discovering this sacred
item in the Nottingham Castle Museum in the United Kingdom in 2018,
I was in touch with authorities at the Glenbow Museum, who promised
to seek its return to its rightful owners. *Photo by the author.*

as Boas and David Mandelbaum[130] is worthy of the study that it is
finally receiving.[131]

Indigenous delegation members visiting the Vatican in 2022
were aghast at how many Indigenous ceremonial objects are sitting
in Vatican museums or vaults. A medicine pouch that I came across
in Nottingham, England, is another such example. It is incredible to
think that European-background missionaries so attached to chalices

---

130   Wiebe, *Big Bear*, 200.

131   For a generally positive evaluation of the work of early anthropologists with
      Indigenous groups on the prairie, see Noel Dyck, "Cultures, Communities
      and Claims: Anthropology and Native Studies in Canada," *Canadian Ethnic
      Studies* 22, no. 3 (1990): 40. See also Brenda Macdougall, "Speaking of Metis:
      Reading Family Life into Colonial Records," *Ethnohistory* 61, no. 1 (2014): 28.

and robes, crosses and Bibles, could find it so easy to take sacred objects from others and fail to see the hypocrisy in it.[132]

BY THE END of our NWMP walk, we began most mornings with smudging, led by Richard. On later walks, Sharon Pasula, or Sky Dancer Louise Bernice Halfe and Peter Butt, also led us in smudging and in times of prayer. In their words, they acknowledged the Land. They also acknowledged the sacred relationship of the speaker—and of the others present, Indigenous and non-Indigenous—with all creation.

Those of us who are not Indigenous must re-examine, engage with, and challenge our own ideas of a split between sacred and secular, even as we engage with and support Indigenous spirituality. Behind the TRC Calls to Action was the implicit understanding that, in order to make restitution for the sins of the past, and in order to be proper treaty partners, we must engage in land restitution and recognition of sovereignty (there is no substitute for that) and understand that these actions are not only political and social but also constitute part of a *spiritual* healing. The Calls to Action invoke a spirituality that respects land and calls Canadians and their institutions to admit responsibility for past and present actions. As Blair Stonechild notes, "the more important principle of behaviour was the establishment of positive and respectful relations, not just with other humans but also with the spirit world and with other living things in Creation."[133]

Within that spirituality is a moral imperative that comes from honestly facing what Canadian colonial society has done and too

---

132 Matthew R. Anderson, "Strangers on the Land: What 'Settler-Aware' Biblical Studies Learns from Indigenous Methodologies," *Critical Theology* 1, no. 2 (2019): 10–14.

133 Stonechild, *The Knowledge Seeker*, 79.

often continues to do to First Nations, Métis, and Inuit Peoples.[134] A first step, as Eva Mackey has pointed out, is for those of us who are settler descended to see ourselves as living within a context of Indigenous sovereignty overall.[135] Such an honest assessment will result in Canadians pressing our own governments to live up to the agreements made, not only because it is legally necessary, but also because it is the right thing to do. It is healing.

When Hugh and I walked into the kilometres-wide gorge that is the Frenchman River, sometimes still called the Whitemud River in its western reaches,[136] it had been less than two months since the funeral for my mother. Knowing that I was to walk from Wood Mountain to the Cypress Hills, and especially that I would be walking along the Frenchman, my brother and sister and I had refused the box that the funeral home had wanted to sell us for her ashes. I had found a potter named Zach Dietrich, who worked with prairie clays. His studio sits along the service road on the outskirts of Moose Jaw. Zach confirmed that he did have clay from the Whitemud near Eastend, very close to where our mother grew up. Whitemud clay makes a very special kind of pottery, he told me. Yes, he had made urns before. He was happy to make one for us.

In June 2015, after a funeral in Swift Current, we buried the ashes of Shirley Yvonne Golling in Whitemud clay, at the cemetery by the turn of the Swift Current Creek. At the graveside, after placing the urn into the ground, our family, which had inherited much of

---

134   Aubrey Jean Hanson notes how often settler Canadians' desire for "recon-
       ciliation" masks a corresponding desire to forget the wrongs committed by
       settler governments, institutions, and individuals. See Aubrey Jean Hanson,
       Literatures, Communities, and Learning: Conversations with Indigenous Writers
       (Waterloo: Wilfrid Laurier University Press, 2020), 25.

135   Eva Mackey, *Unsettled Expectations: Uncertainty, Land and Settler Decolonization*
       (Winnipeg: Fernwood, 2016), 129.

136   The name Frenchman River might have gradually replaced the name Whitemud
       River to match the name Frenchman Creek used for the same river south of
       the American border.

its musicality from her, sang the old gospel songs that she loved as we shovelled in the earth.

My mother was a complex individual. She could be stubborn, opinionated, and argumentative. More often than not, however, she was kind, and it was this trait that came to the fore with the dementia that afflicted her for years before she died. She had been expelled from high school for "rebellious behaviour," had worked as a secretary in the office of Saskatchewan Premier Allan Blakeney, had been an early wave feminist in the Women's Division of the provincial NDP government, and had ended her working career as a greeter at Walmart. At her funeral, I said the following:

> Shirley married a boy from the neighbouring farm, Rob Anderson, who was, not coincidentally, the best friend of her cherished brother Carl. Like her, Rob was the youngest of eight children, he dashing, to her vivacious. They made a fine couple. But their mettle was tested almost immediately. Their first child, Kandace, was a happy young thing, playing on the farm. Their second child was also a girl, Karen. She was born with a hernia. The local doctors told Shirley and Rob that surgery to correct this condition was minor, and that they might as well proceed with it, so that little Karen could grow up to wear a bikini without embarrassment. When she was eight months old, Shirley and Rob took their little girl into the hospital in Shaunavon. They never saw her alive again. Karen died in surgery. In my opinion, neither of my parents ever fully recovered from that fateful decision and that terrible loss. My father retreated into his work and his solitude, and my mother into the long, deep grief of decades.

I never knew my sister Karen. Her grave is in the municipal cemetery on the hill just south of Shaunavon, not far from the Frenchman River valley. As a parent, I cannot imagine the grief of anyone who loses a child, especially after making such a decision. Years after our parents had divorced, we children would drive each

Harold Steppuhn, 2017. *Photo by the author.*

of them, independently, to the grave to place flowers. From their deathbeds, both of our parents expressed their desire to have some of their ashes scattered by the lonesome little grave. There is something about that place that has ownership of our family.

That evening, as storms rolled down the Frenchman River valley, Hugh and I were joined by others. The Greens returned with their horses. Harold, the lanky, seventy-nine-year-old hydrologist from Swift Current, also returned. This time he brought with him a 1970s aluminum-framed orange backpack. When pressed, he told us that it was his goal, day by day, to carry everything that he needed, including food, water, and shelter, on his back.

Don Bolen also arrived at our camp that evening. Don is the Catholic archbishop of Regina. He is a liberation theologian and a spare, slim, and friendly priest who talks quietly but passionately about poetry and social justice (it was Don who accompanied the Indigenous delegation to the Vatican in 2022). As a Lutheran pastor sometimes sent to ecumenical meetings, I had met him in meetings in Montreal and Toronto, and he had expressed interest in hearing of my plans for a prairie pilgrimage. He grew up in Gravelbourg and knew the territory around Shaunavon well. Unfortunately, his schedule that July allowed only two days of walking, and his arrival coincided with the first major rain. He had just enough time to set up his tent between downpours.

I managed to make a hot meal for myself. When the next shower hit, I sat sideways in the back of my brother's van, the raised back gate providing a roof, eating my tandoori and vegetables from the pot while I watched hard, fast pellets of water bounce off my tent fly.

All that night lightning and thunder rippled up and down the great valley. The Greens' horses were anxious, banging their trailer continually. Our tents were drenched. Hugh and I held an early morning consultation and decided to scrap our day's plans. It was one of the trail sections that he knew less well, and there was no road access to it. After nearly twenty millimetres of rain, the high grasses along the river would soak us. Any earth that we would cross would clump like huge weights on our boots. We were sodden and dispirited.

Fortunately, our planned stop that evening was a place with shelter—Valley View Bible Camp, a few kilometres away on a main highway. A rental group had just finished their family reunion. They were packing up as we arrived early to hang our wet tents and sleeping bags in the mess hall. More walkers showed up. Kathryn Scott, an educator and community worker in the Northwest Territories, had been a classmate of mine in high school, and she had walked the St. Olav Trail with me and others in Norway. She wanted to see what walking closer to home felt like. Since we had an unplanned rain day, I decided to drive the short distance into Shaunavon to visit my sister's grave. Don volunteered to come along.

The *Shaunavon Standard* of May 7, 1958, contained a brief notice under the title "Funeral Held for Infant." In part, it reads, "Karen Judy, eight-month old daughter of Mr. and Mrs. R.G. Anderson of Illerbrun, SK, died in Shaunavon Union Hospital, Tuesday, April 29th. Funeral services were held Friday, May 2."

Most of the graves at the Hillcrest Municipal Cemetery are marked with domed slabs of aging concrete. The slabs are topsy-turvy, tilting this way and that in the knotty earth. This is a truly prairie cemetery: there has been no attempt to create what would be an out-of-place suburban park with manicured lawns and flowers. Instead, the cemetery is a bare hilltop of prairie grasses with little tree cover, swept by winds from the west. Candace Savage writes that

> the special genius of the grassland ecosystem is its ability to ride the extremes of a midcontinental climate—a meteorological rollercoaster of blazing heat, brutal cold, sudden downpours, and decades-long droughts—by storing precious moisture and nutrients in the ground. As much as ninety percent of the biological activity in the grasslands takes place in the soil. When this life force puts up shoots, the vegetation may look meagre and stunted, but it is bursting with energy.... Transferred up the food chain, this vitality takes on animal form and becomes manifest in the blue of a butterfly, the bright eye of a snake, the eerie voice of a curlew echoing over a lonely landscape.[137]

On my last visit with my mother to the cemetery before she died, a small herd of bison watched us from behind a nearby fence while I guided her toward the spot. Outside the cemetery gate, a hawk hovered against the wind. For me, my mother's final years brought a kind of unexpected blessing. Her three-pack-a-day smoking habit left her with lungs that could barely bring in oxygen, resulting in a series of minor strokes that bit by bit took away her memory. Her second husband, Harold, did all he could to keep her at home, but eventually we children had to move her to the Swift Current Care Centre. In an irony typical of small towns, my mother had worked at the centre briefly. Some of those who ended up taking care of her in her final years had once been colleagues and welcomed her "home." By this time suffering from full dementia, she loved to sit by the nurses' station, where she could enjoy the commotion and sip the occasional beer that we would pour for her. From that spot, she could be wheeled outside for a smoke every now and then but still keep an eye on whatever else might be going on.

Although her mind slipped, her hearing never did. Our mother still made sharp, if not always contextual, comments, fixing whichever of us children were with her with a look of surprise, derision, or, increasingly, happiness. Her smile came back. The loss of memory was also a releasing of her inner regrets and grief. She stopped drinking and eventually smoking. As her memories faded, she came to the kind of peace that had so eluded her since the death of her second daughter.

Normally, I would have brought flowers for Karen's grave. That day in Shaunavon none were to be found. Don and I stood looking at the miniature grave of crumbling and slightly cracked concrete. For some reason (I know not what), it must have been the fashion in the 1950s to top the grave cement with crumbs of green and brown glass. The glass is still there, the edges of the concrete now orange with lichen. Dark grey clouds scudded overhead, and there was a fragrance rising from the wet earth.

"The prairie is full of bones," writes Sky Dancer Louise Bernice Halfe. "The bones stand and sing and I feel the weight of them as they guide my fingers on this page."[138] The last remnants of the storm were still moving through. I was about to turn to go when Don asked me if I normally said a prayer or something. "Yes," I answered, embarrassed. "We can do that together, if you like," he quietly suggested. So we each said a prayer and gave a blessing. I wondered what the mourners in 1958 would have thought of a brother not yet born, and a Catholic archbishop, giving a blessing to the grave so many decades later.

The next day the mud meant that we had to give up on trying to walk along the river and instead skip a leg of the Trail. We started from the road allowances just north of the valley. To the west and south, we could see Old Man on His Back Plateau, with the Frenchman River

138   Halfe, *Blue Marrow*, 2.

valley immediately to our backs. We should have waited, perhaps, another day to walk. Unfortunately, as Euro-Canadians have always been, in a country that doesn't respect such artificial deadlines, we were on a schedule. The roads were more dirt here than gravel. With almost every step, our boots brought up half a pound or more of sticky, grass-laced clay. Although the ditches were easier to walk, there we soaked ourselves in the tall grasses. Kilometre after kilometre, our group struggled until—sore-legged, wet, and cold—we finally crossed Highway 37. We were edging into the Rural Municipality of White Valley and up across the Whitemud River plateau, as shown in the Geological Survey maps from 1885.

It was country that I knew well because I had once married into it. From the valley's edge along the highway, I could see where my brother had worked one summer on an exploratory oil rig and where I had ridden a tractor with my then father-in-law. I was amazed then, and still am, at how, one lunchtime, on a break from harvesting, I witnessed my father-in-law and a neighbour conduct a sale of twenty-five thousand dollars' worth of farm machinery. What was amazing was how they did it on the shake of a hand, without either of them directly mentioning the piece of equipment.

Such an admirable custom works fine as a way of negotiating—if both partners of the deal have roughly similar access to power (money in this case) and if both understand the terms (one could say the cultural language, spoken and unspoken) of the other. Two farmers shake hands on a sale worth tens of thousands of dollars: such negotiations are successful only if both partners of the agreement understand what is at stake and are exercising what can sometimes be called "good faith." A deal on a handshake is a sign not only of trust but also of shared culture and goodwill. Such ease in dealing is probably also proof of a community that would punish, in its own way, either member of this arrangement who reneged on it.

None of these conditions, unfortunately, was true in the signing of Treaty 4 and Treaty 6. As Paulette Regan notes, "Morris and his fellow treaty negotiators, along with various Indian Affairs bureaucrats, . . . viewed treaty making simply as the legal mechanism required to access

Indigenous Lands for settlement purposes. In undertaking treaty negotiations, they went through the ceremonial motions required of them, but with no apparent understanding of, or appreciation for, . . . [Indigenous] sinews of diplomacy."[139] Treaties had never been for the extinguishment of title. That had never been the purpose, ever, in Indigenous history. Title itself was a foreign concept. Treaties were for making kin; their purpose was to make relations and share spaces for living: this was the way that Indigenous leaders saw it then and continued to see it.

If there was cultural misunderstanding in 1874 at Fort Qu'Appelle, and in 1876 at Fort Carlton, it was the government negotiators' misunderstanding of Indigenous conceptions of treaties, protocols, and sovereignty. Peter Erasmus, a witness of the Treaty 6 signing, makes the same point from the vantage of the nêhiyaw: "Our approach to the Governor's tent was delayed by certain ceremonial proceedings. . . . [L]et me say that these ceremonial practices had a deep significance to the tribes."[140]

Nor were the government negotiators true even to their own legal traditions. In the Treaty 7 documents are over eighty major mistakes in the names of the Indigenous signers, showing that the government translators "were not real Blackfoot speakers. The names of the Nakota chiefs, who spoke a Siouan language, were recorded in Cree."[141] Sheldon Krasowski, in his book *No Surrender*, underlines the point made by Regan and Erasmus by showing how the lack of a Pipe Ceremony for Treaty 4 negotiations at Fort Qu'Appelle in 1874 meant that the Indigenous parties to the treaty afterward considered the negotiations to remain open.[142]

---

139   Paulette Regan, *Unsettling the Settler Within: Indian Residential Schools, Truth Telling, and Reconciliation in Canada* (Vancouver: UBC Press, 2011), 158–59.

140   Erasmus, *Buffalo Days*, 240.

141   Sarah Carter, *Aboriginal People and Colonizers of Western Canada to 1900* (Toronto: University of Toronto Press, 1999), 125.

142   Sheldon Krasowski, *No Surrender: The Land Remains Indigenous* (Regina: University of Regina Press, 2019), 155.

Many now agree that the Crown never properly included or explained its understanding of the so-called surrender, or extinguishment of title, clauses. For the Indigenous Nations, the purpose of the treaties was to enter into reciprocal relationships; for the government (and the business interests behind it), it was to secure "extinguishment of Indigenous title" for the purposes of resource exploitation. The government representatives took part in "relation-making" ceremonies without, in fact, making relations.[143]

In light of the deliberate obfuscation and the omission of mention of the all-important "surrender clause" by government negotiators, Krasowski's conclusions are stark:

> By analyzing Treaties One through Seven as an interconnected whole, and arguing against the cultural misunderstanding thesis, I demonstrate that Indigenous Peoples did not surrender their land through the treaty process. Indigenous Chiefs agreed to share their land with settlers in exchange for treaty benefits offered by the Canadian government, including annuity payments, reserved lands, education, and assistance with the transition to agriculture. But they certainly did not surrender the land. It was to remain Indigenous.[144]

For those under the impression that the Indigenous Peoples might not have completely understood what Canadian government negotiators meant in the treaties, but signed them and are responsible nonetheless (the "cultural misunderstanding thesis"), both Regan and Krasowski join Indigenous commentators in noting the cultural misunderstandings that took place among the commissioners and the intentional duplicity of the government's treaty negotiators.[145]

If such a deal had occurred between the two farmers noted above, then it wouldn't have been a deal at all. It would have been a theft.

---

143   Harold Johnson, *Two Families: Treaty and Government*, Saskatoon: Purich Publishing, 2007, 25-27.

144   Krasowski, *No Surrender*, 2, 158.

145   Krasowski, *No Surrender*, 158. See also McIvor, *Standoff*, 110.

A PERSONAL RECONCILIATION

LATE THAT AFTERNOON we arrived at the farmyard of Curt and Lori Gronhovd. Our ranks changed yet again: Don Bolen left for Saskatoon, and Madonna Hamel arrived from Val Marie to join us for the balance of the walk to Fort Walsh. James Page had come as well; while in Val Marie, I had arranged with my remaining grant funding for the accomplished photographer to document some of our pilgrimage.

The truth was that I barely noticed the comings and goings: seeing Lori and Curt brought a flood of memories and being at their farmyard even more. I had been married over thirteen years to Curt's sister Wanda—she and I had dated in the last year of high school and married while barely into our twenties. I had not seen Curt and Lori, or the farm, in many years. Lori was still every bit as gracious and friendly as I remembered, and Curt was still the wiry, smiling stoic with the thoughtful comments.

They welcomed me with hugs. Soon we were sitting around the familiar kitchen table talking about our walk and—naturally enough for farmers—about the precipitation. I told them of some of the recent happenings with my kids, and they brought me up to date on theirs. Our group of pilgrims had fallen into a routine when talking to farmers. Hugh and Harold took the lead in conversations about crops, moisture, and the look of the fields that we had walked by. Being "the professor from Quebec," and a Lutheran pastor, I got involved in more personal topics and sometimes more sensitive ones: economics, government policies, history, religion, and Canada's dealings with First Nations.

Despite my personal history in that house, I had forgotten that one of Everett Baker's NWMPT posts stands only half a kilometre away, in the neighbouring farmyard that once belonged to another family whom I knew, the Aadlands. While we talked about the trail, Lori poured rhubarb wine from the Cypress Hills and told us not to bother with our rations; she had cooked enough lasagna for the group. My cousins Darlene and Ken, from a farm nearby, arrived to add freshly baked buns, ham, and potato salad to the feast. We chatted amiably long into the evening, the sky turning auburn while Hugh and Harold compared notes with our hosts.

When the party broke up, Curt took me aside: "Why bother with a tent?" he said. "Just stay here in the house." The divorce was ancient history. But it had not been easy on any of us. Nonetheless, they had opened their home to me. I fell asleep thankful at how acknowledgement of a difficult past, and the steps to move on from it, might come to all of us in ways that we don't expect.

The next morning there were homemade buns and sliced ham for our lunches. The sun had mostly dried the road. We set out west, then turned north on a dirt lane. Overnight I had received a message from Deanie Aadland in Edmonton. She had written a long email reminding me of how important the neighbouring farm was to her family and asking me if I would stop a moment and say a prayer as we passed Baker's post in their former yard. I did and caught up with the others just as we came to the next of Baker's posts, which happened to be beside White Valley Lutheran Church.[146] The little country church was unlocked. We went in, careful not to disturb anything. Kathryn Scott sat at the piano and played some old hymns from memory. The acoustics were great; soon Kathryn, Madonna, and I were trying to remember the words. Madonna has sung in professional bands and performed in one-woman shows. She has the actor's knack of being completely interested, and present, in whatever is happening at the moment. It was fun to hear her high soprano added to Kathryn's earthy alto and to add in my unpractised baritone. Hugh and Harold enjoyed the concert for a couple of minutes and then gently moved our trio out the door and back onto the route.

Westward from the white church, the land slopes downward toward a distant horizon. It was possible to walk far ahead and still be visible to the folks behind. Soon enough that is exactly what our group did. We stretched out over a kilometre or more. Finally, we came to a junction, where we caught up with each other and turned,

---

Anderson, *Settling Saskatchewan*, 315.

winding more steeply down into the Whitemud River valley. Near the trough of the valley were steep banks of Whitemud clay, still wet from the storm. As gravel trucks thundered past us on their way to a nearby pit, Madonna and I sank our hands into the banks of cool clay. I tried to imagine that this was the earth in which my mother had so recently been buried.

That night we camped in the Wade Duke farmyard, finding spots for our tents and for the gazebo in the tall grass between the farmstead's hedges. Our hosts were again hospitable, offering us their toilets and water to wash up and inviting us for cookies. A neighbour, hearing of the pilgrimage, came by in his half-ton. His rambling commentary, delivered out the truck window with the motor running, indicated something of the social gap starting to trouble some prairie villages, which these days are going through yet another kind of demographic and cultural change.

Val Marie and Eastend are both examples of a fairly recent trend—rural rehabilitation through an inflow of low-income artists and other former city dwellers who can no longer afford to live in overpriced urban areas.[147] I had enjoyed Diane Chabros's mural art in Val Marie, spoken at Prairie Wind and Silver Sage, and stayed at the Convent Inn, all revitalization initiatives helped in part by "new" people moving to the village. Similarly, Eastend has a thriving artistic community and the Stegner House artistic retreat, in addition to potters and painters, the ranks of local artists increasingly supplemented by those who have moved in from elsewhere.

There can be tensions initially between the locals and low-wage artists who leave the city and come to the country for cheaper living or greater flexibility, people such as Madonna and James. This is true particularly when such folks bring with them their city habits and expectations. "These artists," the farmer said, cocking his hat as if what he was about to say was a confidence between him and me, then scratching his head, "these artists and writers and

---

147   See Lyz Crane, "Artists as Revitalization Agents," *Communities and Banking* 22, no. 3 (2011): 11.

such. They move in here, and they just don't understand. You play a little joke on them, and they go off and call the police."

Because of the recent rain, and because we were in the valley, that night the insects were fierce. I fell asleep plugging my ears against clouds of mosquitoes whining around the tent entrance. Farther away the coyotes started their yapping, making sure that we would not miss our usual evening lullaby.

EASTEND

THE DUKE FAMILY dog must have liked us. The next morning when we set out, he trailed us for kilometres across the flats. We tried to get him to go home, until finally an annoyed Wade arrived on an all-terrain vehicle to fetch him. As we climbed back out of the Whitemud River valley, the smell of sage again became prominent. The path intersected more and more rings—circles of stone that had once held down the edges of a nêhiyaw, or Nakota, or perhaps Niisitapi lodge tent. At first, discovering a ring had been so new and exciting that we would call our discoveries out to each other. By day thirteen, we had seen so many rings that I found myself not bothering to walk the few steps to a hilltop to check, certain that I would find evidence of habitation on almost every elevated spot. Indicative of the possible numbers is Claire Thomson, who points out in her short article on Lakota history on these territories that winter camps were chosen only if they had enough wood for approximately five months and for three to four hundred lodges.[148]

In *A World We Have Lost*, Bill Waiser includes an aerial photograph taken after the first snowfall in the Cabri Hills, about 160 kilometres north of where we were that day.[149] The photograph underlines the truth of what we were discovering: the prairie is anything but empty. One can see outlined against the dusting of snow in the aerial photo that the ground in that area is remarkably

---

148   Thomson, "Lakota Place Names," 38.
149   Waiser, *A World We Have Lost*, 72.

crowded with overlapping stone circles, evidence of dense habitation over millennia. The first Europeans to settle on the prairie used words such as *bleak, empty,* and *untouched* to describe the land, when the more accurate word would have been *emptied.* Clifford Sifton, an early Canadian immigration minister who aggressively pushed settlement in this region, printed posters that advertised the prairie to prospective farmers throughout Europe as "virgin territory" (reinforcing yet again the masculine trope of domination of a frontier). Travellers still see southern Saskatchewan as fly-over country, speeding away the kilometres east or west along the Trans-Canada Highway or passing overhead at thousands of metres. To do so is to buy in uncritically to the myths that, while walking slowly across the land, what our eyes showed us simply was not true. Many people have lived here. For millennia, Indigenous families and Nations have made it home. Ironically, the land is far emptier now, post-settlement, than it ever used to be.

For colonization to occur, a territory *must* be empty—the emptier the better so as to rewrite it with the occupiers' history.[150] But actually to believe, in the twenty-first century, that the prairie was ever empty is to ignore the depopulations that occurred with European-brought disease, the starvation and death that accompanied the wanton destruction of the bison, and the forced removal of Indigenous groups onto reserved lands. We Canadians are finally realizing that our self-satisfaction is hypocritical. We might pride ourselves on a history that avoided American-style armed violence against Indigenous populations, but Canada has not been "Canada the good" with Indigenous Peoples. The truth is that Canadians avoided only outright warfare (and then not always, as 1885 illustrates) because successive Canadian governments and bureaucrats waited for disease and starvation to do their dirty work.

As we followed cattle paths along the river and over the arms of the plateau, we came across not only many lodge rings but also

---

150   Andy den Otter, *Civilizing the Wilderness: Culture and Nature in Pre-Confederation Canada and Rupert's Land* (Edmonton: University of Alberta Press, 2012), 24.

a group of stones arranged in a turtle effigy, where we were led in silence and prayer. One of Baker's posts stands not far away; I like to think that Baker knew the turtle was there. We kept ascending and descending the valley, sticking relatively close to the Frenchman/ Whitemud River through patches of wolf willow. After we crossed yet another fence, we stumbled across a large flock of sheep. Two sheepdogs lay sleeping in the middle of the bunched animals. They awoke only when the sheep, mistakenly thinking that we were driving them, began pouring through a ragged hole in a nearby fence. Surprised at the turn of events, we tried to keep our distance. But the damage was done. The ranchers no doubt had their work cut out that evening bringing the flock home.

The afternoon was so hot that the only relief we could find was a metre or less of shadow cast by the large bales that we occasionally passed. In those moments, we pressed our backs against the prickly straw, our legs sticking out into the sunlight. Thankfully, carrying enough water for the day was no longer such a problem. By this point, we had an accompanying car that would meet us from time to time to fill our canteens and water bladders.

Mid-afternoon we climbed over a rise and saw our first views of the Cypress Hills, blue and hazy in the distance. Eastend was not far across the plain, a dozen kilometres or so. Our plan, however, was to angle northwest, following the posts to Chimney Coulee. We would camp near the one-time Cowie trading site, Métis settlement, and NWMP post and proceed into town the following day.

Hugh and I were walking down a newly cut gravel road, chatting, when my phone rang. The sound shocked me. After a week and a half, I had forgotten that my phone was even on; I was keeping it charged only to use as a camera and for evening messaging. As I stopped to take the call, I happened to look down. There, at the end of my boot, was an arrowhead. The protocol normally would be to leave such an object undisturbed where it lies. But because it had been scooped somewhere in a gravel pit, and dumped out of context on this new road, I was able to examine it. It was not an unusual or a particularly old arrowhead. But I still treasure it as a memory of our journey. In her article on pilgrimage in the ancient Mediterranean, Jenn Cianca notes that one of the first documented Christian pilgrims, Egeria, "refers numerous times to the gift[s] of *eulogiae* (gifts of blessed objects) that she and her fellow travellers [were] given" as a sign of their pilgrimage.[151] I had been given a *eulogia*.

When we finally arrived in the shade of Chimney Coulee's cottonwoods and trembling aspens, our group was in fine spirits. We decided not to head into town for restaurant food. James had brought a dish of fresh beans from Val Marie, and we each added something to the meal. We ate and sang and visited into the evening, enjoying the fragrant smells and birdcalls of the prairie coulee. As darkness descended, owls swooped through the trees. I spent time looking up, marvelling at how little of the night sky one can see in Montreal. The stars hung low, and the sandy reef of the Milky Way stretched from one horizon nearly to the other. On his journeys along the Qu'Appelle Valley, Norman Henderson fairly preached the virtues of a prairie night sky: "Drunk with wealth and noise, we forget God's gift of silent stars—yet who at end of life could defend this disregard before the Lord of Earth and Heaven?"[152] That evening the coyotes sounded closer than ever.

The next morning George Tsougrianis arrived at Chimney Coulee, along with Stew and Cyndi Tasche, who had also driven out for the day. George is an amiable, spare, and hard-working film-maker—he shot and produced the award-winning documentary in 2022 on James R. Page and the Grasslands National Park titled *Wild Prairie Man*. George is one of those people who rarely stops moving. For most of that morning, he filmed us: jumping into and out of his car to get close-ups and walking footage, and driving ahead for long-distance shots, while James took wildlife photos closer by.

151   Jenn Cianca, "Written by the Body: Early Christian Pilgrims as Sacred Place-makers," *International Journal of Religious Tourism and Pilgrimage* 7, no. 1 (2019): 16.

152   Henderson, *Rediscovering the Prairies*, 119.

Stew grew up in Eastend and has an intense personal interest in the Cypress Hills and in sharing the history of that region, including its Indigenous history. Both he and his wife are artists— Stew a producer of musicals, Cyndi an accomplished painter. Stew was the driving force behind *The Cypress Hills Would Never Be the Same*, a musical featuring an original script and score, acting by locals, live music, and a storyline that both celebrates local history and subverts the usual pioneer accounts by including nêhiyaw, Niisitapi, and Nakota storylines.

Since we were road-walking that day, and it was extremely hot, we were thankful that the distance to town was shorter than our usual daily distance. For the sake of a view, we turned off the road before town and sat for a few minutes on a hill overlooking Eastend. "There used to be only one house there," Stew pointed to the closest part of town. "And no trees." We watched the poplars by the river sway in the breeze. Eventually, we skidded and stepped down a cattle trail through shale and cactus. Although there was a bridge not far away, we decided to cross into Eastend by fording the shallow creek, then passing up through the bull rushes into the town, mud clumping to our boots.

Like Val Marie, Eastend has seen an influx of artists in recent years. Unlike some other prairie villages, Eastend seems to have developed quite successful alliances between long-time locals and newcomers. Whereas Val Marie can boast the nearby Grasslands National Park, Eastend has not only the Stegner House arts and writing retreat (named for the writer Wallace Stegner) but also the T.rex Discovery Centre. There, among other fossils, one can see Scotty, the largest complete *Tyrannosaurus rex* skeleton in the world.

When we arrived, there was a boil-water advisory. I stopped by Whitemud Foods, the local grocery store, to buy water for the last few days of our walk. At the cashier, two elderly women were peering out the window and discussing the sign on the side of Hugh's van.

"Saskatchewan History and . . . something," one of them was saying to the other. "I can't quite make it out."

"Folklore," I told them. "It's Folklore."

Unfazed, they asked me if I was with a government agency.

"No," I responded.

They nodded.

"I'm with a group that just walked into town," I continued. "We walked from Wood Mountain."

They seemed to be less impressed than confused. "Good for you, I think," said one of the women.

In the local motel, the bed was too soft compared with my normal camping mat. I tossed and turned and didn't manage to sleep until the small hours. When I saw Harold at Jack's Café the next morning, he informed me that he'd had the same problem. He'd ended up setting up his tent at midnight in the local campground and sleeping there despite having booked and paid for a room.

At Jack's Diner for breakfast, Max and Barb Mirau slid into the booth beside me. I didn't recognize them, but Max told me that they were friends with my father. They asked about him and promised to visit him in the nursing home the next time they passed through Herbert. Over eggs and bacon, Max regaled me with stories of my dad's time on the Swift Current police force, in the 1960s.

As the day went on, more familiar faces arrived, registering for a full day of Saskatchewan History and Folklore Society presentations. My brother and sister-in-law came from Regina, politely overlooking the dried layers of mud and grime on their van. Kristin Catherwood from SaskCulture was there, along with a colleague from the National Film Board, who showed a short movie about the prairie. Simone Hengen, an educator from Regina, had come to walk with us; she told us how a curriculum on the treaties was now becoming mandatory in Saskatchewan classrooms. My cousin and aunt from Swift Current drove down, and friends Gwenanne and Allen Jorgenson from Waterloo, Ontario, arrived mid-afternoon, having flown out with their camping gear to join in the final segment.[153]

---

153   Allen later wrote about this time of walking in Jorgenson, *Indigenous and Christian Perspectives*.

It was a reunion for Kathryn, Gwenanne, Allen, and me. We had walked the St. Olav Way from Dovrefjell to Trondheim, Norway, in 2013, the first Scandinavian-background Canadians to do so as a group.[154] Walking the St. Olav Way had been instructive. When I had walked through Norway with other Scandinavian-background Canadians, I'd been surprised that I *hadn't* felt like I belonged there. I took that as a sign that the mountains and fjords of my father's parents were more important to my past than to my present. As beautiful and awe-inspiring as the Norwegian mountains were, they did not speak to my heart like poplars lining a prairie coulee.[155]

That night the SHFS hosted a banquet and presentation at Jack's Cafe. Candace Savage was the guest speaker. She drew a good crowd and talked about her book *A Geography of Blood*, and about the historic and ongoing injustices against Indigenous groups, who nonetheless continue to find new vitality politically and artistically. Afterward, she stood under one of the few streetlamps and chatted with us while we all swatted at mosquitoes.

Candace has links to Nekaneet First Nation,[156] other than Wood Mountain the only First Nation close to the trail. Both Wood Mountain Lakota First Nation and Nekaneet First Nation can be called "resistance reserves." Both were formed by those who refused to leave years after the main groups of Lakota at Wood Mountain, and nêhiyaw/Nakota at the Cypress Hills, were forced from where they had been promised land. Wood Mountain Lakota

---

154 Matthew Anderson, "Walking to Be Some Body: Desire and Diaspora on the St-Olaf Way," *International Journal of Religious Tourism and Pilgrimage* 7, no. 1 (2019): 62–76; Jorgenson, *Indigenous and Christian Perspectives*, 71.

155 See Raymond Aldred and Matthew R. Anderson, *Our Home and Treaty Land: Walking Our Creation Story* (Kelowna: Wood Lake Books, 2022), 119–21.

156 *Nekaneet* is a word formed by the omission of the first syllable of *kâ-nîkânît*, which means "Leader" or "Foremost Man," the name of the nêhiyaw Chief who headed the group in the late nineteenth century. See Jean L. Okimâsis, "As Plain(s) as the Ear Can Hear," in *Plain Speaking: Essays on Aboriginal Peoples and the Prairie*, ed. Patrick Douaud and Bruce Dawson (Regina: Canadian Plains Research Center, 2002), 29.

First Nation was made a "temporary" reserve in 1910 and finally granted official status in 1930.[157] Nekaneet First Nation was made a reserve in 1913, but compensation for land promised and never given didn't happen until 1992.[158] Both First Nations were reluctantly recognized by Canadian governments when, after decades, refugees and resisters simply wouldn't go away.

Hugh had tried to contact the Nekaneet without success. Richard had contacted Nekaneet through nêhiyaw friends in Regina, but his links were stronger with other groups. We started the walk knowing that we would have some time with the Wood Mountain Lakota but without any plan to visit the Nekaneet. It was disappointing. However, expecting a First Nation to automatically host us would only have been to repeat the all-too-familiar demands of colonizing cultures. Our task as a group made up primarily of settler-descended Canadians was to educate ourselves, to connect with the land and its history in ways that might help us to be better dialogue partners with Indigenous Peoples, and to publicize the trail as a way of reminding other Canadians about a past that's been suppressed. Not to automatically expect Indigenous hospitality.

We chatted with Candace long into the evening. I mustered the courage to tell her how her book about the Cypress Hills had affected and inspired me. To my delight, she signed my copy. Late that night Hugh, Madonna, and I sat on lawn chairs in the middle of the empty motel parking lot and talked quietly about history, the new group of walkers, and (for some reason that I no longer remember) maritime TV shows. Around midnight, a white-tailed deer edged around the corner of the building just yards away, hooves clicking on the asphalt. When one of us made a slight noise adjusting a chair, it raised its head and looked at us with unconcern, then moved on.

157 Anderson, *Settling Saskatchewan*, 31.
158 Savage, *A Geography of Blood*, 163.

TO CYPRESS LAKE

> *The disappearance of the Buffalo has left them not only*
> *without food, but also without Robes, moccasins and*
> *adequate Tents or "Teppees" to shield them from the*
> *inclemency of the impending winter. Few of their lodges*
> *are of Buffalo hide, the majority being of cotton only, many*
> *of these in the most rotten and dilapidated condition....*
> *[This is] a terribly insufficient protection against the wind,*
> *frost and snow of the severe winter of this exposed region....*
> *It would indeed be difficult to exaggerate ... the urgent*
> *necessity which exists for some prompt and sufficient*
> *provision being made for them by the Government....*
> *[U]nless speedy and adequate measures are taken ... the*
> *results will be disastrous and even appalling.*

—DR. AUGUSTUS JUKES, NWMP PHYSICIAN[159]

> *It must be recollected that Dr. Jukes has not had much*
> *experience with Indians.*

—EDGAR DEWDNEY[160]

THE NEXT MORNING we were again a large group. It was sad that, after so much glorious prairie shortgrass, the first day's journey for so many new pilgrims was spent walking on gravel roads. There was a more scenic, treed path along the Eastend reservoir, but walking on the road helped us to stick close by the old trail and Baker's posts. Having had a day and a half off, and because my feet were starting to flatten and expand, I found myself facing familiar walking challenges.

---

159   Augustus Jukes to Edgar Dewdney, October 21, 1882, Library and Archives
       Canada [hereafter LAC], RG 10 C-10134, vol. 3744, file 19506-2.
160   Edgar Dewdney to John A. Macdonald, October 21, 1882, LAC, RG 10, reel
       C-10131, vol. 3744, file 19506-2.

For any long-distance walker, these are issues common whether one is walking the Meseta or Moose Jaw: swollen toenails, chafing heels, forgetting the sunscreen.

Once again the day was brutally hot. Except for vapour trails, the sky was empty. The horizon was empty of *anything*, even fencing, the only sounds muted conversations and our boots on the gravel. Kathryn had had the good sense to bring a parasol. She chatted while she strolled, the most comfortable of any of us; I have always admired the easy and generous way that she moves through the world. I was thankful that Richard had left me his Australian hat. But I was aware that he would soon be back and need it.

When we finally arrived at the abandoned farmyard that Hugh had arranged for our tent sites that evening, there was a problem: it didn't seem to be abandoned. A new truck sat outside a house that clearly had been recently renovated. No one was home, but our phones showed a wifi network. We conferred and decided to set up our tents in a thicket of overgrown poplars, aspens, and caraganas about a kilometre north. There we tramped down the long grasses, their scent and that of clover sticking to our legs. The evening turned into one of those gloriously long, russet sunsets for which the Prairies are famous. I made a large pot of curried beef stew from my rations. Our new group of pilgrims watched the light linger while crickets sang and nighthawks dove.

When we set up our tents, we had to choose between sides of a barbed-wire fence. We decided on the north side. When I stuck out my head from my tent the next morning, I realized that we had been fortunate: four very large bulls were watching our tents from the south side of the barbed wire.

After that surprise, we set out for another day of trekking. First it was back down into the last arm of the Whitemud River valley, an expanse that opened before us like a walker's dream. Hugh informed us that it was the Dry Coulee Grazing Co-op, a pasture pooled into a commons by a group of ranchers, the type of arrangement that Trevor Herriot and other prairie conservationists advocate because it better preserves prairie habitat.

We were walking into ranching country. On the undisturbed grass, we came across at least a dozen lodge rings. Skulls of old bulls leered at us from the earth, horns curling around toward their eye sockets. Once I walked by a double line of stones that looked like it might mark a grave. Some plains funerary rites took place on elevated stands,[161] whereas other sites—such as a large cemetery near Swift Current, with burials for at least two thousand years—demonstrate that interments were also common.

As had happened near Pinto Horse Butte, with such a wide expanse of prairie grass and no clear markers, our group slowly spread out. Hugh had said to head west. "Eventually, you'll hit a rail line," he'd told us. "That'll be the southwest line—a private branch used by locals. Turn left there." We were to follow it south, where Hugh had told us that it would eventually lead to the Lois and Roland Lacelle farmyard.

Unfortunately, on the open prairie, one loses track of both time and distance. We kept walking and walking. A Swainson's hawk circled above. I remembered what a farmer had said in Val Marie: "The gophers gone means the hawks went away. Used to be so many gophers they had patches on them. Some kind of sickness. Now they're gone."

At some point, we realized that Hugh and Simone, who had been walking more slowly, were no longer behind us. We skidded down a steep, scrabbly hill of river stones and cactus and emerged onto a muddy alkali plain. Had Hugh told us about this? No one seemed to remember anything about the reservoir that we now saw to the north. We kept it to our right, following a beaten-down fenceline along a dank irrigation ditch, our noses full of a sour alkali smell. Eventually, confused, we conferred. We were still heading west, but was it the right path? Either Hugh and Simone were lost (unlikely), there had been some kind of accident and they were delayed (less unlikely), or we ourselves had strayed (most likely). As had been the case throughout most of the trail, there was no mobile phone

---

161   Ahenakew, *Voices of the Plains Cree*, 43.

coverage. At least we were a group of four: if we were lost, then we were lost together.

Then we heard a shout. Far ahead and on a ridge to the south, two tiny figures waved. Hugh and Simone had decided to take a shortcut and walk straight across the hills. We followed the irrigation ditch in their direction until we were intercepted by curious horses. They took no interest in the celery that I offered but stood still for tufts of grass from Gwenanne, a farmgirl. Soon we were all reunited at the Lacelle farm, where we were greeted with fresh water and cookies. As we sat around their kitchen table, Lois informed us that she was from Simmie. That was my family's home village: I had driven grain into the Simmie elevator with my mother, had walked, hunting, with my father and my uncle through many of its coulees. Lois and I knew people in common. But most of our mutual acquaintances were the old folks, long passed. "Yes, it's sad," Lois commented, "so much has changed. All those communities are gone now." The Lacelle yard was well organized, its lawn edging and hedges immaculate. We were fortunate to have soft grass on which to pitch our tents.

That evening we drove down an empty Highway 13 to Robsart, a hamlet billed in Saskatchewan tourist literature as "a real-live ghost town." Apparently, no one had mentioned the ghost town advertising to the young family whom we met. While three children chased their dog down the broken wooden sidewalk, their father watched a football game on a TV that he had brought outside their trailer. "We moved here because it's cheap," the young man told us. "And look at the million-dollar view!" He was right. The sun was beginning another long, red-hued descent toward the distant purple humps of the Cypress Hills.

Robsart boasts spectacular abandoned buildings—the Beaver Lumber store, the Community Club, and the remains of what in its day must have been an elegant two-storey home. But it was no more a ghost town than hundreds of other prairie hamlets no longer the lively communities that they were in the 1930s to 1960s. All failed when roads became better and economic changes took away rail lines and favoured large, mechanized grain farms with few workers instead of the smaller, mixed farms and denser populations of the early to mid-twentieth century.

Robsart reminded me of Simmie. Older than I was, Lois remembered Simmie as a lively village, its hotel full, cars and trucks lined up in winter, their motors idling to keep the children warm while the adults visited. She remembered the Simmie general store where I used to get dime candy and the Lutheran church where I preached my first sermon. Simmie, like Robsart, was another hamlet disintegrating in an economic eddy as prairie society changed, its past marked by the yearbooks shelved in nursing homes and basements across Saskatchewan.

I once met an American who had driven down the highway after his arrival in Saskatchewan expecting to have coffee in one town on the map and lunch in another. He was surprised that so many of the names on the map were, as he put it, "not really there." "Why are these towns still on the map?" he asked me. "Because people want them to be," I answered. He was unsatisfied, but I believe that I spoke the truth. Yet, when one thinks of "place" and "space," does holding on to the name of a hamlet that has mostly disappeared actually keep the place alive, in the Cresswellian sense?

As Indigenous writers such as Chelsea Vowel have pointed out,[162] rural depopulation that began in earnest in the Prairies in the late 1950s[163] plays havoc with the very notion of "settler." Indigenous prairie groups have remained on the land vastly longer than the so-called settlers, so many of whose children and grandchildren, like me, migrated away again. The other demographic change that is increasingly obvious is that Indigenous birth rates have generally led to a younger, more dynamic Indigenous population across the Prairies. Indigenous groups make up an increasingly important minority of the prairie population, both numerically and culturally.[164]

---

162   Chelsea Vowel, *Indigenous Writes: A Guide to First Nations, Métis, and Inuit Issues in Canada*, The Debwe Series (Winnipeg: HighWater, 2016), 163.

163   John Herd Thompson, *Forging the Prairie West* (Toronto: Oxford University Press, 1998), 178. See also Anderson, *Settling Saskatchewan*, 387.

164   Thompson, *Forging the Prairie West*, 180.

In Robsart, I took photos by an old split-windshield Ford half-ton that reminded me of the trucks in which my uncles taught me to drive. We toured the "ghost town" until it was time to return to our camp at the Lacelle's farm. The next morning, to our delight, Lois had cooked a breakfast of bacon and eggs to share with us. We spent most of the day walking along roads, passing fields of ripe durum wheat, barley, and dry-smelling hay. Both Hugh and I had been doing various radio and local newspaper interviews as we walked. That afternoon was my first interview in French. It went well enough, but I found it tough work. The others laughed when I emerged drenched with sweat from the truck where I had taken refuge from the wind for the interview.

That day Richard was driving out to rejoin us, and Kathryn was with us her last day before heading back north. Kathryn and Allen and I walked together for kilometres, singing every old jazz standard or gospel song that we could think of, our feet falling naturally into rhythm. We had done the same through Norway, a terrain as mountainous as that day's walk to Cypress Lake was flat.

Certain songs just seem to have the cadence for walking. In his memoirs of prairie travel, Norbert Welsh remembers how the Métis traders also sang as they went along: "On their long trips westward . . . the leader of the brigade lifted his voice. . . . Instantly the tune rang down the long, swaying line of carts, and straightaway, the musical voices of the prairie voyageurs drowned the doleful wailing of the Red River carts."[165] Kathryn and I were singing "This Is My Father's World," with its optimistic line "all nature sings and 'round me rings, the music of the spheres," when we startled crows scavenging the corpse of a dead coyote. "Hmm," commented Allen, who teaches theology at Martin Luther University College. "That's part of God's world too."

That evening we arrived at the east end of Cypress Lake, a place both horrific and holy. As with so many other places along the trail, my memories of Cypress Lake stand in sharp contrast to what I later

---

165   Weekes, *The Last Buffalo Hunter*, 175.

learned of its Indigenous history. The twentieth-century reservoir is larger than the lake was during Welsh's bison-hunting days. As a child, I fished in Cypress Lake with my family. I remember our fifty-five-horse Johnson outboard motor cutting through the water as we sped back and forth looking for the best places for pickerel and pike. I remember how sparse the trees seemed to be along the shoreline. Already in his journals of 1871–72, Cowie had noted the unprotected nature of the terrain around the lake.[166]

I had no idea of Cypress Lake's terrible past. It was only when I read Savage's *A Geography of Blood*, about the winters of starvation in the 1870s, that I personally experienced how remembering the past can change who we are in the present. Hugh, like me, had read Savage's book. In March 2015, he wrote in an email to me, "I hadn't realized that Cypress Lake existed back in the 'terrible times.' I always thought that it was created by installing a dam on the Frenchman in the 1920s or '30s. You had indicated an overnight stop there during the trek, and I wasn't sure why. In light of my new awareness, I think it is important to do so."

When we arrived after our twenty-two-kilometre day of walking, the wind had calmed, and the lake sat still as glass. A small group of black-clothed Hutterite Brethren men were fishing from the dock. The air hummed with insects; in the shallows, I could see minnows and a dragonfly nymph, and blue damselflies flitted over the mirrored water. It was spectrally quiet, and the small campground was nearly empty. Richard put down tobacco. We took turns at the lake's edge, talking about history and inevitably about present-day government policies and Canadian attitudes.

Noga Collins-Kreiner, a scholar of pilgrimage, has explored the meaning of what she termed "dark pilgrimages" to places of death, horror, or disaster.[167] Among such pilgrimage destinations are the 9/11 monument in New York, Holocaust memorials, and, for young

---

166   Cowie, *The Company of Adventurers*, 433.

167   Noga Collins-Kreiner, "Dark Tourism As/Is Pilgrimage," *Current Issues in Tourism* 19, no. 12 (2016): 1185–89.

Australians, the Gallipoli site in Turkey. Jim Miller, who started the Dakota 38 horse and walking trek in the northern United States, did so in response to a vision that told him to commemorate the thirty-eight Dakota men executed in the largest mass hanging in American history, by the government of Abraham Lincoln.[168]

Cypress Lake would certainly qualify as such a place in Canadian history if more non-Indigenous people actually knew its story. The arrival of the CPR line in Maple Creek in the first months of 1883 coincided with a series of callous, sometimes criminal, misdeeds by government representatives and several years of famine following the final collapse of the bison herds. The famine of the early 1880s was exacerbated by government policy that actually cut relief when it was most needed. Its effects were made more severe by officials, led by Dewdney, more worried about speculating on property, profiting from contracts, and ensuring their political survival than saving lives.[169]

These men helped to create a perfect storm of human misery. Indigenous groups that had already signed the numbered treaties, many of which had taken land farther north, had been forced by hunger, and the provision of poor or no agricultural equipment, to return to the prairie to seek bison that were no longer there. Dewdney played a high-stakes and deadly balancing act with their lives. He turned a blind eye to groups moving south of the border to hunt because it meant less relief on the reserves and more money for his coffers. Yet he kept watch lest these disgruntled groups of hunters return north and join Mistahimaskwa (Big Bear) at the Cypress Hills in his holdout for more just conditions.[170] At this point, fully half of the population that had signed the treaties were not on reserve lands even if they had been on the reserves earlier. The main reason was

---

168   The movie *Dakota 38*, about the pilgrimage, can be watched in full at https://youtu.be/1pX6FBSUyQI.

169   Daschuk, *Clearing the Plains*, 122.

170   E. Brian Titley, *The Frontier World of Edgar Dewdney* (Vancouver: UBC Press, 1999), 47.

their search for food, even though one of the clearest provisions of the treaties had been famine relief.[171]

Food had become the blunt instrument of government policy. Through government inaction, the Cypress Hills became an epicentre of starvation. The overburdened post at Fort Walsh had become a de facto refugee camp. In early 1882, Dewdney reported that about thirty-five hundred Indigenous people were in the Cypress Hills, not including the thousands more who had moved south of the border temporarily, to seek bison unsuccessfully along the Missouri River, and who could be expected on their return to congregate at Fort Walsh seeking emergency rations.[172]

The solution? One would think that it would have been to provide food, which the government was capable of doing and obliged by treaty to offer. Instead, Dewdney recommended closing the fort with its relief supplies completely so that the "greater Indian nation" that Mistahimaskwa envisioned as the best means for Indigenous survival did not become a reality.[173] Dewdney argued that, if a cluster of reserves formed near the Cypress Hills, then it would interfere with government plans to open the south of the province to settler farmers. He gambled that the loss of life would not spark central Canadian outrage and that eventually hunger would force the remaining nêhiyaw and Nakota to move north and east again. In the meantime, Cypress Lake became a hunger camp and a place of starvation and death.[174]

"Within a year, 5,000 people were expelled from the Cypress Hills," notes Daschuk.[175] Perhaps even Dewdney had had enough of death; in 1881, he had petitioned the prime minister, unsuccessfully, to appoint him to the Senate and allow him to leave the prairie. Prime Minister Macdonald would have none of it. He double-appointed

---

171   D. Aidan McQuillan, "Creation of Indian Reserves on the Canadian Prairies 1870–1885," *Geographical Review* 70, no. 4 (1980): 385.

172   McQuillan, "Creation of Indian Reserves," 385.

173   Titley, *The Frontier World*, 47.

174   Savage, *A Geography of Blood*, 145.

175   Daschuk, *Clearing the Plains*, 123.

Dewdney, adding the responsibility of being lieutenant-governor of the North-West Territories.[176]

This was also a tipping point in the role of the North West Mounted Police. Instead of acting as occasional allies of the First Nations against the Americans, beginning in 1882 and with the expulsion of Mistahimaskwa and Payepot from the Cypress Hills, the police were increasingly used as armed guards. Their job was first to make sure that the people were placed onto reserves and then to keep them there. Cecil Denny, who had been part of the March West, retired from the force in 1882. He was immediately appointed by Dewdney as the Indian Agent in Fort Walsh and tasked him with closing it. In contrast to the pages and pages of his memoirs devoted to the earlier trek, and to his "glorious" NWMP adventures, his comments about Fort Walsh say much by being so brief: "I succeeded after tedious negotiations," Denny noted, "in persuading them to move to their different reserves, the Crees to the north and the Assiniboines to the east."[177]

For me and others of our group, the stop at Cypress Lake became penitential. As Trevor Herriot reminds prairie Canadians, "the work of atonement . . . stands before all prairie people."[178] Ray Aldred says that, "when you journey on the land, you're remembering your ancestors, and you're thinking about your grandchildren. This is why you do this."[179] Those ancestors spoke loudly at Cypress Lake. The failure of the Canadian side of the treaties never seemed to be more true than at the site of the Cypress Lake hunger camp.[180] There many of the nêhiyaw ancestors had starved and frozen to death,

---

176   Titley, *The Frontier World*, 48.

177   Denny, *The Law Marches West*, 170. On accusations against Denny of "arrogance, ignorance, drinking and womanizing," see Titley, *The Frontier World*, 50. For an Indigenous perspective on the expulsion from the Cypress Hills, see Abel Watetch, *Payepot and His People* (Regina: Canadian Plains Research Center, 2007), 8–9.

178   Herriot, *Towards a Prairie Atonement*, 80.

179   Aldred and Anderson, *Our Home and Treaty Land*, 8.

180   Savage, *A Geography of Blood*, 145.

and my cultural forebears—Dewdney, Denny, and the Canadian government—had made their unbearable plight far worse, doing little to nothing except profiting from it. It was a solemn evening despite the brightness that lingered over the lake.

That night hard gusts of wind rattled the exposed flats, shaking our tents. The next morning there was heavy dew on the fly. Richard led us into a hollow by the beach and attempted to lead a smudge. Whether the sweetgrass was too green, or the site would not allow it, the smudge would not take. Instead, we sat in a circle on the sand, sheltered by the bank, while Richard led a blessing. I looked at the tufts of overhanging grass and thought about Inspector Walsh, who had written about the groups then at Wood Mountain: "Following this want of food, and the eating of diseased horses, an epidemic appeared, which marked its results by the many graves now seen. . . . The conduct of those starving and destitute people, their patient endurance, their sympathy, and the extent to which they assisted each other, their strict observance of law and order, would reflect upon the most civilized community."[181] It was on July 1, 1880, that Dr. John Kittson of the North West Mounted Police wrote in anger about the insufficient rations provided (at Fort Macleod) during that time: "Gaunt men and women with hungry eyes were seen everywhere seeking or begging for a mouthful of food, little children were ever on the look out for the small barrels to dredge out the solid part and fight over the 'tid-bits'; morning and evening many of them would come to me and beg the very bones left by the dogs in my yards."[182]

That morning, after the others left, I stood by the shore for some time watching minnows skitter over the sandy bottom. I wondered if the reason that we were not taught these stories growing up was simply because they might have spoiled our fishing.

---

181   Daschuk, *Clearing the Plains*, 118.

182   "John Kittson to N.T. Macleod, Indian Agent, July 1, 1880," in Report from D[r]. Kittson of the Northwest Mounted Police Stationed at Fort Macleod, Concerning the Insufficiency of the Rations Issued to the Indians in the Northwest Territories, LAC, RG 10, vol. 3726, reel C-10126, file 24811, Mikan 2059165.

RIGHT: Twelve-year-old Mistatim Awâsis (Horsechild) and twenty-six-year-old William Bleasdell Cameron, 1885. *Photo courtesy of the Saskatoon Public Library (PH-87-100).*

BELOW: Indigenous walkers on one of the Saskatchewan History and Folklore Society excursions to the Cypress Hills, 2020. *Photographer unknown.*

THE FRONTIER ADVENTURE GENRE

IT'S IRONIC THAT for the frontier "hero" to play the solitary cowboy he so badly needs other people. Canadian tales of the frontier, such as Cameron's *Blood Red the Sun* or Cowie's *The Company of Adventurers*, were set inevitably against an exotic Indigenous backdrop. (With typical dark humour, Thomas King says that there were only three options open to Indigenous characters in settler depictions: "the bloodthirsty savage, the noble savage, and the dying savage."[183]) The term "frontier" itself is inescapably colonialist: it implies an "inside" that wants to expand and a dangerous "outside" that must be conquered. Whether the travels of Marco Polo to the east or those of Christopher Columbus or Jacques Cartier to the west, frontier stories are always told for the benefit of empire's insiders—the audience "back home."

Without Indigenous Peoples to help colour their frontier tales, Cameron, Cowie, and others on the prairie were just small-time employees of a distant company, cogs in the machinery of a system that valued profit more highly than life. Yet, if you had asked them, they might have said that they were men "made by the frontier." Their books certainly give this impression.

In fact, whatever reputations these men enjoyed, they owed a lot to the Indigenous individuals and groups that they met. Men who had already established their reputations did not generally go to the frontier. Dewdney, Denny, and others were what postcolonial theorist Homi Bhabha called "mimic men."[184] Whatever else they might have been, most were hustlers, men on the make: entrepreneurs of their own fortunes and reputations who leveraged their frontier experiences to gain wealth and respectability back in their home societies.

In 1885, Cameron dressed himself for a photo with Mistatim Awâsis (Horsechild), the twelve-year-old son of nêhiyaw leader Mistahimaskwa (Big Bear). The photo was taken in Regina during

---

183 King, *The Inconvenient Indian*, 34.

184 Homi Bhabha, "Of Mimicry and Man: The Ambivalence of Colonial Discourse," *October* 28 (1984): 128.

the trial of Mistahimaskwa and others.[185] I have set it alongside a photo from the Saskatchewan History and Folklore Society's 2020 walk, in the Cypress Hills, to contrast Cameron's posed photo with an example of real, uncaricatured, and contemporary Indigenous presence on the prairie.

In *Settler Colonialism*, Lorenzo Veracini states that settler colonialists typically seek two overlapping goals. The first is to suppress local Indigenous populations (through disease, starvation, imprisonment, or other means of pushing them off their lands). The second is more subtle. We see it clearly in the photo of Cameron as a cowboy: it is for the settler to perform his own indigeneity.[186] This self-performed indigeneity is where "frontier adventure" really came, and comes, into its own.

In the seventeenth century, Kelsey adopted several literary clichés in his journals that set the tone for later frontier writings: (1) the story revolves around a solitary hero, white and male (the Scotsman didn't know how to travel by himself across the vast territories southwest of Hudson Bay, but he makes it sound as if he did); (2) he presents the wilderness not as home but as other, a dangerous place, one to be tamed; and (3) the narrative lists his "sufferings," the trials and tribulations that he had to overcome, including the unfaithfulness of the "Indians," before his safe return.

De La Vérendrye, the Americans Lewis and Clark, and HBC workers Henday, Smith, and Waggoner, among others, wrote similar recollections.[187] Additionally, there is a small collection of Canadian settler autobiographies dealing with the crucial decades of the 1870s and 1880s on the prairie. They include the accounts of Isaac Cowie,[188]

---

185 Remarkably (and showing the "entanglements" typical of colonialism), there is another photo of Cameron and Mistatim Awâsis taken sixty-two years later, in 1947. See https://digital.scaa.sk.ca/ourlegacy/permalink/28301.

186 Lorenzo Veracini, *Settler Colonialism: A Theoretical Overview*, Cambridge Imperial and Post-Colonial Studies Series (Houndmills, UK: Palgrave Macmillan, 2010), 95.

187 See Waiser, *A World We Have Lost*, chapters 4 and 5.

188 Cowie, *The Company of Adventurers*.

Cecil Denny,[189] Henry Halpin,[190] William Bleasdell Cameron,[191] and John McDougall.[192]

Prior to walking from Wood Mountain to Cypress Hills in 2015, I had never heard of any of these books. Although the ideal western Canadian hero was white, Anglo-Celtic, and Protestant, three of my four grandparents spoke a language other than English. As a bookish and socially awkward kid, I wasn't attracted to the violent, repressive, and bravado masculinity performed in these cowboy accounts. I preferred science fiction to westerns.

At the same time, and despite their faults, some of the frontier writers occasionally slip, indicating what they really thought. Even while rendering his Métis compatriots in fantastic and lurid detail, Cowie writes about settlers owing them "a debt that can never be repaid."[193] Similarly, in the midst of casting himself as a typical cowboy, or ranger-style hero, Cameron nonetheless summarizes the crushing disintegration of pre-settlement prairie society as resulting from "the white man's . . . cupidity and looseness and contempt."[194] Both men put the blame for the demise of the bison herds squarely on the newly arrived Euro-Canadians and Americans.

Yet, even at their most sympathetic, both writers lament a time that they say is no more and a people who, in their narratives, seem to be doomed to disappear. Dallas Hunt echoes Thomas King: "In the archives of settler nation-states like Canada," she writes,

---

189   Denny, *The Law Marches West.*

190   David Elliott, *Adventures in the West: Henry Ross Halpin, Fur Trader and Indian Agent* (Toronto: Natural Heritage Books, 2008).

191   William Bleasdell Cameron, *Blood Red the Sun* (1927; reprinted, Calgary: Kenway Publishing, 1970).

192   John McDougall, *George Millward McDougall: The Pioneer, Patriot and Missionary* (Toronto: W. Briggs, 1888); John McDougall, *On Western Trails in the Early Seventies: Frontier Life in the Canadian North-West* (Toronto: W. Briggs, 1911); John McDougall, *Pathfinding on Plain and Prairie: Stirring Scenes of Life in the Canadian North-West* (Toronto: W. Briggs, 1898).

193   Cowie, *The Company of Adventurers*, 29.

194   Cameron, *Blood Red the Sun*, 191.

"Indigenous peoples are often . . . presented as always already disappearing from the landscape."[195] In accounts such as Cowie's and Cameron's, Indigenous people are used as props and quickly ushered backstage when they no longer spotlight some heroic trait of the Euro-Canadian protagonist. Not coincidentally, the collapse of the mythological "old west" and its people was not tragic for the hero, whose stories thus became even more valuable, since they defined a bygone, never-to-be-reproduced age. Contemporary Indigenous Peoples trouble Canadian history precisely because they offer alternative narratives.

Duncan Campbell Scott was an early-twentieth-century bureaucrat and poet who claimed that he liked working for Indian Affairs because it wasn't an onerous job, and it allowed him time for his writing.[196] Scott was one of the commissioners who negotiated Treaty 9. He has become as infamous for his post at Indian Affairs as he was once famous for his poetry. His poems idealized the "noble savage" while his day job involved eradicating the same people whom he so romantically pictured.[197] In 1920, he wrote that "our objective is to continue until there is not an Indian that has not been absorbed into the body politic, and there is no Indian question, and no Indian department."[198]

To call Scott a racist pure and simple, however, would be to miss the subtler, *structural* racism wrapped in a seemingly generous, but ultimately suffocating, Canadian nationalism. Scott could and did advocate forcefully on behalf of Indigenous individuals. He strongly critiqued those who took advantage of people on reserves. Yet all the while (like Pierre Trudeau and Jean Chrétien much later) Scott imagined the dissolution of Indigenous Peoples and the assimilation of their identities into the larger, British- and French-led, population. Taiaiake Alfred writes that "framing indig-

195 Hunt, "Nikîkîwân," 26.
196 Angus, *Children of the Broken Treaty*, 12.
197 For more on Scott, see Angus, *Children of the Broken Treaty*, 5–12.
198 See Joseph, *21 Things*, 8.

enous people in the past as 'noble yet doomed' relics of an earlier age allows the colonial state to maintain its own legitimacy by preventing the fact of contemporary indigenous peoples' nationhood to intrude on its own mythology."[199] Put another way, "Indians" of the past can be romanticized and forgotten; contemporary First Nations have real sovereignty, real cultures, real money owed to them, and real treaty demands.[200]

As far as I can remember, my parents and most of my adult relatives did not speak ill of Indigenous Peoples or use the terrible stereotypes with which Canadians so often miseducated their children, the kinds of attitudes that David Robertson discusses in *Black Water*.[201] Instead, I grew up with a prejudice toward Indigenous groups that might seem to be more benign but certainly is not: I grew up with the mistaken notion that they were *gone*.

My brother and I usually spent a week or two of our childhood summers working on the family farm. I remember a few occasions when my uncles came in for lunch with an arrowhead or a stone hammer found while out moving the cattle. The items were always treated with deference. I recall sitting around the table as these arrowheads or stone hammers were shown and discussed. I was told that I should respect them because they were from the people who had once been on the land. It says something about both the very parochial nature of the area and time in which I grew up, and my own childish ignorance, that the underlying impression that I was left with as a child was that, like the ancient Egyptians of the Bible,

---

199   Taiaiake Alfred, *Peace, Power, Righteousness: An Indigenous Manifesto*, 2nd ed. (Oxford: Oxford University Press, 2008), 83.

200   The prairie writer Wallace Stegner is a good example of such romanticism: "I wish I could have known it [Indigenous history] early, that it could have come to me with the smell of life about it instead of the smell of books, for there was the stuff of an epic there, and still is for anyone who knows it right." Stegner, *Wolf Willow*, 112. On the problems of his romanticized account of the history of the prairie region, see Savage, *A Geography of Blood*, 60–65.

201   David A. Robertson, *Black Water: Family, Legacy, and Blood Memory* (Toronto: HarperCollins, 2020), 179ff.

the Indigenous Peoples of my corner of Saskatchewan, although memorable, had disappeared forever.

The problem was that *no one asked what had happened to them or where they had gone.* Nor did I ask these difficult questions. Only as an adult, and only because of the resistance and the blossoming culture of their descendants, did I come to realize that avoiding such questions was our family's way of covering over the deep and unconscious guilt of taking something that was another's. Only as an adult did I find out that there had been what James Daschuk—based upon overwhelming evidence—terms an "ethnic cleansing" of the plains.[202] It took place on the same Cypress Hills where I loved to camp with my family.

The tools of that cleansing were mass starvation and false promises. They included a prime minister who signed treaties guaranteeing Indigenous sovereignty and agreeing to give Indigenous leaders their choice of location, only to stand in Parliament on March 24, 1882, and promise Canadians that there would be "no Indians left" between the railway and the American border.[203] This was precisely the area of my patrimony.

Whether or not they were conscious of it, the fact that my parents and my uncles and aunts did not address questions of "where are they now?" was because the land that I thought of as our family's heritage had been taken, violently and dishonestly. Meanwhile, the descendants were and are demanding that the treaties be honoured. Raymond Aldred, for instance, writes that "Canadians are finally beginning to educate themselves about how the Treaties were broken, from the beginning, by the governments who signed them, and about the true story of how they are ongoing, practical, and political documents of kinship-making."[204]

In recent years, I have been struck by how the basic ingredients of a pilgrimage are similar to four things that many Indigenous

202   Daschuk, *Clearing the Plains*, 123; McQuillan, "Creation of Indian Reserves," 385.
203   Daschuk, *Clearing the Plains*, 123.
204   Aldred and Anderson, *Our Home and Treaty Land*, 48.

writers identify as important simply to being human: land, relations, spirituality, and stories.[205] Unfortunately, the way that we Canadians have tended to write our history respects none of them well. There has been far too much emphasis on the "me" in the story, a selfish or idealistic idea of place, and almost no thought given to remembering relations established by treaty, much less any idea that the treaties were in any sense "sacred."

A brief self-locational statement here: I realize that the stories of our prairie walks could be understood as yet another example of the "frontier adventure" genre. I hope that by paying attention to all my relations, to the community nature of our walks, to integration with the Land rather than mastery of it, and to the good that writing might bring to various communities I can avoid this. I also attempt to highlight as much as possible, in a Canadian account, the methodologies and research of Indigenous scholars.[206]

"The contemporary Canadian writer," notes Laura Smyth Groening, "is caught in an ironic situation, because of her or his irreconcilably conflicted feelings about Canada's ambiguous past."[207] I certainly believe that my grandparents were courageous people. Yet I have learned about the horrendous clearing of the plains that prepared their arrival, and about the ongoing police actions in the twenty-first century against Indigenous groups, supposedly on my behalf as a Canadian. This continues to happen when nations such as the Wet'suwet'en are simply exercising their sovereignty, often against commercial agents of economic "development" not so different from the economic forces that caused such suffering a century and a half ago.

So how should we Canadians now think about who we are on this land? Kiera Ladner states that what is necessary for Canadians

---

205   Aldred and Anderson, *Our Home and Treaty Land*, 30.

206   See Sharanya, "A Manifesto to Decolonise Walking," *Performance Research* 22, no. 3 (2017): 85–88.

207   Laura Smyth Groening, *Listening to Old Woman Speak: Natives and AlterNatives in Canadian Literature* (Montreal and Kingston: McGill-Queen's University Press, 2004), 108.

"is a political project. It is a social project. It is a legal project. It is a historical project. It is a language project . . . of being and becoming—a project allowing all peoples and all nations to exist, while determining how it is that we live together on these Indigenous lands."[208] Denise Nadeau critiques reconciliation as a "very fuzzy concept and one that often serves to maintain the status quo," and she suggests that respectful coexistence might be another way to think about the goal of settler self-education.[209] Aldred believes that all people on this land must adopt certain Indigenous values yet not lose their separate identities.[210] For his part, David Garneau points out that the very concept of reconciliation falsely posits a once-existing harmony. He notes that "the present Reconciliation narrative should be recast as a continued struggle for conciliation rather than for the restoration of something lost (that never quite was)."[211]

If there is a way out of our identity ambiguity, then it should begin by recognizing that some uncomfortable, action-inducing truths must come before reconciliation and that reconciliation, if and when one can even discuss it, will consist of much more than the "limited-liability guilt-management" gestures currently being practised.[212] The past cannot be forgotten just because it reflects badly on us. In the same way, the future must be a future in which what it means to be Canadian has fundamentally changed.

---

208   Kiera Ladner, "Proceed with Caution: Reflections on Resurgence and Rec-
      onciliation," in *Resurgence and Reconciliation: Indigenous-Settler Relations and
      Earth Teachings*, ed. Michael Asch, John Borrows, and James Tully (Toronto:
      University of Toronto Press, 2018), 246.

209   Denise M. Nadeau, *Unsettling Spirit: A Journey into Decolonization* (Montreal
      and Kingston: McGill-Queen's University Press, 2020), 259.

210   Aldred and Anderson, *Our Home and Treaty Land*, 129–31.

211   David Garneau, "Imaginary Spaces of Conciliation and Reconciliation,"
      in *Arts of Engagement: Taking Aesthetic Action in and beyond the Truth and
      Reconciliation Commission of Canada*, ed. Dylan Robinson and Keavy Martin,
      21–41, Indigenous Studies Series (Waterloo: Wilfrid Laurier University Press,
      2016), 32.

212   Roger Epp, *We Are All Treaty People* (Edmonton: University of Alberta Press,
      2008), 123.

Horses and lodge ring at the Cypress Hills, 2015.
Photo by Madonna Hamel.

Walking hardly solves such systemic and generational problems. But it can be one of those small ways in which we can start. By walking, our group was attempting to pay attention. By consciously retracing traditional trails, we tried to offer an alternative to the usual Canadian story of how to interact with the land. We Canadians have to be content being uncomfortable and unsettled for some time yet. We need to spend some time feeling an unhomeness, willing not know to exactly who we are, while we embrace the treaties and find our origin stories where they truly belong.[213]

---

213   Aldred and Anderson, *Our Home and Treaty Land*, 121–23.

CYPRESS LAKE TO FORT WALSH

> *The cascade of ecological destruction that began with the removal of the buffalo and the buffalo-hunting economy, and continued with the tearing up of the prairie and the suppression of fire, has left the remaining islands of native grass vulnerable to a chain of cause and effect that has altered everything from the microcosm of soil biota to the macrocosm of weather patterns under climate change.*

—TREVOR HERRIOT[214]

AS WE CONTINUED our route, we stuck close to the south side of Cypress Lake. The walking was easy, and we passed through pasturelands fragrant with late summer's yarrow, prairie onion, and bluestem. At the west end of the lake stood a solitary tree. It contained an eagle's nest but no eagle. After crossing a fence, we hiked upward and over more rumpled terrain toward Cottonwood Creek and Cottonwood Coulee.

On the hills, we discovered more lodge rings. I saw something white poking up from the earth and eventually managed to dislodge it with my boot. It turned out to be a piece of Medalta pottery. I remembered my mother and aunts having items made by this prairie factory. There wasn't an old farmstead in sight, and I wondered at the mystery behind this orphaned piece.

From a nearby hill, a group of horses watched our arrival at the Cottonwood Coulee ranch. After we set up our tents, Clinton Brost took us upstream, deep into the poplars, to the site of the NWMP post established over a century ago. As we stood at the remains of the post, a giant stag watched our group intently from a hundred metres away. I struggled to find my camera. By the time I had retrieved it, he was gone.

---

214   Herriot, *Towards a Prairie Atonement*, 85.

The Brosts were friendly but busy. After our tour, we returned to our tents to find that the horses, which run relatively free in that part of the country, were busy nibbling at the peg ropes. "Keep an eye on them," Clinton warned. "There was some guy from the city here a year ago. He lost all the mouldings on his car. The horses chewed 'em right off—and it was a rental!" He laughed hard at that. After Clinton left, we agreed that we should park our vehicles inside his yard.

The next morning we were to walk up and over the edge of the central block of the Cypress Hills escarpment, from the Brost ranch to the Lou and Roger Parsonage spread. Like other ranchers in the area, the Parsonages were some of the first Euro-Americans to settle this part of the country. Like the nêhiyaw, Nakota, and Anihšinápēk before them, they were dismayed at the flood of people that followed. The attitude is still there: "If there's one thing I can't stand," said one cattleman to me during our walk, "it's a farmer." I never asked him where Montrealers might place on his list.

The Cypress Hills were sacred to Indigenous groups, who for that reason did not settle permanently in them but shared them as a kind of international boundary.[215] Yet by the 1880s some ranches had already been established in the Cypress Hills area, building upon the herds that the North West Mounted Police had kept at Walsh.[216] In his memoirs, Erasmus notes that, when he was sent by the government to try to persuade Mistahimaskwa to go to a northern reserve (a commission from which he resigned because of the hunger that he witnessed), he ate an unusual meal: "True, I ate buffalo meat at Big Bear's camp in the Cypress Hills," he wrote. "But it tasted a great deal like beef—so much so that I didn't consider it polite to inquire too closely as to its source."[217] During the years of starvation at the Cypress Hills, likely motivated both by

---

215   Aldred, "A Shared Narrative," 202; see also Aldred and Anderson, *Our Home and Treaty Land*, 108.

216   Stegner, *Wolf Willow*, 133.

217   Erasmus, *Buffalo Days*, 268, 301.

humanitarian concerns and by poaching, settler ranchers offered the government their cattle at cost to feed the starving nêhiyaw and Nakota. The offer was refused by Dewdney. No one knows why, but he had financial links to the Montana firm of I.G. Baker that supplied meat at a substantial markup to the government.[218] Had Dewdney accepted the ranchers' offer, it would have saved lives. But it also would have undercut their—and his—profits.

There is no simple story in remembering settlement and no turning back the clock on some of the changes that occurred. As both Herriot and Savage have pointed out, ranching is often better than farming for climate change because it tends to better respect the native grasses and soils that constitute such effective carbon sinks. This is especially true when ranchers join together to herd cattle in a large common pasture of prairie grass.[219]

The next morning I left the Brosts early. While the others finished their breakfasts, I spent an hour by a nearby makeshift corral watching a young woman tame a horse. Horse taming is mesmerizing. The horse was on a rope, trotting quickly and nervously in circles around the inside of the enclosure. Its ears were back, its head high, its front hooves occasionally coming off the grass. With one hand on the rope, the other on a woollen blanket, the tamer kept talking in a low voice, she the pivot to the horse's constant motion. As I watched, she began to swat the horse's buttocks and flanks with the blanket. Round and round the horse ran—hundreds of times around the circle. Patiently, with each revolution, the trainer kept the blanket on the horse's back just a little longer.

My mother's brother, my uncle Carl, "broke" horses—as they used to say—for his neighbours. I remember seeing the animals out in the corral by the tall aspen and Manitoba maples that my grandparents had planted. They were wild, bucking ponies. My mother's father

---

218 Daschuk, *Clearing the Plains*, 115.

219 Henderson, *Rediscovering the Prairies*, 111, is somewhat less enamoured of cattle pastures, having had to endure both nervous cattle and dangerously hidden barbed wire on his journeys by canoe and travois.

would tease us kids: "If you're not good, you'll have to go out there and ride that one after supper!" In the months before he died, my father often wanted to talk about his first horse, the one that would go out on the trapline with him. He told me how the horse had never had a rider, and how he kept leaning against its flanks every day a bit longer, giving more of his weight each time, until one day he was riding it.

I watched the tamer's patient interactions with the horse as long as I could, then joined the others as they passed on their way up into the hills. It was a day of prairie walking through sage mixed with some of the usual grasses: western wheatgrass, blue grama grasses, spear grass, prairie wool, and needle-and-thread. By lunchtime, we'd come across more lodge rings than we could count. This was hard evidence, in stone, of the importance of the Cypress Hills to the prairie First Nations and stark witness of their contemporary absence—apart from the Nekaneet—from their lands.[220]

Without cell phone coverage, and kilometres from vehicles, we did not know, and could not have realized, that Environment Canada had issued an extreme weather warning for the furrowed hills and draws that we were traversing that day. It was reporting possible tornadoes around Robsart.

When we climbed onto the Cypress Hills plateau, it became extremely windy. I stopped to take a photograph. The wind lifted my baseball cap, and within seconds it was fifty metres away, rolling into the distance like a prairie thistle. There, on top of the escarpment, we found ourselves on a treeless plain, glowering black thunderclouds bunching to the west. Again there were lodge rings everywhere. We had stopped to take a look at one particular rock formation and were wondering if it might be a turtle effigy when a herd of horses came galloping from the north, turned, and circled at high speed around the edge of the horizon behind us. Madonna was trailing our group of walkers and hadn't noticed the horses. I can still picture

---

220   In a promising development, First Nations have recently begun purchasing land near the Cypress Hills once more.

the moment when she decided to go back and look at one particular circle of stones and to her surprise came face to face with a dozen of the regal creatures, standing against the dark sky. She wrote to me later that this was a transformational and spiritual moment for her.

There was a bolt of lightning and a long roll of thunder, and the horses wheeled away, headed at a high gallop toward the valley and shelter. We had no such speed or luck. Unfortunately, at that point, we seemed to be the tallest objects on the horizon. Allen and Gwenanne had gone ahead. They returned to report that they had found a shallow draw. It was not deep enough to be a real coulee. But it offered a bit of shelter, perhaps three and a half metres in depth. We filed in and discussed whether, if the lightning got close, it would be better to spread out and whether we should sit, or crouch, or how best to manage. I hadn't noticed cattle around. But when the storm hit, we certainly heard them: every crack of thunder was followed by frightened bellowing from somewhere nearby.

We crouched and waited out the hard, pelting rain and the roaring thunder. We were fortunate. The storm blew through relatively quickly. Apart from being soaked in the chilling wind that followed, we were okay.

That evening was our last before reaching Fort Walsh. The last (or first) of Baker's posts stood near the Parsonage ranch. We met more horses roaming the hills. When eventually an all-terrain vehicle appeared, Roger Parsonage got off to welcome us and to tell us that we could set up our tents near the lee wall of one of his corrals. Richard and Allen and I tried to string tarps against the boards to give our tents a break from the now ever-present gales. Harold had walked from Fort Walsh to meet us, again carrying everything in his old orange backpack. He passed on news of the tornado and told us that the temperature was forecast to fall to just above zero, colder where we were, on account of the altitude. I thought about the times when it had snowed in August in Saskatchewan.

As it turned out, there was no snow. However, the night was extremely cold, windy, and uncomfortable. Just before daybreak, I left the tent and warmed up in my brother's van with Gwenanne, Allen,

Richard, and Madonna, all of us drinking hot drinks and awaiting sunrise. We were wearing every item of clothing that we had brought just to keep warm. As the sun came up, we watched Harold emerge from the thin plastic tube that he used as his tent (open at both ends). The seventy-nine year old set up a camp stove and—squatting on the frozen ground—made coffee, then stood to drink it. It should have come as no surprise when, a few days later, Harold mentioned that in his early life in the United States he'd been a ranger.

Just after breakfast, Roger dropped by. It was only nine in the morning, but he already had a Colts cigarillo between his teeth. His voice was low and so quiet that I could barely understand what he was saying unless I stood right in front of him. When I did, I was surprised at how passionately he talked about the land, about not tearing it up for agriculture, and about preserving its past.

Parsonage might have looked like the Marlboro man, but his words were about ecology and preservation. "You know," Richard said to me as we walked around the ranch, "he kind of reminds me of an Elder. He talks like an Elder. He even looks a bit like one." Richard scratched his head. "I dunno," he said almost to himself, "maybe the Land makes Elders when there's no one else around."

As we were packing our tents to leave, Roger asked Hugh, "Would you like to see the house?" Hugh had no idea what he meant or what we were about to witness. Out of politeness, he agreed. It turned out that "the house" that Roger wanted to show us was where he'd grown up, now empty, but a building that he was keeping in shape to safeguard memories of the earliest ranching days. At the door, he took his cigarillo out of his mouth. For a minute, he glanced this way and that, clearly trying to figure out what to do with it. Apparently, taking a lit cigar into the house of his parents was not what one did, even after they were long dead. Then, with a look of slight irritation, he spit into his palm and ground the cigar out in it.

After the tour, we finished packing up, said our goodbyes, and started for Walsh. Our final day's trail was not long; it was to take us uphill along what is called locally "the gap" (about twelve hundred metres above sea level) to the northeast. We planned to pass the

intersection with Four-Mile Coulee, where in the 1870s there was a
Métis settlement of some sixty families.[221] From there, it was a short,
sharp descent to Battle Creek and finally along the creek valley to the
historic fort. Dave and Esther Green met us on horseback when we
reached the ridge. They had come from Fort Walsh to accompany
us the final few kilometres.

Norbert Welsh talked about finishing a Métis hunt and meeting
James Walsh in 1875 close to where we met the Greens:

> I put up a house for the winter in what was called the Four-
> Mile Coulee. The Indians called it Wa-pa-tou-nis-ou-see-
> peesis. . . . One day we were busy baling and packing our
> meat when three red coats rode up. One of them stepped up
> and spoke to me in English, asked me if there was anyone in
> the brigade who could speak English. . . . He told me that he
> wanted two interpreters, one that could speak English and
> French, and one that could speak English and Blackfoot. I
> told them I could get them for him. Then I told him that my
> name was Norbert Welsh. "I'm Major Walsh so we might
> be related," he replied.[222]

For the first time in hundreds of kilometres, we were entering
a very different ecological zone. The Cypress Hills have plants and
animals reminiscent of the Rocky Mountain foothills. We were now
in a lodgepole pine woodland (the reason for the lodgepole name
had become obvious to me after so many lodge rings, although I
had never associated the tree name with the tent dwellings before
the walk). When we descended again to Battle Creek, we entered
woods of white spruce.[223] Animal life in the hills is also unique. Even
though grizzly bears have long been hunted out, the park is a place

221   Norbert Welsh talks about building part of the settlement there in Weekes,
     The Last Buffalo Hunter, 84–85.
222   Weekes, *The Last Buffalo Hunter*, 84.
223   Padbury, Acton, and Stushnoff, *Ecoregions of Saskatchewan*, 175.

where you often encounter moose or elk—until recently one of the only places on the prairie where this was so.

It is approximately 280 kilometres between Fort Walsh and Wood Mountain along the trail as Baker and the volunteers of the early 1960s marked it.[224] Unlike the Métis and the North West Mounted Police, we were obliged to walk the edges of fields that the trail goes straight through so as not to disturb the crops—cropped fields aren't easy to walk in any case. As a result, according to Hugh's calculations, by "squaring the corners" so often, we had walked about 350 kilometres by the time we reached Fort Walsh. It seemed to be a bit surreal finally to be arriving at our destination. Dave and Esther rode ahead to alert the staff at the fort. We walked slowly along the last bit of Battle Creek to allow the red-coated summer workers time to assemble outside the walls. As was common by this time, several interested horses also showed up as onlookers.

The red-suited "North West Mounted Police" (Parks Canada interpretive staff in costume) awaited our approach. On arrival, we all shook hands solemnly. I had no idea what we were supposed to do next. Hugh had the papers given to us in Wood Mountain. He handed them to the "officer in charge." This seemed to be a good thing, but afterward we all simply stood around again, unsure of what should come next. Both Hugh and I had arranged for photographers for our arrival, and they were busy snapping photos. As we smiled for the cameras, Hugh suggested to the "officer" that, since he and I had been "commissioned" at Wood Mountain by the Royal Canadian Mounted Police, we should now be "decommissioned."

"I've never decommissioned anyone before," laughed the interpretive staff person. He scratched his forehead under his white plastic helmet. "I'm not sure how to do it." Then, seeing that we were waiting, he sighed and did something with his hand that looked oddly like the sign of the cross. "I hereby decommission you," he announced.

---

224   Garrett Wilson, "The NWMP Trail Fort Walsh to Wood Mountain," in *Fort Walsh to Wood Mountain: The North-West Mounted Police Trail*, ed. Mike Fedyk (Regina: Benchmark Press, 2010), 38.

We all shook hands again. It seemed to be the default action with which we all felt the most comfortable.

Just in time I remembered that I had some ritual work of my own to do: the envelope with earth from Walsh's grave. Taking the staff member aside, I asked where I could spread it. His eyes widened. "From Walsh's grave? You could put it down by the flagpole."

We followed the red coats into the fort. They marched in formation while we straggled along behind them. The palisades, like the buildings inside the fort, were impressive, but they are no more original than the summer staff whom we were following. Fort Walsh was abandoned in May and June 1883, just when it was most needed for famine relief. In 1942, the Royal Canadian Mounted Police repurchased the area around the former NWMP post and partially reconstructed it, using it as a training ground for the horses of the RCMP Musical Ride. RCMP Commissioner Stuart Wood "had a keen interest in NWMP history, and ordered that the new buildings at Fort Walsh be replicas of the Fort's original buildings."[225] When the RCMP ceased operations at Fort Walsh in 1966, it turned the fort over to Parks Canada, which designated it a national historic site. Parks Canada then constructed the palisades, furnished the buildings in the style of the 1880s, built an interpretive centre overlooking the valley, and hired interpretive staff of the sort whom we were just then trailing into the fort.

So, whereas we had been commissioned by actual police at one end of the trail, we were met at the other end by genial actors. As a welcome to us (and a treat for the small crowd of tourists), they loaded and fired the ceremonial cannon. That seemed to be the end of the official welcome.

We walkers were all slightly stunned at having arrived. I hung around for the tour of the buildings but soon found myself back at the centre point of the grounds, lounging around the flagpole. When Hugh showed up, I put down the earth from Walsh's grave.

---

225   Fedyk, "History, Memory, and the NWMP Trail," 9. See also James De Jonge, "Reconstructions of a Different Kind: The Mounted Police and the Rebirth of Fort Walsh, 1942–1966," *Saskatchewan History* 49, no. 1 (1997): 22–32.

"Are you coming?" asked Richard, passing by. "We're going to do a final smudge." On a last-minute whim, I held on to some of the earth.

Despite the "decommissioning," our walk had not actually been a historical re-enactment in the manner of some previous celebrations of the trail.[226] Richard decided that—like the nêhiyaw, Niisitapi, Anihšinápēk, and Nakota, who would have camped outside the fort—our final smudge should also take place outside the palisades. Given how much time we had spent on the land, the outside simply felt more comfortable. As we sat in a circle, and Richard brought around sweetgrass, I put down the last of Walsh's grave earth. Walsh had spent most of his time outside the fort too. It seemed to be right.

TWO DAYS AFTER our arrival at Fort Walsh, after a laundry break in Swift Current, Hugh picked me up, and we drove back to the Jensen ranch. His plan was that the two of us would finish the one segment of the trail that we had been forced to miss because of the heavy rain. We would walk several kilometres through the grasses and brush along the Frenchman River valley, then turn and try to cross the river near the location identified on old maps as Stone Pile Crossing—if we could find it. From there, we would trek more or less straight across the valley, trying to pick up the historic trail, following it up through the coulees to the north highlands.

Within a few hundred metres of leaving the cultivated areas, Hugh discovered a stone hammerhead. It takes a trained eye to spot such a find, since at first glance it looks like any other fist-sized river rock. Hugh picked it up and turned it over, showing me where the stone had been chipped away to give it heft in the hand and how the base of it had been flattened for use in hammering in pegs for securing tents or stretching hides. We returned the rock to its place.

It was heavy going through the buckbrush, chokecherries, and tall sage along the river. Fortunately, it was partly overcast, and the day wasn't hot. The only sounds were our footsteps and the occasional cricket or the cry of a hawk overhead. A kilometre or so along, we came across one of Baker's missing posts. The cattle had been at it, and it was listing badly. Hugh noted the GPS coordinates. He would return with volunteers later in the fall to paint and straighten it. Another kilometre on we came to a bend in the river that Hugh was pretty sure meant that we were almost to Stone Pile Crossing. There was another of Baker's early 1960s posts, its paint faded. It was leaning but still standing.

The Saskatchewan History and Folklore Society has a program for donations toward maintenance of the markers. Supporters are encouraged to donate and to have their names inscribed on plaques atop the trail posts or the names of others whom they wish to honour or remember. I'd been thinking for some time of making donations for my brother and sister and myself. This looked like a good spot. "Wait," Hugh advised. "We still have a few missing posts to find before the day is out."

A herd of horses were grazing on the other side of the river. After a brief reconnaissance, we found the spot where they and the cattle had beaten a path to the water's edge for crossing. To cross a river safely, Hugh advised, take the route that the livestock use. I removed my boots, rolled up my pants, and waded across without incident. We could see another of Baker's posts in the distance, amid a low area of thick, blue-green sagebrush and cactus. Partway we discovered an ancient wooden post, stuck stoutly in the ground. Two bleached wooden arrows had been hammered into the post, each pointing to some destination at right angles to each other. Coils of rusted wire and some broken glass lay at its base. Unfortunately, the old boards were washed clean. Any writing that might once have been on them was long gone: they were signs that said nothing and pointed to unknown destinations. Baker's post was still there, but it was equally mute, the 1960s concrete fractured at the top.

We decided that this must have been the Stone Pile intersection or at least close to it. This was one of the historic junctions of the Traders' Road. It was there that the road met north-south traffic to

Before the smudge, outside Fort Walsh, August 7, 2015. *Photo by James R. Page.*

and from the Milk River basin on the south side of the "medicine line" border. Stone Pile had been an important intersection for Métis traders and, briefly, one of the many NWMP customs posts strung along the north side of the international boundary.

After more GPS readings and notes, we headed north, zigzagging to avoid a set of unused corrals and low alkali areas, slivers of white edging black banks. One of Baker's posts lay forlornly on its side, knocked over completely by cattle, after years of serving as a rubbing post. For a while, we lost the trail, then picked it up at the base of a deep coulee, heavily wooded with poplars. A steep ascent brought us to the next post atop the highlands.[227]

From this spot, it seemed as though you could see the whole world. The Jensen ranch sat to the southeast. Straight south and a hundred metres below us, I could barely make out where we had just stopped at the posts of Stone Pile Crossing. West was the highway

---

227   This spot might be the place called High Descend by the Lakota. See Thomson, "Lakota Place Names," 37.

and beyond that a cascade of chalky, striated dirt bluffs, fingers of the highlands extending into the river valley, the creases between them green with trees. Thirty-two kilometres or so to the north, not so far in prairie terms, was my sister's grave, where my parents wanted some of their ashes to be spread. It was the closest that the trail came to the cemetery. Lisbeth Mikaelsson, in her article on pilgrimage, notes "the importance of . . . the fusion of the outward and inward journeys" to contemporary pilgrims' feelings of a "successful" pilgrimage.[228]

I leaned against the weathered concrete. It held firm. "What about here?" I asked Hugh, putting my hand on the worn post. "Is this one free for sponsorship?"

He nodded. "If you want it. I'll put a sign on it this fall."

"I'd like that."

We hiked west past another post, one coulee over, that shared a similarly beautiful view of the valley and then up an ascent until, eventually, we reached the beginning of cultivated fields, where we had left one of the vehicles.

Soon I was back in Swift Current and then Montreal. Six months later I found out that Hugh had sponsored the post beside mine, looking out over the same valley. It was a fitting tribute to our friendship. It was also a fitting end to the half-crazy project that we had undertaken of walking and remembering one of the most important of the old trails stretching across Treaty 4 prairie.

For Further Reading

For a contemporaneous nêhiyaw description of some of the ceremonies listed in this chapter, see Edward Ahenakew, *Voices of the Plains Cree*, ed. Ruth M. Buck (Regina: Canadian Plains Research Center, 1995), 46–47 and 94–95, as well as the description in Mary Weekes, *The Last Buffalo Hunter: As Told to Her by Norbert Welsh* (1939; reprinted, Saskatoon: Fifth House, 1994), 47–50. For an alternative view of Alexander Morris and his negotiations concerning Treaty 4, see

---

228   Lisbeth Mikaelsson, "Pilgrimage as Post-Secular Therapy," *Scripta Instituti Donneriani Aboensis* 24 (2014): 266.

Robert J. Talbot, *Negotiating the Numbered Treaties: An Intellectual and Political Biography of Alexander Morris* (Saskatoon: Purich, 2009). Gina Starblanket has written a perceptive piece about the treaties in "The Numbered Treaties and the Politics of Incoherency," *Canadian Journal of Political Science* 52, no. 3 (2019): 443–59.

On White Valley Lutheran Church, see Alan B. Anderson, *Settling Saskatchewan* (Regina: University of Regina Press, 2013), 315.

The events at Cypress Lake were not a natural tragedy. They could have been prevented. Dr. John Kittson was only one of a number of people who alerted the government to the plight of the people at the "hunger camps." See "John Kittson to N.T. Macleod, Indian Agent, July 1, 1880," in Report from D[r]. Kittson of the Northwest Mounted Police Stationed at Fort Macleod, Concerning the Insufficiency of the Rations Issued to the Indians in the Northwest Territories, LAC, RG 10, vol. 3726, reel C-10 126, file 24 811, Mikan 2059165. (Note the names of Edgar Dewdney and John A. Macdonald on this document as well as a 1915 postscript page from Duncan Campbell Scott noting that he had found Kittson's report among the collected letters from Dewdney to Macdonald.)

For more on Duncan Campbell Scott, see Charlie Angus, *Children of the Broken Treaty: Canada's Lost Promise and One Girl's Dream* (Regina: University of Regina Press, 2017), 5–12, and Mark Abley, *Conversations with a Dead Man: The Legacy of Duncan Campbell Scott* (Madeira Park, BC: Douglas and McIntyre, 2013).

On "liminal men" or "mimic men" and the ways throughout history that such individuals have been drawn to the edge of empire to make their reputations and their fortunes, see Homi Bhabha, "Of Mimicry and Man: The Ambivalence of Colonial Discourse," *October* 28 (1984): 125–33, especially 128. On how empires require a "frontier" or "contact zone" for self-definition, and the complex interactions between centre and periphery of this construct, see Mary Louise Pratt, *Imperial Eyes: Travel Writing and Transculturation* (London: Routledge, 1992), 6–7.

Chapter 3

THE FORT BATTLEFORD TRAIL, TREATY 6

S ANYONE WHO HAS DONE IT KNOWS, THERE'S something addictive about long-distance walking. That's probably why Hugh and I started talking about the possibility of highlighting another traditional prairie trail shortly after we finished the first.

It turned out that, through the Saskatchewan History and Folklore Society, Hugh was also responsible for what was called the Swift Current to Fort Battleford Trail. I had always known this route simply as the Battleford Trail. Over the fall of 2015 and into the next spring, whenever I was out to Saskatchewan, I took breaks from visiting my father at his care home to discuss with Hugh the possibility of making this our second trek. We had been fortunate in how much local press coverage there had been of the Traders' Road walk. We wondered if we could repeat that public interest and education. Meanwhile, under its executive, including Hugh, the SHFS continued to move more consciously toward highlighting both the history and the ongoing presence of Indigenous Peoples. In its workshops and seminars, it began to seek more and more Indigenous participation and leadership.

In June 2016, I met Hugh and Harold at a Swift Current coffeeshop, and we discussed the Battleford Trail in detail. I had lined up a pilgrimage that summer with a group of Icelanders on the Bær to Skálholt path in Iceland.[1] Both Hugh and Harold were keen to come along. We decided that it would be best to wait one more year on the Battleford Trail.

When I spoke with my brother about the walk to Battleford, he raised his eyebrows. "Do you mean the Dairy Queen trail?" Swift Current has a "linear park" that still contains some of the old cart tracks. That park is a small, fenced-off section[2] of old grassland, sitting along the service road of the Trans-Canada Highway, right beside a Dairy Queen fast-food restaurant.

"That's the one," I told him.

"You'll be needing a vehicle again, I guess?"

We—or I should say Hugh—began planning in earnest. We agreed that this time he and the SHFS would lead the project, making official what had become the facts on the ground in any case. I would be free to concentrate on recording sound, researching, and writing.

Then, on August 9, 2016, twenty-two-year-old Colten Boushie, a young nêhiyaw man from Red Pheasant First Nation, was shot and killed by Gerald Stanley on Stanley's farm, near Biggar, Saskatchewan. The shocking killing took place along our planned walking route. Stanley was charged with second-degree murder.

Stanley's trial polarized Saskatchewan communities. It led to a flood of racist invective against the very family and community that had lost a son.[3] Shortly after the killing, I was in Swift Current visiting my father. When I contacted Hugh about the walk, he thought that

---

1   Eygló Svala Arnarsdóttir, "Priests Mark Pilgrim Route in Iceland," *Iceland Review*, December 18, 2012, https://www.icelandreview.com/news/priests -mark-pilgrim-route-iceland/.

2   "Battleford Trail Wheel Rut Area," Canada's Historic Places, 2006, https:// www.historicplaces.ca/en/rep-reg/place-lieu.aspx?id=4979.

3   Gina Starblanket and Dallas Hunt, *Storying Violence: Unravelling Colonial Narratives in the Stanley Trial* (Winnipeg: ARP Books, 2020), 24.

it should still occur. I agreed. Without knowing how tensions might play out, such a project seemed to be more appropriate than ever.

NEW SHOES

THAT AUTUMN MY father's blood pressure dropped precipitously. My father went into a coma several times and began spending regular periods in the hospital. His liver was causing him trouble as well; everything seemed to be off. My brother began driving to Herbert (where our father had been placed in nursing home and hospital care) weekly from Regina, my sister went as often as she could make it, and I began flying to Regina even more frequently from Montreal. There was no longer much chance to get our dad into a car and out where he could enjoy the land. We were simply trying to ensure some quality of life for him. Not that his enthusiasm for music, or conversation, had abated: if not on the hospital wing, he was always delighted to play the keyboard with his one good hand or talk about his early days on the farm.

I asked him about his father, about his mother, and about the Anderson homestead near the Great Sand Hills. It had always struck me as odd that the government had granted an allotment to my grandparents so close to an area where farming was—and is—nearly impossible. Moreover, the Sand Hills are holy to the prairie First Nations, a place where the Niisitapi and other groups believed that the spirit went when you died, to hunt forever among the dunes.

The place where George Marjus Anderson and his new wife, Kamilla Arneson, received a homestead in 1911 is north of the hamlet of Webb, just east of Antelope Lake. As usual, the grant was conditional: in order to be granted complete title, the family had to fulfill a number of conditions, including erecting a building and successfully harvesting crops. The homestead was the southeast quarter of section 21, township 15, range 17, west of the third meridian, or SE-21-15-17-W3. In GPS coordinates, it can be located at 50° 16'12"N 108° 17'45"W.

The much higher wheat prices of the first decade of the twentieth century,[4] combined with a boom in railway construction, meant that farming was attractive. My grandfather and grandmother were part of a flood of immigrants who arrived in Saskatchewan in those years in response.[5] They were northwestern Europeans who, like George, had already acculturated to the plains—just the type of settler whom the government of Canada and Minister of Immigration Clifford Sifton wanted.[6]

But poor farmland is poor farmland. Whereas the first decade of the twentieth century had been exceptional, the second decade was marked by drought. Records show that one of the first buildings erected on the Anderson homestead was not a granary but a blacksmith shop for shoeing horses and repairing machinery. Soon George was not so much farming as blacksmithing. He moved the forge and family to Webb, along the CPR line that had been built only thirty years earlier. A few years after that, they moved again. They purchased a farm farther south, near other Norwegian settlers.

My father did not know much about that first land grant or the Sand Hills. When he was born, the family was already on the new farm, southwest of Simmie.[7] However, my grandfather was still a blacksmith. Dad told me that one of his earliest memories was of being shoeless. He said the word in Norwegian—*barfod*—and laughed. "I hurt myself going *barfod* all the time," he said. "I was running like always and stepped on hot metal near the forge."

Back in 1882, the Sand Hills—in fact, the whole vast commons that had been the Northern Plains—was surveyed out from under

---

4   Arthur S. Morton, *History of Prairie Settlement* (Toronto: Macmillan, 1938), 125.

5   Morton takes care to point to the prosperity as a draw equal to, or more effective than, the immigration policies of Clifford Sifton, then head of the Department of the Interior. Morton, *History of Prairie Settlement*, 125–26.

6   Starblanket and Hunt, *Storying Violence*, 42.

7   My grandfather was likely attracted to the area near Simmie by the presence of other Norwegian farmers who had moved there via North Dakota. See Alan B. Anderson, *Settling Saskatchewan* (Regina: University of Regina Press, 2013), 316. This was also the reason for the Lutheran church there.

the feet of the prairie First Nations. That year ninety-two survey parties crossed the territory.[8] They laid out the township divisions that soon would be turned into farms such as the one promised to my grandfather and grandmother. That summer hundreds of men on train crews laid tracks westward from Regina. They reached the Swift Current Creek in December 1882. Immediately, the Canadian Pacific Railway set to work building a railyard, shops, and a roundhouse that would serve to move freight—and settlers, especially Europeans—into the area.[9] In his memoirs, Cecil Denny is either disingenuous or completely oblivious when he notes that "the Indians, too, became uneasy over this army of invasion, and its peaceable purposes had to be explained to them."[10] Denny's remark is notable for its ignorance, an example of the incredible blindness of privilege, then and now.

The nêhiyaw and Nakota understood this "army of invasion" and its "peaceable purposes" well enough. David McCrady reports that, as far back as the British-American survey of 1873–74, Lakota and Anihšinápék groups who encountered the surveyors wanted reassurance that the whites were not surveying the land for a rail line.[11] I remember driving with my mother and father past a hamlet called Piapot, named for the Indigenous leader Payepot,[12] on the Trans-Canada Highway between Swift Current and Maple Creek.

---

8   Garrett Wilson, *Frontier Farewell: The 1870s and the End of the Old West* (2007; reprinted, Regina: University of Regina Press, 2014), 425.

9   Gordon Errett Tolton, *Prairie Warships: River Navigation in the Northwest Rebellion* (Victoria: Heritage House, 2007), 114.

10   Cecil E. Denny, *The Law Marches West* (1939; reprinted, Toronto: J.M. Dent and Sons, 1972), 175.

11   David Grant McCrady, *Living with Strangers: The Nineteenth-Century Sioux and the Canadian-American Borderlands* (Toronto: University of Toronto Press, 2010), 56.

12   I use the name Piapot to refer to the town, as well as to the First Nation, both of which use this spelling of the leader's name. However, most contemporary sources, and Indigenous writers, have moved to the spelling Payepot. I use the old spelling when describing stories from my parents since they would have said it this way at the time.

Even though we'd heard the story from them dozens of times, my parents would never fail to tell us children what had happened there. Cigarette in hand, my mother would lean back from the front seat, pointing and saying "That's where old Chief Piapot sat down on the railway tracks to stop the train." For some reason, he was always "*old* Chief Piapot." "He had to be carried off," she would announce with satisfaction. For people who had only ever benefited from the railway, my parents seemed to feel an odd solidarity with this bit of resistance history. To many among the underdog western farmers and ranchers, Payepot somehow became "one of us": a local prairie hero, the incident absorbed into prairie lore, without any deeper appreciation of what his resistance had actually meant for the Nakota whom he was trying to protect.[13]

At the time of Payepot's attempted railway blockade, it had been three years since Edgar Dewdney had agreed with the nêhiyaw and Nakota that they would pick reserves in the Cypress Hills.[14] In that short time, not only was the promise broken, but also groups who had agreed to treaty were not receiving their promised rations. Children

---

13   My parents were hardly the only settlers to focus on Payepot's act of resistance but ignore the wider picture:

> While emphasizing a particular angle of the historical situation, the narrative focus within the display case [of the local museum] largely skirts some important historical events and questions. For example, while Payepot seems to be celebrated as a local hero, there is no mention of the forceful displacement to which he and his people were ultimately subjected. Likewise, although the mythology of his peaceful protest on the railway tracks is featured prominently (both visually and textually), there neither is mention of the eventual failure of his peaceful efforts to restrict the opening of his homeland to Euro-Canadian settlement.

Tobias Sperlich and Lace Marie Brogden, "'Finding' Payepot's Moccasins: Disrupting Colonial Narratives of Place," *Cultural Studies ↔ Critical Methodologies* 16, no. 1 (2016): 11

14   Bill Waiser, *A World We Have Lost: Saskatchewan before 1905* (Calgary: Fifth House, 2016), 507.

and adults were dying from hunger[15] and hunger-related diseases.[16] The surveyors were everywhere, and the railway was arriving and would only bring more settlers.

Far from *not* understanding, Payepot was ahead of his time. With our twenty-first-century eyes, we can discern in Denny's account how the Nakota and nêhiyaw were practising a form of non-violent resistance. Their ultimate cooperation with a foreign law was the only thing that allowed the police to displace them:

> A large Cree camp, of which Chiefs Piapot and Long Man were the heads, sat down squarely on the line of construction and halted the advance. They announced that they were there to stay and that they would not allow the work to continue. The railway authorities appealed to the Lieutenant-Governor, who communicated with the nearest police post. . . . A sergeant and two men went to the camp and gave the Indians a half an hour to move, promising should they fail to do so to pull down the tents. The Indians threatened and wasted some powder [meaning shooting into the air] but showed no intention of moving, so the three men proceeded calmly to flatten the tents. . . . [N]ot a hand was lifted against the dauntless trio by the swarm of angry Crees surrounding them.[17]

Denny misses the point entirely. (I cannot imagine what it must have been like to have had to deal with this man for relief rations.)

---

15   According to Edward Ahenakew, Dewdney made similar promises to Chief Thunderchild, the last to sign Treaty 6: "What I can do, I will do humbly. You will not starve under me." Dewdney was wrong on both counts. Edward Ahenakew, *Voices of the Plains Cree*, ed. Ruth M. Buck (Regina: Canadian Plains Research Center, 1995), 11.

16   "At Fort Walsh, a camp of 1,500 Cree [in 1880] came down with dysentery and diarrhoea and NWMP medical officer George Kennedy found himself treating 150 cases a day. He reported that 'quite a number, principally children, died.'" Wilson, *Frontier Farewell*, 389.

17   Denny, *The Law Marches West*, 176.

The fact is that from the Cypress Hills to the Oka Crisis,[18] and into this twenty-first century, there has been a consistent double standard when applying the law.[19] Canadian authorities have *always* counted on Indigenous Peoples to cooperate with laws that they themselves do not respect.

Shortly after Payepot and his band were coerced into taking a reserve far to the east near Fort Qu'Appelle, over a hundred members of his band were reported to have died from eating rancid bacon supplied by the government.[20] Dan Kennedy (Ochankugahe) reports that over one-third of the band died of malnutrition after Payepot was forced to move to his first reserve.[21] This was the "benefit" of cooperation. When he then refused to stay in a place of death, the group was reluctantly granted a spot farther south. When Payepot later allowed one of the "forbidden" cultural ceremonies of his people, in order to grieve the incredible toll of deaths, the government—illegally even in light of its own laws—stripped him of his status as Chief.[22]

Even then the group's troubles with Canada were far from over. Immediately after the First World War, their territory was again lost, this time when the government illegally expropriated Indigenous reserve land, supposedly protected under treaty, to give to returning war veterans.[23] Bob Joseph notes that, in "the period from 1896 to 1911, 21 percent of reserve land in the Prairie Provinces was surrendered to accommodate western expansion."[24]

---

18   Leanne Simpson and Kiera L. Ladner, eds., *This Is an Honour Song: Twenty Years since the Blockades* (Winnipeg: Arbeiter Ring, 2010).

19   Bruce McIvor, *Standoff: Why Reconciliation Fails Indigenous People and How to Fix It* (Gibsons, BC: Nightwood Editions, 2021), 112.

20   Waiser, *A World We Have Lost*, 509. See also Abel Watetch, *Payepot and His People* (Regina: Canadian Plains Research Center, 2007), 8–11.

21   Dan Kennedy (Ochankugahe), *Recollections of an Assiniboine Chief*, ed. James R. Stevens (Toronto: McClelland and Stewart, 1972), 57.

22   Watetch, *Payepot*, 35–37.

23   Sarah Carter, "'An Infamous Proposal': Prairie Indian Reserve Land and Soldier Settlement after World War I," *Manitoba History* 37 (1999): 9–21.

24   Bob Joseph, *21 Things You May not Know about the Indian Act: Helping Canadians Make Reconciliation with Indigenous Peoples a Reality* (Port Coquitlam, BC:

The next time I flew west from Montreal, our father informed us that he needed to go into Swift Current to the denturist. With his intravenous pole and increasing immobility, not to mention the occasional blackouts that he was experiencing, the journey seemed to be almost impossible to manage. He had also decided that he would like to go shopping. No matter what any of us said, including his doctor and the nurses, he was not to be put off. Finally, my brother arranged to rent a minibus to take our father and me into town. Unfortunately, it was a very hot day, the bus had no air conditioning, and the mall where the denturist was located had its air conditioning set extremely cold.

Dad decided that he needed a new pair of shoes. To this day, I am ashamed to remember how short I was with the idea. "New shoes?" I asked, incredulous. "What do you need new shoes for? The ones you have look fine." We ventured down some store aisles, but my father didn't like the pairs on the shelves and wanted to find something else from the clerk. I was annoyed. We had left his sweater on the bus, which had dropped us at the mall and left for another appointment. It was a big store, and of course there were no staff in sight. The process of trying on shoes would not be easy with his advanced Parkinson's and his wheelchair. And I was already noticing my father shaking from the air conditioning.

I couldn't decide whether he was better off outside the mall in the heat (and complaining) or inside it in the chill (and freezing). He preferred inside. Always a socialite, even if he was uncomfortable, at least he would meet people whom he knew and could visit with them.

Finally, we arranged his dentures and purchased some new shoes—my father had insisted—and the driver returned. She and I managed to manoeuvre him and his wheelchair back into the bus. As soon as we were on the highway, my father fell asleep. As the air gusted through the open windows, I kept checking his forehead, which had become clammy. I phoned my brother to tell him that our suspicions had been confirmed—the trip clearly had been too much.

Indigenous Relations, 2018), 69.

Two weeks later, on August 24, 2016, my father died in the Herbert Hospital with my brother by his side and my sister there shortly after. His funeral was in the same church as my mother's, the church that I grew up in, at the top of Swift Current's Central Avenue. The church is named St. Olaf's after a Norwegian king who lived a thousand years ago and almost certainly was no saint but to whose grave pilgrims travelled for centuries. Some of my father's former Swift Current police colleagues were at the funeral. My stepmother's Lebanese Canadian family attended as well. It was symbolic of how multicultural prairie society really is, even when people don't realize it: my stepmother's hummus was featured alongside white bread egg sandwiches, and baklava sparkled from where it was tucked in among the Nanaimo bars and puffed wheat squares.

My father had vacillated on whether he wanted to be buried in Swift Current or in Shaunavon beside my sister. Eventually, he had settled on the Swift Current location, at the cemetery by the twist of the creek. As we had done for my mother, we had an urn made of Whitemud clay, reserving some of the ashes for later. It had been a bit of a chore finding a plot near enough my father's parents, and his best friend, our uncle Carl, without placing our father right beside our mother.

As those who have lost their parents know, there is an emptiness that comes when the previous generation is gone. After we shovelled earth over my father's grave, we joined the others at the church for the reception. One of my cousins hugged me and asked whether, with both parents gone, I would still come out west for "those walks—you know, the ones you do." She went on quickly, as if I might get the wrong idea: "I mean," she added, "they sound nice. They're good. Important. Hope you don't give that up."

For Further Reading

For more on Payepot and the Piapot First Nation, see its website at https://piapotnation.com/history-2/. On how western Canadians "took over" and appropriated the memory of Payepot's resistance, see Tobias Sperlich and Lace Marie Brogden, " 'Finding' Payepot's

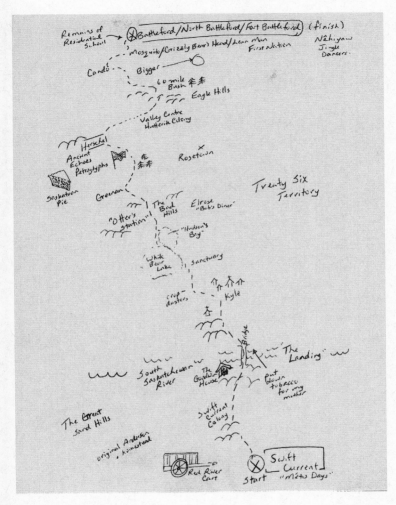

Sketch by the author of the Swift Current to Fort Battleford Trail.

Moccasins: Disrupting Colonial Narratives of Place," *Cultural Studies ↔ Critical Methodologies* 16, no. 1 (2016): 7–17.

For an Indigenous memory of promises of food aid made by Dewdney and others but never kept, see Edward Ahenakew, *Voices of the Plains Cree*, ed. Ruth M. Buck (Regina: Canadian Plains Research Center, 1995), 11.

For more on how the government of Canada started expropriating Indigenous reserves for its war veterans, see Sarah Carter, "'An Infamous Proposal': Prairie Indian Reserve Land and Soldier Settlement after World War I," *Manitoba History* 37 (1999): 9–21.

SWIFT CURRENT TO FORT BATTLEFORD

> *Loose ends and ongoing stories*
> *are real challenges to cartography.*
>
> —DOREEN MASSEY[25]

I MET JAMES DASCHUK, author of *Clearing the Plains*, in 2015. His encyclopedic demonstration of how nineteenth-century Canadian policy constituted an ethnic cleansing of the Indigenous population of the prairie region has influenced many of us permanently. Building upon fact after fact, he showed how the way for European settlement was prepared by unchecked disease, facilitated famine, and political manoeuvring that took almost no account of Indigenous lives.

Jim's office is close to the University of Regina's gymnasiums. Jim and I could hear the dribbling of basketballs as we walked down the long hall. We hadn't yet walked our first pilgrimage, and I was trying to sell him on accompanying us along the Traders' Road. Would he like to come along?

"Would love to," he answered. "But I can't get away."

It would be an important social statement, I urged (I was also thinking that it would help to publicize the walk, one of my goals). "With what happened, it's kind of our own Trail of Tears," I argued.

At that, Jim stopped. "Trail of Tears?" He corrected me: "No. It wasn't. Not if you mean a forced exodus. The North West Mounted Police Patrol Trail wasn't that. Maybe for Sitting Bull. But Cypress being emptied was far worse. The Nakota and the nêhiyaw were forced to walk north and east, hundreds of kilometres, sometimes

---

25   Doreen B. Massey, *For Space* (London: SAGE, 2005), 222.

in terrible conditions and starving. Men, women, children—many died, either wintering in Cypress or on the way to Battleford or Qu'Appelle. If anything qualifies as our Trail of Tears, it's those walks."

That conversation was ringing in my ears a year later as Hugh and I continued our discussion of a trek north from Swift Current. One of the most significant differences between the Battleford Trail and the Traders' Road was that walking to Battleford involved moving into, and through, an area where there is far more *contemporary* Indigenous presence than there had been on our southern route. According to estimates, almost 40 percent of the population of the North Battleford area is Indigenous.[26] Many of the First Nations around Battleford consist of the descendants of precisely those expelled from the Cypress Hills at the end of the nineteenth century.[27] Although there have been tentative steps recently toward regional, government-to-government cooperation,[28] for over 150 years mistrust and animosity have marked relations between settlers and Indigenous Peoples in the area. If we decided to walk this trail, then we would be walking into what Gina Starblanket and Dallas Hunt call "a geography . . . deeply structured by racial violence."[29]

It is a fact too little appreciated by almost all Saskatchewan residents that the present and past of the Battleford–North Battleford region are inextricably woven together.[30] The shooting of Colten Boushie in 2016 cannot be separated from the events of the 1880s. The reverse

---

26 Paul Seesequasis, "The Stanley Verdict and Its Fallout Is a Made-in-Saskatchewan Crisis," *Globe and Mail*, February 12, 2018, https://www.theglobeandmail.com /opinion/the-stanley-verdict-and-its-fallout-is-a-made-in-saskatchewan-crisis /article37945105/.

27 Anderson, *Settling Saskatchewan*, 25–30.

28 In 2019, the City of North Battleford and many of the neighbouring First Nations signed a "Sacichawasihc agreement" pledging government-to-government cooperation. See Kaitlynn Nordahl, "Battleford, Surrounding First Nations Commit to Working Together," *Eagle Feather News*, June 28, 2019, https://www. eaglefeathernews.com/news/battlefords-surrounding-first-nations-commit -to-working-together.

29 Starblanket and Hunt, *Storying Violence*, 26.

30 Seesequasis makes just this point in "The Stanley Verdict."

is also true. Anyone looking at the late-nineteenth-century history of the area is irresponsible if not keeping contemporary events such as Boushie's killing foremost in mind. The choices made by our ancestors had—and have—ongoing consequences. Ours will as well, for good or ill.

On May 12, 1883, Battleford's *Saskatchewan Herald* announced on its cover page that "advices from the south bring the intelligence that over a thousand Indians are on their way to Battleford to be assigned to reservations in this district."[31] Two years later Battleford was the site of the largest mass hanging in Canadian history: the execution in the morning of November 27, 1885, of eight nêhiyaw and Nakota.[32] In defiance of its own laws, the government made the hanging a public event. Indigenous students forced to watch the hangings came from the Battleford Indian Industrial School, one of the many residential schools set up as part of Canadian government policy the year before.[33] We realized that walking toward Battleford would be very different from walking on the Traders' Road. It would be a dark pilgrimage in many ways. We kept revisiting the question of whether, given events, such a project would be wise. Ultimately, we kept returning to our hopes that, by pointing toward a different form of being together on the land, we might be in solidarity in some small way with those who oppose hatred.

Before setting out on the Swift Current–Fort Battleford Trail, I was asked by my friend Dr. Raymond Aldred to go to British Columbia to

---

31   *Saskatchewan Herald*, May 12, 1883, 1.

32   The first-person recounting by William Bleasdell Cameron of the hangings was, for him, uncharacteristically subdued. His death cell conversations with Wandering Spirit might indicate that he was suffering from survivor guilt. See William Bleasdell Cameron, *Blood Red the Sun* (1927; reprinted, Calgary: Kenway Publishing, 1970), 204–12.

33   Joseph, *21 Things*, 52. See also Waiser, *A World We Have Lost*, 563–64. Waiser mentions that many Indigenous residents were brought in to witness the executions but does not mention the Industrial School students. Seesequasis, "The Stanley Verdict," notes that the bodies were simply thrown in a mass grave after the execution.

teach a short course in the Indigenous Studies program that he heads at the Vancouver School of Theology (UBC). I was to teach on the topic of journeying. Both Ray and I knew that, as a settler-descended Canadian, I couldn't teach about "Indigenous Journey." He advised that I should present global and especially Christian traditions of pilgrimage and that the students and I could learn together as they made connections to practices from their various home nations. It was one of my first attempts at what Denise Nadeau calls "making space rather than taking space,"[34] and I am forever thankful to my students and to Ray for the learning experience.

His teachings about kin making through treaty have been deeply formative for me. In a book that we authored together, he writes that

> the land now reminds us of [our] covenant. It warns us to remember the Treaty, and what is so often called the climate crisis, in its totality, is part of that warning. Part of living in a good way, with your relatives who are Indigenous peoples, is recognizing the specificity and holiness of this land, this place. Askíhk is never a general, abstract thing. It is always a specific relationship with a specific land, with specific animals, and trees and plants, and relations. In order to live long in this land, journeying on this land—you have to live in a way this land lets you live.[35]

During the class at UBC, I spent more time listening than lecturing. The students identified themselves as Stoney, Wood Cree, Plains Cree, Métis, Nisga'a, Haida, and a sprinkling of settler-descended Canadians and Americans. Their experiences, languages, and politics differed widely. I learned much from the discussions among Indigenous students—especially their careful ways of disagreeing with each other and giving space to others and the social repercussions

---

34   Denise M. Nadeau, *Unsettling Spirit: A Journey into Decolonization* (Montreal and Kingston: McGill-Queen's University Press, 2020), 67.

35   Raymond Aldred and Matthew R. Anderson, *Our Home and Treaty Land: Walking Our Creation Story* (Kelowna: Wood Lake Books, 2022), 77.

the rare times that that didn't happen. I was touched when, on the last day of class, one of the students from near Hudson Bay gave me a beaded necklace for my own future journeys.

Two learnings in particular stand out when I reflect on my time with this group. First, all agreed that the land is an active partner in any journey. The Land (they often capitalized the word in this usage) is part of the "web of relations" that must be recognized. European traditions have tended to be blind to any relations to land other than the obsessive pursuit of acquiring and exploiting it. I took away from my student teachers that, if I was really serious about my own spirituality as a Canadian who grew up on Treaty 4 territory, I must come to know and count the land, and its original peoples, as well as its other-than-human beings, as my relations.

Second, the students taught me that it is always important to seek permission. For the most part, they didn't use the word *permission* but words such as *blessing* and *offering*. The point was that, if you are entering a new territory, you should put down tobacco, sage, or sweetgrass and recognize by protocol the Indigenous Peoples who belong there. This is "the good way," they said, echoing the Lakota Elder at Wood Mountain two years earlier. The good way, they told me, is to announce one's intentions and seek the blessing of the Land as well as that of the ancestors.[36] They recommended the practice as a way of honouring not only the Land but also its non-human beings. I made it my business to get tobacco for the Battleford Trail.

A year after the killing of Colten Boushie, and the arrest of Gerald Stanley, he was still awaiting trial. Stanley had been freed nine days after the killing on bail that included the conditions that he remain within six and a half kilometres of his home and that he have no contact with Boushie's family. Tensions remained high throughout Saskatchewan, particularly between farmers and First Nations in the Biggar-Battleford area.

---

36   Nadeau, *Unsettling Spirit*, 228, comments that "the protocol of asking permission creates a framework of respect and reverence for the land and spirits."

While I was in Vancouver, Hugh was busy making the final plans for our route, lining up overnight camping spots, and getting permissions from landowners whose fields or pastures we would be crossing. He made contact with First Nations along the route and with Métis organizations in the southwest. The plan was to repeat the format of our journey two years earlier by punctuating our walk with presentations or gatherings in communities along the way. Hugh secured invitations to Kyle, Fiske, Cando, Mosquito First Nation, and Biggar, and he was working on our reception at Battleford. This time there would be no "commission"—in fact, Hugh had quite different ideas.

The night before our departure, Hugh called us walkers together for a meeting in a restaurant beside the fenced-off historical ruts. Visiting Swift Current felt odd. It had been a year since my father's passing and two years since my mother's. With both parents gone, my whirlwind of flights west had slowed. I felt adrift, as if I had little business being in Saskatchewan. I was thankful for Hugh's solid direction of the pilgrimage. As I parked my brother's vehicle to join the others, I looked up at the sign above the park from which we would be leaving the following morning. I couldn't remember ever seeing that sign, even though it had been there since my youth: Battleford Trail Ruts.

We were a much larger group than had started out from Wood Mountain two years earlier. As we ate pizza, Hugh unfolded maps and handed out information. In general, because there was more cropped farmland and less pasture along the Battleford route, we would do more road walking than we had on the previous trek. We would also cover slightly longer distances, averaging twenty-two kilometres a day.

Harold was there sitting by Hugh. He grinned and indicated that he planned to do the whole walk, "if my wife doesn't mind, and she doesn't seem to." I was very happy to discover that my friend Richard Kotowich was also planning to walk most of the way to Battleford. He and I had been in touch ever since the walk to the Cypress Hills.

Archbishop Don Bolen was back as well. This time he had booked time off for the entire journey.

Among the new pilgrims were Ken Wilson and Christine Ramsay, professors from the University of Regina who had signed up through the SHFS. Christine is an artist as well as a professor. Ken (her partner) and I share many interests, and I was looking forward to meeting him after corresponding several months by email. We are similar except in size—he is a giant not only in stature but also in his encyclopedic interest in the intersections of walking, art, pilgrimage, literature, and decolonization. In 2016, Ken had undertaken a symbolic walk similar to ours from Wood Mountain: he had walked solo the length of the Haldimand Tract in south-central Ontario to raise money for a museum dedicated to residential schools.

Fred Ludolph was also at the meeting, fresh from the airport. He is from Waterloo, Ontario, and like me a Lutheran pastor. Decades before, he had come to the Prairies for the last of his university years. When he heard about our Battleford plans, he asked to join in as a way of marking his sixtieth birthday and reconnecting with the west. Fred is one of those people who has a story for every occasion, and sometimes for none, but always delivered with a country humour hard to resist. The group was rounded out by Connie Sykes, an activist schoolteacher and a United Church lay minister from Frontier, Saskatchewan, with an avid interest in history, environmentalism, justice, and decolonization.

We had hardly planned it that way, but the group bound for Battleford included three Protestant ministers and a Catholic archbishop. We Christians realized that we bore a special responsibility to listen, and not to speak, especially when Indigenous fellow walkers were speaking. We knew that we had to speak honestly about the churches' roles in Canada's oppression of Indigenous Peoples and the churches' responsibilities in helping to make things right.

It was the unholy alliance of church and state that brought into being the horrors of the residential "schools," an action for which the Truth and Reconciliation Commission called the churches to specific repentance and restitution.[37] European Christian mission-aries almost always supported the imperial project. Most of them blindly conflated the gospel with European civilization, ideologies, and languages—as if being "Christian" meant a certain haircut or type of shirt. Now many Canadian churches are trying to act more in solidarity with First Nations, Métis, and Inuit.[38] But for most of Canadian history, Christians in Canada have been actively—even zealously—complicit in trying to "Europeanize," assimilate, and neglect or abuse to the point of death the people whose homeland they were colonizing.

Indigenous writers such as Raymond Aldred and George Tinker critique this default mixing of Christ and culture. They and others have developed Indigenous theologies that move in very different directions from European expressions of the faith.[39] As a scholar and teacher of early Christianity and Second Temple Judaism, I have spent much of my professional life trying to understand Jesus in his *first*-century, *Jewish* context. Jesus was not European at all. Neither was his movement.

However, most European-background Christians were never taught that the essence of Christianity did not somehow originate in England, France, or Germany. Nor do they realize that the cul-tural baggage that we tend to think of as Christian (robes, crosses, Bibles, crucifixes, hymns, candles, organs, etc.) are not Christian

---

37 See Truth and Reconciliation Commission, *Honouring the Truth, Reconciling for the Future: Summary of the Final Report of the Truth and Reconciliation Commission of Canada*, 6, http://publications.gc.ca/collections/collection_2015/trc/IR4-7-2015-eng.pdf. For a brief summary of some of the responses of "mainline" Canadian churches, see Nadeau, *Unsettling Spirit*, 94–97.

38 See Aldred and Anderson, *Our Home and Treaty Land*, 23–24.

39 See Robert Allen Warrior, "Canaanites, Cowboys, and Indians: Deliverance, Conquest, and Liberation Theology Today," *Christianity and Crisis* 49, no. 12 (1989): 261–65; George E. "Tink" Tinker, Clara S. Kidwell, and Homer Noley, *A Native American Theology* (Maryknoll, NY: Orbis, 2004); and Allen G. Jorgenson, *Indigenous and Christian Perspectives in Dialogue: Kairotic Place and Borders* (Lanham, MD: Lexington, 2021), 24–25.

but European cultural "wrapping." Once a person grasps the fact that Jesus was a Jew, and that Christianity had not even emerged as a separate faith when Paul wrote his letters, it helps to illuminate just how much the European Christianity of the missionaries was itself a European "indigenization" of the (Jewish) faith of Jesus's and Paul's day.

This shows in turn how hypocritical it was (and is) for European-background Christians to critique Indigenous appropriations of the faith. In a process analogous to what European peoples once did, Indigenous Peoples also sometimes make this faith their own.[40] In the process, they also transform it in ways different from those of Europeans.[41] On more than one occasion, I have heard Ray say that some folks should ask themselves what it means to be white and Christian before asking Indigenous Christians what it means to be Indigenous and Christian.

Given our feelings about this history of oppression, and the differences in belief and practice within the group, it was no surprise that the one ceremony we all gravitated toward was the Indigenous-led smudging. Whereas it would have been inappropriate for those of us of European backgrounds to take on this ceremony as our own,[42] the nêhiyaw and Métis leaders of our smudges seemed to be able to include us all in an expression of relationality that encompassed our walk, the land through which we travelled, the ancestors whom we remembered, and each other.

THE FORT BATTLEFORD TRAIL

UNLIKE THE TRADERS' Road/NWMPT, which ran east-west along a continental ridge, the Battleford Trail follows a rough line north and south. It was never a traditional path in the same way as the

---

40   Aldred and Anderson, *Our Home and Treaty Land*, 58–61.

41   Matthew R. Anderson, "'Aware-Settler' Biblical Studies: Breaking Claims of Textual Ownership," *Journal for Interdisciplinary Biblical Studies* 1, no. 1 (2019): 42–68.

42   Jorgenson, *Indigenous and Christian Perspectives in Dialogue*, xviii–xix.

Métis Red River cart, part of send-off, Swift Current, August 3, 2017.
Photo by the author.

Traders' Road. Rather, it was a settlement-driven freighting route important both to settlers and to the Métis as well as a path that saw Canadian military use during the Riel Resistance.

The trail ascends the west bank of the Swift Current Creek and meanders north-northwest onto rolling terrain, proceeding forty-eight kilometres along a large glacial moraine until it approaches the South Saskatchewan River. There it descends steep slopes before arriving at Saskatchewan Landing. The Landing, as locals call it, is a relatively short crossing point of Lake Diefenbaker and the South Saskatchewan River valley.

From there, the trail ascends again, this time along the north bank of the river just west of the highway. It continues west of the Coteau Hills to pass Kyle en route to Sanctuary, close by the eastern shore of Whitebear Lake. Following this northward, the trail angles west again and climbs a ridged moraine crossing into the southern end of the Bad Hills. The Bad Hills are an undulating landscape (mostly pasture now) formed from extensive ground deposits left by the last glacial retreat. We planned to camp overnight in the hills, three kilometres east of Bad Lake, a ten-square-kilometre lake without an outlet. Bad Lake, Harold wrote to me, is thought to have originated from a huge, broken-off section of glacial ice buried under moraine deposits, which left a large internal basin upon melting. From there, he added, I should expect that we would trek "across remnants of a proglacial lake ending at Eagle Creek, and the village of Herschel."[43]

Herschel might be a rural hamlet but has given its name to the ubiquitous backpacks of many an urban walker. From Herschel, the trail moves northward again, between the Bear Hills to the east and Eagle Creek to the west. Then it crosses undulating and hummocky land before advancing into the Eagle Hills, with the Neutral Hills indicated to the west on older maps. After crossing the Eagle Hills, the trail traverses the Lands of the Mosquito–Grizzly Bear's Head–Lean Man First Nation before descending once more, this time into the North Saskatchewan River valley. The town of Battleford and its twinned city of North Battleford are on opposite sides of the river at that point. Battleford was our destination.

Prior to the walk, Ken Wilson and I shared what few readings we could find on the Battleford Trail with each other and with the other trekkers. Our research suggested that over the years this trail, like the Traders' Road/NWMPT, had different identities. By the nineteenth century, the edges of a wide causeway defined the shifting borders of the Niisitapi to the west and the Nakota/nêhiyaw to the east, with regular diplomacy, and occasionally incursions, taking place in both directions.[44]

---

43   Harold Steppuhn, email to the author, March 25, 2019.
44   Peter Erasmus went through this area on his first trip to what is now northern Alberta. He relates the story of his horse (and himself) being spooked by the bodies left behind by a skirmish between Niisitapi and nêhiyaw. See Peter

The town of Battleford came into existence in 1874, the same year that the North West Mounted Police arrived farther south. That summer surveyors chose "a popular Cree camping place on a ford near the mouth of the Battle River as their headquarters."[45] The location made sense: it was a branch of the trail from Winnipeg to Edmonton and on the route from Fort Carlton to Fort Pitt. A telegraph line soon followed. Two years later Ottawa chose Battleford as the capital of the newly created North-West Territories (a large area including present-day Saskatchewan and Alberta). The rail line that everyone expected seemed to be imminent when it was surveyed though Battleford.[46]

Buoyed by news of the coming railway, hundreds of settlers began arriving, along with substantial numbers of Métis families. For six years, Battleford enjoyed a boom. It quickly became the second-largest town in the North-West Territories,[47] with a gossipy weekly newspaper, the *Saskatchewan Herald*. Settlers and Métis alike, especially those who had speculated on land, awaited the promised rail link.

However, Edgar Dewdney, who had substantial personal real estate interests in the south, and was an ally of John A. Macdonald, successfully lobbied for the new capital to be the settlement at Pile-of-Bones, later renamed Regina. A second shock to those at Battleford came with the decision to route the Canadian Pacific Railway closer to the border with the United States. Arthur Morton, in his *History of Prairie Settlement*, notes that the disappointment over the rerouting of the railway initially led Canadian settlers around Battleford to support Métis grievances.[48] The solidarity, however, didn't last long.

The citizens of Battleford were devastated by the news. They realized that they would need a trading route to the CPR line. By

Erasmus, *Buffalo Days and Nights*, ed. Henry Thompson (Calgary: Fifth House, 1999), 24–25.

45   Waiser, *A World We Have Lost*, 492.

46   Morton, *History of Prairie Settlement*, 62–63.

47   Waiser, *A World We Have Lost*, 493.

48   Morton, *History of Prairie Settlement*, 73.

December 1882, rail construction had reached the hamlet of Swift Current. Battleford's merchants were ready with wagons. The March 17, 1883, issue of the *Saskatchewan Herald* announced that, "as soon as it is practicable to cross the plains, Goodwin Marchand will go south to lay out a traffic route between Battleford and Swift Current."[49] This is the first specific mention that I could find of the route that we were about to walk. Two weeks later the newspaper noted that Marchand would lead "thirty-five horses, and also a scow nine feet by eighteen—large enough to carry two carts at a time—with which to cross the South Saskatchewan."[50] His group successfully crossed the river and exchanged freight at the Swift Current Creek rail depot. They then returned by the same route, building a bridge at Eagle Creek for others. They arrived in Battleford just before Queen Victoria Day, their arrival timed to be part of her birthday festivities.[51] Within weeks, Métis freighters, settlers, mounted police, and even Victorian tourists began taking the trail.[52]

Nineteenth-century overland freighting from Battleford to the new railway line farther south created the ruts that we were to follow. The heyday of the trail didn't last long. In 1890, after eight years of wagon freighting to Swift Current, a second rail line reached the more northern village of Saskatoon, and Battleford's merchants no longer needed the southern route. The Battleford Trail fell into a quieter rhythm, used mostly by local farmers and ranchers.

Like Marchand, many, perhaps most, of the original overland freighters were Métis. The morning that we set out on our walk, as

---

49   *Saskatchewan Herald*, March 17, 1883, 1.

50   *Saskatchewan Herald*, March 31, 1883, 1. When the first party of freighters finally set out on April 20, one of the travellers with them was William Bleasdell Cameron, the only male settler to survive the later killings at Frog Lake and the author of *Blood Red the Sun*.

51   *Saskatchewan Herald*, May 26, 1883, 4.

52   The same issue notes that "two young fellows came down from Edmonton last week, and after spending a few days here they left for Swift Current. They sold their blankets and overcoats and started on foot. Their supplies consisted of 2$ worth of hardtack and four cans of corned beef."

our group gathered at the Trail Ruts site, I was surprised to find myself in a good-sized crowd of people, many of them dressed in traditional clothing. Hugh had coordinated with Barb Parchman, a Métis historian, that our departure should coincide with the Métis Culture Days in Swift Current. I was delighted: there was a horse pulling a Red River cart of the type that would have been used for carting goods to Battleford (the freighters also used heavier ox-drawn wagons). Barb had arranged for the construction of the Red River cart, commissioned from an expert builder in Manitoba, using traditional types of wood.

After Hugh welcomed the crowd, Richard spoke about the walk and the importance of retracing the paths that were once lines of colonialism and violence against Indigenous Peoples. Swift Current RCMP Staff Sergeant Gary Hodges gave a prepared speech about the use of the trail by the North West Mounted Police and its place in policing history. Métis Elder Cecile Blanke[53] told us about the ongoing importance of the active Métis community in southwestern Saskatchewan, pointing out the Métis and Treaty 4 flags rippling in the breeze above our heads (just that morning Hugh had hoisted them above the entrance).[54] All in all, it was quite the send-off.

While the Red River cart was manoeuvred into position, Richard and Hugh put down tobacco on behalf of our group. Then we began walking. It was hard not to feel great: we stepped alongside the century-and-a-half-old tracks accompanied by a traditional Métis

---

53   See Cecile Blanke, *Lac Pelletier: My Métis Home* (Saskatoon: Gabriel Dumont Institute, 2019). An interview with her that gives a helpful perspective on the racism that caused the "hiding" of Métis through the twentieth century especially can be found in "Blanke, Cecile, Interview," January 30, 2012, in *Gabriel Dumont Institute, Virtual Museum of Métis History and Culture*, 5–6, https://www.metismuseum.ca/resource.php/13725.

54   Hugh's letter to the mayor of Swift Current suggesting that both the Treaty 4 and Métis flags should flank the Canadian flag at the flag court at the top of Central Avenue for National Indigenous Week (leading to June 21) never received a reply. At the time of writing, the Canadian flag was accompanied rather by the American and British flags.

reel (a type of traditional dance tune) played on fiddle and guitar, with the Red River cart bouncing along beside us. Hodges and Blanke hugged and posed for a photo. I thought about how that same trail had witnessed events that had so badly alienated Métis communities from the police.

Briefly, we numbered about thirty: part pilgrimage, part parade. Most intended to go only as far as the city limits. We walked down Walsh Trail street, parallel to a city roadway called Cowie Crescent. Swift Current's city planners, like the city overall, and like my family, tended to look for their symbols to the south and west, rather than the north, where we were headed.

To a settler descendant like me, the history of the Cypress Hills, even with its starvation winters, still somehow feels like a more personal past. It's a mistake, of course. But the myths of the southwest have been framed powerfully to reinforce that connection. By walking to Battleford, however, we were walking toward the present. My mother's sister, my aunt Isabelle, then in her mid-eighties, had helped me to tie some of the tobacco pouches that I was going to give when we stayed on Mosquito First Nation. It was the first time that she had done such a thing; she was enthusiastic, wanting to do it in the right way. I asked her about her days as a schoolteacher in one-room schoolhouses near Maple Creek, just north of the Cypress Hills. "Were the winters cold?" "Oh, yes," she answered. One of her jobs was to get the fire going every morning so that the pupils wouldn't freeze during their lessons. How did she get to work? By walking. Or on horseback. Sometimes, if the snow was high, she told me, the farmer whom she stayed with would harness a team and take her in a cutter. I asked her if they used bison hides. "Robes," she corrected me. "They're called buffalo *robes*. Yes, we used them. But they're all gone now," she added sadly. Just like those old-timers.

I thought about how the tobacco pouches that she was helping me to tie embodied an attempt to live out values of responsibility, respect, and relationality with Indigenous Peoples. I remembered how they were the same values that she and my uncle had so promoted, in a different way, as part of the prairie cooperative movement.[55]

When we passed the corner of her street, Cypress Drive, my cousin took my aunt's arm and turned to walk to her apartment. Nowhere in Swift Current is very far from the open plains, and a few minutes later we hit the sharp dividing line between city and prairie. This is one of those distinctions that someone from an urbanized environment has to see to believe: there is a sharp edge to prairie towns and cities. It is a place where the sidewalk ends, and beyond it is the wide-open world of wind and sage, no buildings in view. I stopped a moment and remembered standing with my aunt and watching the aurora borealis dance from exactly that spot just a few months before. I thought about the scene in W.O. Mitchell's *Who Has Seen the Wind* in which, at the threshold of the prairie, the protagonist, Brian, experiences a feeling of the transcendent that he cannot describe but knows contains deep truths. Looking out at the prairie, I sometimes get that feeling as well.

The Red River cart kept up with us for a time. We took turns riding it with Indigenous storyteller and community leader Joseph Naytowhow. We took photos and traded jokes and pleasantries. When the cart turned back to rejoin the festivities in the city, that was that. We walkers were alone. Not long after, we stopped. In a ditch by the side of the road, Richard led our now much smaller group in a smudge. We shared our hopes for walking, why we were there, and what we were asking the Land for permission to learn.

Leanne Betasamosake Simpson writes that "the starting point within Indigenous theoretical frameworks . . . is different than from within western theories: the spiritual world is alive and influencing; colonialism is contested; and storytelling, or 'narrative imagination,' is a tool [for] . . . visioning other realities."[56] If you asked any of us

---

55   Not that the cooperative movement was in any way above racism toward Indigenous Peoples; see F. Laurie Barron, *Walking in Indian Moccasins: The Native Policies of Tommy Douglas and the CCF* (Vancouver: UBC Press, 1997).

56   Leanne Betasamosake Simpson, *Dancing on Our Turtle's Back: Stories of Nishnaabeg Re-Creation, Resurgence and a New Emergence* (Winnipeg: Arbeiter

how these walks might contribute to addressing past injustices, or to decolonizing Canadian history and Canadians, we wouldn't necessarily have been able to give a clear answer. But all of us knew, instinctively, that the place where we might at least *begin* to "vision other realities" would be on the land. We hoped that it might teach us the stories that we needed to hear. "It's a way Indigenous peoples know well—of experiencing askîhk, of letting the land do the teaching."[57]

The walking was hot and dusty. Soon the only sounds were splashes of quiet conversation and our feet crunching gravel. We followed Hugh up into the hills, keeping with the historic tracks a while, then losing them again. After a cross-country trek through ankle-high grasses filled with cow parsnip, we rejoined the old tracks by a solitary, twisted, Manitoba maple, from which a large and motionless hawk watched us. Not long after, we passed a little-known Indigenous burial area used for millennia; there we stopped and put down tobacco again.[58]

About an hour later, just when the sun was beating down its worst, we were greeted by Hutterite girls in an all-terrain vehicle. It was a surprise that Hugh had arranged and a welcome one on such a hot day: in the shade of one of their buildings, the Swift Current Colony Hutterites had set up folding tables, on which were iced tea and freshly baked cookies. As we visited, they teased us about taking so many photos (it was the first day of our walk, after all). They asked us when they might see photos of themselves and their colony on social media. The iced tea was delicious. I asked them for their recipe—was it something German? They giggled and pointed at each other until one of them told me that it was a mix from a can.

Then we were off again, finally arriving nineteen kilometres from Swift Current at the farm of Rennie and Henry Funk. Henry, the creases in his face dirt-lined from a day of construction, came down

Ring, 2011), 40.

57   Aldred and Anderson, *Our Home and Treaty Land*, 18.

58   The Gray Burial Site is a National Historic Site but because of its sacred nature remains less publicized than some others.

Swift Current Hutterite Colony hosts, August 2017. *Photo by the author.*

the driveway to greet us carrying a big pot of homemade chili and rice. While the others set up tents amid caraganas and maple trees, I found a spot between two trees and hung a hammock. Wrens chattered nearby. At 9 p.m. exactly, coyotes started to yip, welcoming us back onto the prairie.

The next morning Kristin Catherwood of Heritage Saskatchewan drove up to conduct interviews. Kristin is a filmmaker and an infectious enthusiast of all things prairie: she had walked briefly with us on the Traders' Road and wanted to document at least some of this second pilgrimage. Later we came across a lovely small lake that Harold told me was likely another one formed by a mountain-sized piece of ice broken off during the glacial retreat. He had turned eighty-one the day before our departure, but there was no keeping him back. Most often he was in front of the group, striding ahead, his tall, angular body listing slightly to the left. At break times, when the rest of us would sit and visit, Harold often sat to the side. If the break was long

Harold Steppuhn, August 2017. *Photo by the author.*

enough, he might put his hat over his head and fall asleep. I saw him catnap in the open sunlight, flat out on stone-rough fields, or with his back against a trunk so deep in a patch of poplars that we had to squint to find him.

THE LANDING

THAT NIGHT WE stayed at the Gord Nodge farm, perched on the edge of the South Saskatchewan River valley. The Nodges once ran a flying club at the Swift Current airport. For years, my father rented planes from them, until Parkinson's took his licence away. Gord's brother is an artist, and the farm was full of odd little sculptures welded together from old farm equipment—pieces that peek out from behind hedges or surprise you when you come around the corner of a building. At times, it was hard to know whether what you were looking at was a pile of old, rusted wire and a radiator core or installation art.

To my surprise, that first day I developed two blisters. On the Traders' Road, I had managed the entire 350 kilometres without blisters at all. I decided to stick some athletic tape on my feet and hope that these ones would go away. I never stopped to think that my boots might have worn out or that the arthritis turning my big toe inward might have changed my footwear needs. My lack of thought turned out to be a mistake that would return to haunt me.

The next day was to be a thirty-kilometre walk, one of the longest of our planned itinerary. We would descend a series of ravines to the South Saskatchewan River. There we would have lunch at the historic site known as the Goodwin House. Then we would cross Diefenbaker Lake at the Landing and climb back up onto the wide plain that leads to the town of Kyle.

The Battleford Trail was used by freighters making overland hauls from Swift Current and then by the Canadian military in their largest-ever domestic action against an Indigenous group. It was that second use of the trail, during the events of 1885, that remains the most contentious.[59]

The largest mobilization of Canadian military ever undertaken for action within the country occurred in 1885.[60] It was a colonial war of pacification against an Indigenous population. That is simple and inarguable fact. The Canadian government moved against the Riel Resistance from three directions. Arriving in Regina from Winnipeg, General Frederick Middleton's troops marched north and west. A smaller force under General Thomas Strange moved north and east from Calgary. Their way was preceded by Father Albert Lacombe, Reverend John McDougall, and Chief Crowfoot, who probably did

---

59   There have been many histories written of the Riel Resistance. One of the most recent, containing a very useful "reception history" of Riel, is Jennifer Reid, *Louis Riel and the Creation of Modern Canada: Mythic Discourse and the Postcolonial State* (2008; reprinted, Winnipeg: University of Manitoba Press, 2012).

60   However, it should be remembered that in September 1666 about thirteen hundred French soldiers participated in an attack on Kanien'kehá:ka villages from their base in Quebec. See Patricia Simpson, *Marguerite Bourgeoys and the Congregation of Notre Dame, 1665–1700* (Montreal and Kingston: McGill-Queen's University Press, 2005), 16.

more good by diplomacy than any of the three military units.[61] A third group under Colonel William Otter marched north from Swift Current along the Battleford Trail.

The Canadian military action in 1885 was similar to the Boer War in South Africa, the Anglo-Zulu war, the British wars in India, and British colonial actions against the Māori in New Zealand. At its conclusion, the prairie Indigenous populations were "pacified," expatriate settlements were safeguarded and reassured, and economic expansion by the colonial power was once again free to move forward.[62]

Like most Canadians, I never managed to wrap my mind around the fact that anything like this belonged to *my* history. British Empire–backed soldiers in pith helmets "subduing" locals—that happened in other places. My ignorance is a triumph of the (literal) white-washing of the accounts. A colonial war is what took place in Canada only twenty-six years before the arrival of my grandparents. One of the main sites of deployment was Swift Current, where it was no coincidence that we were taught the history of countries far away, not the history revealed by the shell casings almost under our feet.

The third major militia to march against Riel arrived by rail in Swift Current at two in the morning on April 11, 1885.[63] Colonel Otter and his troops were scheduled to meet Middleton's Regina group by steamer on the South Saskatchewan River. However, the killing of nine settler men far to the north at Frog Lake, combined with the nervousness of the Battleford colonists, shifted Otter's orders the day after his arrival. While his troops attended "church parade," Otter planned the new route.[64] Eventually, he and his roughly eight hundred soldiers marched along the same trail that we were walking, toward Battleford, where there was a growing nêhiyaw-led food riot.

61   Norman Fergus Black, *History of Saskatchewan and the Old North West* (Regina: North West Historical Company, 1913), 337.

62   Sarah Carter, *Aboriginal People and Colonizers of Western Canada to 1900* (Toronto: University of Toronto Press, 1999), 102–3.

63   Tolton, *Prairie Warships*, 122.

64   Desmond Morton, *The Canadian General Sir William Otter* (Toronto: Hunter Rose, 1974), 107.

G.H. Needler, at the time a member of the Queen's Own Rifles regiment, wrote about their progress on the trail:

> Our column on the march was like a great two-mile serpent winding its way along; coiled to rest at dark and uncoiled again at dawn. When we tented overnight the ground was moist and the frost enough to make it necessary in the morning to lift our rubber sheets with care from the frosty ground to which they clung. Tent pegs were firmly frozen in. By the afternoon of the second day out we reached the South Saskatchewan, where we had two nasty days of cold and rain waiting for the sternwheel steamer Northcote to ferry us across.[65]

Otter believed that he was marching against an Indigenous resistance. Yet at no point was his force ever opposed on their way to Battleford. *There simply was no "Indian Uprising."* It was true that parts of the settlement at Battleford had been looted by starving nêhiyaw and Nakota. But the rioters never stayed, nor did they impede traffic to or from the fort, or communications from it, as a military force would have done.

There simply was no direct link between these food rioters and the resistance except in the hysterical minds of the colonists and of Otter's troops. When Otter arrived at Battleford and found no one there except the colonists, he could have sent for orders. Yet without permission from his superior, General Middleton, Otter turned his troops around and without provocation attacked Poundmaker and his people at their reserve at Cut Knife Hill.[66]

It was a mistake in every way. The so-called Battle of Cut Knife Hill was a near disaster for Otter's force, which sustained injuries. Yet, despite being the ones attacked, the nêhiyaw spared the retreating Canadian troops.[67] The nêhiyaw at Cut Knife Hill had never been

---

65   G.H. Needler, *Louis Riel: The Rebellion of 1885* (Toronto: Burns and MacEachern, 1957), 23.

66   Morton, *The Canadian General*, 116.

67   Waiser, *A World We Have Lost*, 551; see also Blair Stonechild and Bill Waiser, *Loyal till Death: Indians and the North-West Rebellion* (Calgary: Fifth House,

part of any organized opposition to the Canadian government, they had been attacked for no reason, and they had allowed the wounded troops to retreat, yet Poundmaker and his group were later faced with trials, prison terms, and reduced food supplies, all because they had been the "enemy."

If the starving nêhiyaw and Nakota had wanted to take the fort, then they could easily have done so. The property violence that took place arose from food shortages, not from murderous intent. It was a hunger riot that arose only after years of mistreatment. It was never an uprising. As Waiser puts it, "Fort Battleford also came under an *imagined* siege during April and May 1885."[68] The Indigenous rioters never cut the telegraph line that they knew kept the townspeople in touch with the outside world. During the riot, while the Battleford settlers locked themselves inside the stockade, a police courier was dispatched and returned regularly from the fort unhindered.[69]

History has proven that the story that the nêhiyaw and Nakota were allies of Dumont's Métis was a convenient lie. It was propaganda aimed at central Canadian voters, and used by the government to cut its already parsimonious aid to the reserves, while imprisoning independently minded Indigenous leaders.[70] In short, although the resistance was primarily Métis, the government used it to push its ongoing program of subjugation of the nêhiyaw and Nakota.

I was among generations of Saskatchewan schoolchildren shipped from our small towns and cities by yellow school bus to Regina for a tour of the capital. There, after touring the legislative building and the RCMP museum, I and thousands of my classmates watched John Coulter's play *The Trial of Louis Riel*.[71] Jennifer Reid points out that the continuous staging of that play over decades made it a

1997), 142–43. For details of the "Battle" of Cut Knife Hill, see Morton, *The Canadian General*, 114–19.

68   Waiser, *A World We Have Lost*, 540.

69   Morton, *The Canadian General*, 106.

70   See Stonechild and Waiser, *Loyal till Death*, 239–41.

71   Hugh Henry also participated and on his visit was one of the students chosen by the actors to be "part of the jury." He relates how this meant staying silent,

ritual similar to Europe's Passion Plays. As Reid demonstrates, the figure of Riel himself is usefully flexible. In the seemingly endless production of television shows, books, poems, operas, and even a graphic novel in which Riel is featured, sometimes he is portrayed as Métis, other times as a symbol of a pan-western resistance—a group that included western settlers—to central Canadian economic and political exploitation.[72] Riel is sometimes portrayed as a religious crackpot and a lunatic, other times as a master strategist. He became an icon for whatever western Canadians wanted most to love or hate about west-east, Indigenous-settler, regional-central, hinterland-capital dichotomies.

Riel was an international political and religious figure who came to represent a nation. Yet generally he has not been studied from two points of view that would make the most sense: as the leader of one of the nineteenth-century religious movements then sweeping through North America or as the leader of one of the many nationalist movements arising throughout the world during this period.[73]

CACTUS AND LICHEN, spear grass, and low buckbrush blanketed our route as we followed the march of Otter's troops. The smell of sage was almost overpowering as we traced the knife-edged coulees down toward Saskatchewan Landing Provincial Park. Soon we could see a lone building sitting by the water of the South Saskatchewan River.

Goodwin House is an unusual sight on the prairie. It's a fieldstone building standing alone at the south bank of the crossing. For hundreds of kilometres in every direction, there were—and still are—almost

---

and giving the verdict of "guilty" when prompted, for which he received a certificate and photo in appreciation.

72 Reid, *Louis Riel*, 42.

73 Geoff Read and Todd Webb, "'The Catholic Mahdi of the North West': Louis Riel and the Metis Resistance in Transatlantic and Imperial Context," *Canadian Historical Review* 93, no. 2 (2012): 172.

no other heritage stone buildings. Anyone who has driven on this highway knows the place. The house was once about a kilometre southeast of the ferry crossing. With the flooding of the valley after completion of the Gardiner Dam in 1967 (construction began in 1959), the house now stands almost at the shore of Diefenbaker Lake. Largely because of the lobbying of Cecile Blanke, a Métis flag hangs at the site, recognizing not only the Métis freighters and Indigenous ferrymen responsible for the crossing at the end of the nineteenth century but also the Métis craftsmen who helped to build the house and mortared the stone in a landscape where almost every other dwelling was sod or rough wood.

We went down the steep hill on the shoulders of the highway, keeping the Goodwin House in sight. It was built from 1898 to 1900 for Mary Rutherford from Moose Jaw and her husband, former NWMP officer Frank Goodwin. To me, the building could not be a better symbol of prairie settlement. From the outside, it looks European in style, although adapted with porches and a summer kitchen typical of an American ranch layout. Its foundation, however, was dug by two unnamed Indigenous "men with picks and shovels."[74] The stonework was done by a Métis craftsman with the apt name of Larocque. In one of those connections typical of the Prairies, Larocque was the great-uncle of Cecile. For several years, the Larocque family lived just east of Goodwin House, where they ran the ferry and were responsible for mail delivery from Swift Current. According to local sources, Larocque had to build a kiln to reduce local limestone for the cement used in Goodwin House. Local nêhiyaw and Nakota hauled the rocks and squared them for the stonemason. The mortar was reinforced by horse, antelope, and deer hair, gathered from the coulees by Indigenous workers.[75]

In other words, this unique house was built by Métis and, despite its European appearance, built upon an Indigenous foundation. In

74   Margaret Hryniuk and Frank Korvemaker, *Legacy of Stone: Saskatchewan's Stone Buildings* (Regina: Coteau Books, 2008), 40.

75   Hryniuk and Korvemaker, *Saskatchewan's Stone Buildings*, 41.

past years, it served as a boarding house (sometimes for the NWMP), a store, a social centre, and occasionally an Anglican church for those stranded on the south bank of the river by breakdowns, ice, or bad weather. Now it operates as a tourist centre.

We ate sandwiches at a picnic table beside the grand old home, semis roaring past us to get up enough speed for the hill that we had just descended. Upriver, one could imagine the South Saskatchewan, pre-dam, narrower and faster, and the spot to our west (now the Bison Hollow campground) where nêhiyaw, Nakota, and Niisitapi bison hunters forded the river. Métis hunters and traders also crossed it, travelling between the trading posts farther north and the southern bison grounds. In 1883, when Marchand left a flat-bottomed raft at the Landing capable of holding two Red River carts tightly packed, the ferry could sometimes be left on the wrong side for the next group that came along.[76] Alongside the Larocque family, local nêhiyaw operated the ferry for a small fee until eventually the Saskatchewan Coal Mining Company installed a larger, flatbed ferry that ran on a cable.[77] In the early twentieth century, there was briefly an elevated cable-car basket that could carry two or three people, and limited supplies, across the river. It must have been a harrowing ride. A local community history is titled *From Basket to Bridge* in memory of the brave souls who dared it.[78] We were more than happy just to walk.

On April 14, 1885, Colonel Otter arrived at the South Saskatchewan River with eight hundred men and three hundred wagons. There was a strong wind from the west, bringing a cold front and late-spring snow behind it.[79] The tiny ferry could manage neither the human nor the equipment loads. When the paddle wheeler *Northcôte* arrived, Otter's orders were not to take it upriver, as originally planned, but

---

76   Tolton, *Prairie Warships*, 114.

77   Tolton, *Prairie Warships*, 114.

78   Margaret Larson, *From Basket to Bridge: 1905–1980* (Kyle, SK: Kyle Heritage Committee, 1981), 29.

79   "Excerpt of an Unnamed Officer Who Was with Otter," April 14–16, 1885, Canadian War Museum Archives, 58A 1 101.38.

to use it to transport men and goods to the far bank, from where they would continue northward on foot.

The three-year-old hamlet of Swift Current had become a military supply base for Otter's column. Perhaps the first demonstration of the Gatling gun on Canadian soil, one of two imported by the government in 1885 during the resistance, took place by the dirt cliffs where our elementary school sometimes took field trips.[80]

We finished our sandwiches, took one more look at the Goodwin House, and crossed the bridge to the north shore. I held back. I was thinking about a photo that Hugh had sent me earlier that summer of the brief time in the 1950s that the Landing was "between bridges." The blues, greens, and burgundies in the image that I was thinking of are rich and oversaturated, a clue that the photo was originally a Kodachrome slide. The vivid colours almost make you feel the heat of the day, smell the sage, and hear the crickets. Unusual for southern Saskatchewan at that time of year, the land is green in the photo. On the far side of the river, one can see trees planted in a row. The hills in the distance have not yet baked golden.

It must have been warm that day, September 7, 1952. The young people in the photo were from the Swift Current Co-op School. They were on their way to the co-op farm at Matador, north of the Landing. The students stopped to see the wreckage of the bridge, which had collapsed that spring. The young men are in short-sleeved shirts and long pants. The young women would not look out of place in some locales even now: white blouses, pleated and pressed capris, and oxford shoes.

Everett Baker took Kodachrome slides of the school trip. In the group photo, my mother is in the middle, arms over her friend's shoulders. At fifteen years old, she looks every bit the life of the party. Baker took another photo of only her with one of the boys, Arthur Carlson. Freckled, his hair creamed in place, Arthur has the kind of grin that looks like he has just made a joke. His arm is over the

80   Don C. McGowan, *Grassland Settlers: The Swift Current Region during the Era of the Ranching Frontier* (Regina: Canadian Plains Research Center, 1975), 40.

shoulder of my mother. She seems to be sharing the joke—I rarely saw my mother smile that openly. She is posing jauntily, one leg up on a surviving girder. It's a photo typical of the Baker collection. In most of his photos, "it is truly amazing how natural and relaxed the subjects appear to be."[81] Baker somehow captured my mother in all the happy optimism of her youth.

A year or so after her passing, I received an email from Hugh, who had been looking through the Baker archives and come across the name Shirley Golling written on the back of this photo. Hugh had attached the photo with a brief message: "Isn't this your mother?" I had never seen this image before. I could barely believe that it showed up after her funeral. It felt like I was seeing a ghost, but a happy one, an unexpected blessing from the past.

In Baker's group photo, in the middle distance behind the co-op students, and partly submerged, steel girders are tangled together with tree trunks and branches. Posing in front of a disaster has always struck me as odd. This photo is no exception. Behind the smiling students is the catastrophic residue of a spring ice jam that, on April 6 that year, had popped a $1 million, brand-new bridge off its supports, mangling its steel and destroying a century-long hope of merchants and travellers alike. It had taken so many years for locals to get a bridge built across the South Saskatchewan River that its almost immediate collapse must have seemed even more disastrous. Within a year, they started work on its replacement—higher this time.[82]

That day on the Battleford Trek, when I walked over the South Saskatchewan River, I was carrying tobacco. My mother might have been pleased at the idea—for most of her life, she was a three-pack-a-day smoker. At the other end of the bridge, I stepped off the asphalt and, as Richard had suggested, set down tobacco in the shade of one of the struts. I tried to focus on my mother. A car hurtled past headed

81   Finn Andersen, "A Glimpse into the Past through the Eye of Everett Baker (1893–1981)," in *Plain Speaking: Essays on Aboriginal Peoples and the Prairie*, ed. Patrick Douaud and Bruce Dawson (Regina: Canadian Plains Research Center, 2002), 89.

82   Larson, *From Basket to Bridge*, 30.

south toward Swift Current. The driver craned his head to see what I was doing. I ignored him, busy imagining my fifteen-year-old mother standing on that girder in 1952, not knowing yet what would become of her life, young and full of promise and hope. I said a prayer for her, in thanks for her parenting, and for all those overcome by grief and addicted to substances that help to ease the pain of being sensitive and in mourning. I thought about the reciprocity of this land and our family's lives and how the territory still pulls on us.

I realized only later that I had been on the wrong side of the bridge. Maybe it's rationalization, but I put it down to the fact that children almost never get the full stories about their parents right. I had been close.

For Further Reading

On Métis history and ongoing presence in southwestern Saskatchewan, see Cecile Blanke, *Lac Pelletier: My Métis Home* (Saskatoon: Gabriel Dumont Institute, 2019). Cecile was kind enough to meet me on more than one occasion for an interview.

For settler history of the Saskatchewan Landing and of the communities north and south of it, see Margaret Larson, *From Basket to Bridge: 1905–1980* (Kyle, SK: Kyle Heritage Committee, 1981), as well as Don C. McGowan, *Grassland Settlers: The Swift Current Region during the Era of the Ranching Frontier* (Regina: Canadian Plains Research Center, 1975).

In the nineteenth century, on his first trip to what is now northern Alberta, Peter Erasmus went through the Red Ochre Hills, the "Neutral Hills," and the sites of nêhiyaw–Niisitapi conflicts, made more intense by the diminishing bison herds. He relates the story of his horse (and himself) being spooked by the bodies left behind by a skirmish. See Peter Erasmus, *Buffalo Days and Nights*, ed. Henry Thompson (Calgary: Fifth House, 1999), 24–25. Isaac Cowie also mentions the battle site, which he calls a "prairie Golgotha." See Isaac Cowie, *The Company of Adventurers: A Narrative of Seven Years in the Service of the Hudson's Bay Company during 1867–1874* (1913; reprinted, Lincoln: University of Nebraska Press, 1993), 313–15.

Swift Current Co-op School students at the wreckage of the Saskatchewan Landing Bridge, September 7, 1952. The author's mother is fifth from the right. *Photo by Everett Baker, courtesy of the Saskatchewan History and Folklore Society (SHFS_6442).*

The author's mother, Shirley Golling, and friend Arthur Carlson at the site of the collapsed bridge, September 7, 1952. *Photo by Everett Baker, courtesy of the Saskatchewan History and Folklore Society (SHFS_6443).*

Although the Red Ochre Hills are indicated on a map at the front of Rudy Wiebe's *The Temptations of Big Bear* (Toronto: McClelland and Stewart, 1973), it is difficult to track down their precise location. See the excellent blog posts about finding the Red Ochre Hills by Saskatchewan author Joan Soggie at https://www.yumpu.com/en/document/view/53016697/lost-in-the-red-ochre-hills-part-ii-saskatchewan-archaeological-.

Indigenous conflicts over food supply while enduring the extinction of the bison herds must be put into context. Harold Johnson notes that "your family [settlers] tell stories about my family: that we fought a multitude of wars among ourselves, and that our entire existence was premised on war.... The presumption is false." Harold Johnson, *Two Families: Treaty and Government* (Saskatoon: Purich, 2007), 40. Johnson's book is a helpful resource for many reasons, not least for understanding Canadian law not as being "above" treaty but as deriving from treaty.

One of the ironies of Canadian history is that noted twentieth-century Canadian historian Desmond Morton was the great-grandson of General Otter. Morton took on the task of being his ancestor's biographer. He did not see eye to eye with the general, who does not come off well in the book. See Desmond Morton, *The Canadian General Sir William Otter* (Toronto: Hunter Rose, 1974), xvi.

For details on the "battle" of Cut Knife Hill (where in 1885 Otter and his troops attacked an unsuspecting nêhiyawak settlement), see Bill Waiser, *A World We Have Lost: Saskatchewan before 1905* (Calgary: Fifth House, 2016), 551; Blair Stonechild and Bill Waiser, *Loyal till Death: Indians and the North-West Rebellion* (Calgary: Fifth House, 1997), 142–43; and Morton, *The Canadian General*, 114–19.

MISTAHIMASKWA (BIG BEAR)

WHEN WE FIRST decided to walk to Battleford, we had no way of anticipating the killing of Colten Boushie and the pressure cooker of public feelings that would follow. But being on the trail one year later, during the lead up to the trial, put us in the middle of the tensions.

Inviting Battleford-area farmers to join our daily smudges became a political act. I guess it always was, but during that trip it seemed to be more obvious. During my portion of our talks at the town halls and museums, which usually concerned decolonization, I realized even more painfully that, despite growing up on the prairie, I would now be seen as an outsider. And it was uncomfortable for those of us settler descended to accept hospitality from the Mosquito First Nation while Indigenous jurors were being rejected in the selection process for the trial. In many ways, the Battleford walk had become an uncomfortable (and once again powerfully unsettling) learning experience.

It was also a new experience for us because, for the first time on our walks, we were not always welcomed by the farmers whom we encountered. My First Nations or Métis fellow walkers knew well enough the apprehension of approaching a white farmer's home to ask for permission to pick berries or to find some shade to eat lunch. Again and again they told the rest of us that on their own they simply wouldn't risk it, and that summer we came to understand why. Alone they would never have walked the roads and the edges of fields that we could safely as primarily a white group. Such powerful but unwritten rules governing safety and freedom of movement *are what systemic racism looks like in practice.* As an older, white, Canadian man who generally treats the whole world as open, for me these were new learnings.

IRONICALLY, GOODWIN MARCHAND'S and his freighters' inaugural trip in 1883 south on the Battleford Trail coincided with the walk, in the other direction, of the last of the nêhiyaw refugees from the Cypress Hills. In his memoirs, Erasmus states that it was the expulsion that caused him to resign his government post. "Many of the people were in very poor circumstances," he wrote, "with no means of transportation. The officials responsible seemed to be very

reluctant to provide any means of travel."[83] In June 1883, after a winter
of deaths and the closing of Fort Walsh, "Big Bear, with 550 People,
left the Cypress Hills for the last time. They reached Battleford on
July 21. A few elderly [people] were transported on ox carts, but
most . . . walked more than three hundred miles."[84]

Many Canadians have at least heard the names of Poundmaker
(Pitikwahanapiwiyin), his adoptive father Crowfoot (Isapo-Muxika),
Payepot, and Sitting Bull, whom most Canadians think of as an
"American Indian" in unconscious agreement with the historical
revisionism that followed the creation of the international border.
But Mistahimaskwa (Big Bear) is perhaps the First Nations leader
most identified with taking a stand against the Canadian government
during these years.

Although not without problems,[85] Rudy Wiebe has consistently
worked to tell Big Bear's story. Wiebe wrote an influential novel
in 1973 titled *The Temptations of Big Bear*, which, despite its exotic
romanticism, brought Mistahimaskwa to Canadian consciousness.
In 2008, he reworked some of the material into a less flowery account
for the Extraordinary Canadians series, a book titled simply *Big Bear*.
Whether Mistahimaskwa would have been happy to be included
in a list of Canadians, extraordinary or otherwise, is not addressed
in the book.

Wiebe wrote

> Friday, December 8, 1882. On that day of blowing snow over
> Fort Walsh, Big Bear gave an . . . oration explaining how, by
> lies and deceit and promises never kept, six years of Treaty
> Six had stolen from his People the Great Spirit's greatest
> gifts, their independence and their homeland. More support

83   Erasmus, *Buffalo Days*, 268.

84   Rudy Wiebe, *The Temptations of Big Bear* (Toronto: McClelland and Stewart, 1973), 126–27.

85   See the critique of Wiebe's portrayal of Big Bear in Laura Smyth Groening, *Listening to Old Woman Speak: Natives and AlterNatives in Canadian Literature* (Montreal and Kingston: McGill-Queen's University Press, 2004), 106–7.

in tools and skill, and above all, more land, was needed to
live a good and honourable life the way every human being
should live in a good and honourable country. But he could
refuse no longer.... Big Bear made his x.[86]

It took ten more months for the Canadian government to force
Mistahimaskwa and his remaining followers out of the Cypress
Hills. He was not allowed to take the land that he chose despite
having been promised in agreements whose ink was still wet that
he could do just that. Neither was he allowed to settle his people
near Poundmaker, west of Battleford, so that the two could create
an Indigenous "commons" large enough for adequate hunting and
community building. Whatever was written on the treaties, the
Canadian authorities wanted small splinter groups of Indigenous
families on land generally poor for farming. The government told
Mistahimaskwa to forget Poundmaker and that his people would
get rations only at Frog Lake, almost 240 kilometres northwest of
Battleford.

As they struggled north, the nêhiyaw refugees were hardly an
invading army. But that's how they were reported by the settlers
in Battleford, who in one of the more obvious contradictions
of colonialism were nonetheless anxiously awaiting the chance
to sell their flour, wood, and other supplies as relief to the new
arrivals.[87] The *Saskatchewan Herald* (a newspaper never shy to use
racist language or twist the truth) stated that "the first party of Big
Bear's Indians left Fort Walsh for Pitt towards the end of March,
and should therefore be near their destination by this time. Walsh
has been abandoned both as a post of the mounted police and
as a depot of Indian supplies, and has consequently lost its chief

---

86   Wiebe, *Big Bear*, 121–22.
87   Relief was good business for the community. Many issues of the *Saskatchewan
      Herald* in the 1880s contain calls for tenders posted by "the Indian Department."
      For example, the issue of February 3, 1883, states that "the Indian Department
      advertise[s] for tenders for 1200 bags of flour for this District and 300 for the
      Carlton Agency." *Saskatchewan Herald*, February 3, 1883, 1.

attractions for the idle and vicious aborigines who have hitherto lingered around it."[88]

The nêhiyaw likely walked farther west than we did in 2017. However, given the few safe crossings of the river, perhaps they came across the same grandfather stone as we did as we climbed out of the South Saskatchewan River valley. Just north of the Landing, not far off the Battleford Trail, sits a glacial erratic, a truck-sized boulder. The "grandfather's" sides have been rubbed so smooth by generation after generation of bison that we put our cheeks against the surface to cool them on that hot day. Richard placed tobacco and stayed a while after the rest of us had moved on.

Black clouds were banking to the east. As the hours passed, they moved north and then, oddly, curled to our west. For an hour or two, we walked into a little valley of sunshine surrounded on three sides by walls of cloud and into the refreshingly cool wind coming off the weather front. Eventually, a sprinkle of rain followed the breeze. We passed a picturesque Lutheran church where, in my twenties, I had once preached as a student minister.[89] The town of Kyle sat on the horizon. As often happens to walkers in this kind of flat landscape, despite our efforts, the town never seemed to get any closer. After about twenty kilometres, a group left in vehicles to get there before the grocery store closed. The rest of us plodded on, increasingly silent, taking to the ditches to give our feet a break from the asphalt.

By the time we arrived, the rain had stiffened into something more serious. I opted for the hotel. It felt like the best shower of my life. There were new blisters again, worrisome so early in the journey, and they were starting to be painful. That evening our presentation had a good turnout, about forty people. First it was my turn. I felt a bit intimidated since most of the audience's first row was made up

---

88   *Saskatchewan Herald*, May 12, 1883, 2. The writer is unknown but was likely the same as for most of the newspaper's otherwise unattributed content, P.G. (Patrick Gammie) Laurie.

89   On the fate of small Lutheran churches as a result of rural depopulation, see Anderson, *Settling Saskatchewan*, 317, 388.

of my ex-in-laws and their families. But they had come to support me and were an easy audience as I talked about pilgrimage and the necessity of seeing land in a way that recognized Indigenous presence. Hugh read selections from the *Saskatchewan Herald* about freighting in the 1880s. Then he quoted from soldier, traveller, and NWMP diaries, accompanying the readings with historical images of the trail (as usual, the images from the 1940s to the 1960s were the highlight for the audience).

The next day, Sunday, was a "short" day—only nineteen kilometres. We started with a smudge at the museum. On the way out of town, we passed Clearwater Lutheran Church. Fred and I stopped to say hi, and the student minister, Sarah Urano, gave us freshly baked cookies.[90] The trail headed west and then north on soft dirt road. As we walked, munching on the cookies, crop-dusting planes buzzed low overhead. A reporter from the Kyle newspaper drove by in a half-ton truck. She stopped and rolled down her window: "Do you folks have face masks? You really should. It's dangerous to walk too long in this stuff." Since we had been amusing ourselves as we went by composing haikus, I came up with one after the reporter left, her truck trailing clouds of dust:

> They're desiccating
> But we will walk anyway
> We're Round-Up ready.

One of the advantages of a fine-dust road was that you could clearly see animal tracks. There were plenty to identify: deer, badger, partridge, and occasionally coyote. Once the crop-dusting planes were behind us, the smell of canola filled our nostrils. The rain had left the sloughs impassable, so we kept to roads east of the historic route, our walk a kind of etch-a-sketch approximation of the trail. By staying on the roads, we kept our boots dry but trekked farther.

---

90 On Scandinavian settlement in the Kyle area, see Anderson, *Settling Saskatchewan*, 317.

Gravel roads are built with a crown in the middle, sloping gently to each side. When walking on them, it's wise to switch sides of the road from time to time to avoid constantly having one leg higher than the other. In general, road walking results in more frequent injuries from repetitive strain on hips, knees, and ankles. As a result of our road walking, Connie had developed an injury. She decided to take breaks and volunteered her truck for group use. Others began to spell each other off. For the first time on our prairie pilgrimages, we had a consistent support vehicle. From that point on, Connie cheerfully packed extra water and shared her vehicle with whoever might need a break, some shade, or encouraging words. Thanks to her generosity, we found a new way of moving through the landscape.

That night we set up tents in the ghost town of Sanctuary, on the edge of a swollen and eerily still Whitebear Lake. The lake (and a nearby hamlet) were named for a rare albino grizzly supposedly shot in the 1850s during the Palliser Expedition. There are other Whitebear place names, so it is likely that such an animal existed. However, Erasmus, who was with Palliser, mentions nothing about encountering a white bear, although he does relate a harrowing meeting with other prairie grizzlies.[91]

Our evening at the lake was languidly still and hot. The long sunset reflecting across the water made us lazy. We fell asleep to a raucous chorus of crickets and to the sounds of mice scurrying through the grey boards of the abandoned building at our backs. Barn swallows rustled in the rafters. A nearby hawk berated us from her nest. There was a tin cup hanging from a nearby post, purpose unknown.

The next morning warblers, wrens, and sparrows began a ruckus at first light, waking us from our slumbers. After a smudge joined by a local farmer, we headed off. The first part of the walk was spent along the lake, which that year was much larger than normal. Whole corrals had been submerged, the tips of grey posts poking out from silver water tracked by water skitters and other insects. We crossed the lake on a causeway and came across a busy water well at the far side.

91   Erasmus, *Buffalo Days*, 69.

Farm workers were lined up to fill their tanker trucks for desiccating crops and saluted us as we passed. We turned right at the far side of the causeway and followed the far bank, keeping the lake to our east.

After this, we came across another body of water. This was a seasonal slough that for some mysterious reason is called Hudson's Bay by locals; in maps produced by R.C. Laurie's survey of the area in 1886, the slough and a neighbouring one were indicated as "dry lakes" (large sections of Whitebear Lake itself regularly dry out). 2017 was certainly not dry—ducks were everywhere, their feet slap-slapping as they ran across the water to take wing. Vast lines of snow geese and Canada geese wheeled above our heads. Brown-eyed Susans and yarrow lined the ditches, the oranges and browns vivid against the tawny-black of the bearded wheat. Delicate yellow butterflies flitted among the green stalks of canola, dancing in our path. I realized that they were probably one of the targets of spraying.

When we found a patch of cottonwoods, we put down tarps and picnicked. After lunch, I found Harold deep in the trees, napping against a trunk. I asked him about the geological formation of Whitebear Lake and the likelihood that "Hudson's Bay" goes dry many years. When I mentioned the Bad Hills, Harold reminded me that all the rises that we were passing—the Vermillion Hills to the east, the Neutral Hills to the west, even the Eagle Creek Hills ahead—were vast glacial dumps, left by the last retreat of the ice. I asked him about the poplars in which we were resting. He told me that the thicket was all one organism, an ancient, massive, life form putting up new trees as shoots as old trees die. "That's just science," he concluded, laughing quietly. "That's all boring stuff. Now you [he pointed a long thin finger at me], ha ha! You theologians and philosophers and historians . . . you're the real eggheads." After the walk, Connie wrote about Harold:

> Harold's tent was a tube of clear plastic, like from the dry cleaners. It would be set up in 30 seconds, if he could find 2 trees. He was enjoying his supper while some of us were still trying to fit tent poles together. He was settling into

dreamland when we were just finding the can opener for the beans. He waited for the sun to peek over the horizon each morning, then crawled out to wash his face in the dew before it dried. Harold waited patiently while the rest of us ate breakfast, packed up our tents, and scrambled to find enough food to give us energy for the day. More than once, he helped me fold my tent and fill my water bottles. He kept a stone in his mouth (to increase salivation) so he didn't have to carry so much water.[92]

Hours and kilometres later we finally approached Otter's Station, named after the commander who had marched north along our path. After a long afternoon of walking, without seeing a soul, it was surprising to find a group of young people who appeared to be waiting for us. Peter and Sabrina Elliott are local farmers. Their children and grandchildren had travelled home to the farm for the holiday weekend. They had seen us from their window and rushed out to invite us to the shaded porch for a cool drink. As we visited, Sabrina brought out muffins. She introduced us to new Saskatchewan residents, recently arrived from El Salvador.[93]

The forecast that night was for rain. The landowner of the pasture that was once Otter's Station, Carl Sothmann, met us while we peered over his barbed-wire fence. We could see cattle foraging on the pock-marked earth right where we had planned to set up our tents. In light of both the weather and the cattle, we opted to go to Elrose and to a motel instead of camping at Otter's Station. Later, as we shared a brimming pot of lentil stew made by Ken and Christine, she shared the haiku that she had written after needing to take a break from walking:

---

92   Connie Sykes, email to the author, October 8, 2017, part of her Thanksgiving Sunday sermon at the United church in Frontier.

93   On settler mythologies of primacy on the land erasing Indigenous presence while simultaneously operating as anti-immigrant rhetoric, see Sherene H. Razack, "When Place Becomes Race," in *Race, Space, and the Law: Unmapping a White Settler Society*, ed. Sherene H. Razack (Toronto: Between the Lines, 2002), 4.

Blisters are loyal
they come again and again
like blue grama grass

ON SEVERAL OCCASIONS between 1888, when he was elected
to the territorial legislature, and 1890, when the rail line reached
Saskatoon, James Clinkskill travelled by "coach" (really a wagon)
between his lumber yard at Battleford and the rail line at Swift
Current.[94] Fortunately for us, Clinkskill described the trail in detail,
including an intriguing mention of Otter's Station:

> The next [overnight stop], after leaving the river, was Otter's
> Station or the Devil's Gulch. It had been made by digging
> a hole in the sloping bank, with a few boards for walls and
> poles with straw on top for a roof. Its size was about ten feet
> by twelve feet. There were four bunks against the wall, one
> on top of the other. When there were several passengers,
> the furniture, consisting of a table and a bench to sit on, was
> put outside and beds were made on the floor. This place
> was warm, being well made and in a big ravine sheltered
> from the wind. Some fastidious people found fault with
> the accommodation on account of the number of mice
> that would insist on cavorting over your person after you
> had gone to rest.[95]

Bob's Diner in Elrose is an excellent place for breakfast and
considerably more comfortable than Otter's Station must have
been even in its heyday, judging from Clinkskill's description. The

---

94   I'm indebted to Hugh Henry not only for finding the source for me but also
     for pointing out what the dates likely would have been.

95   James Clinkskill, *A Prairie Memoir: The Life and Times of James Clinkskill 1853–1936*,
     ed. S.D. Hansen (Regina: Canadian Plains Research Center, 2003), 72.

owner of Bob's Diner, Salim, originally from Bangladesh, made us tasty omelettes and tea the next morning. His eyebrows arched in surprise that anyone would walk across the prairie, but he was too diplomatic to say anything. On our return to Otter's Station, we were met by Lorne Kelsey, a local farmer. Richard led a smudge near one of the pools of water. He noted that this spring and others like it, before they had settler (and especially military) names, were (and are) significant to the people who for millennia have used the hills for shelter and hunting. As often happened on our walks, Richard and I lingered in discussion as the rest of our group moved off. We were talking about the fact that, although we had seen no offerings in this particular locale, tobacco in little pouches of brightly coloured material can sometimes still be found hanging in the bushes around such springs. Indigenous Peoples haven't forgotten them.

"It's a spiritual place. Can't you feel it? People have been drinking the water from this stream for who knows? Centuries," Richard said.

I'd begun hoisting my backpack over my shoulders and adjusting my straps. Richard gestured for me to stay. He was looking at some rivulets of liquid meandering between the soggy humps of earth. By this point, the rest of our group were examining a slightly caved-in hollow in the side of one of the north hills, probably the location of Clinkskill's stop.

"Water is life. This *spring* is life." Richard spread his arms wide. Under his jacket, he was wearing a blue T-shirt emblazoned with the infinity symbol of the Métis. "Come on!" He surprised me by dropping spread-eagled to the ground. "We can't leave before we drink some."

Everything was sodden. The tufts of grass were muddy, wiped by the hoofs of the recently departed cattle that I feared were likely at that moment grazing—and defecating—upstream. I looked with horror at the slow-moving, muddy liquid. It looked nothing like a spring of life to me, more like a spring of dysentery. Already Richard had his hand in the gravy.

"I don't know," I hesitated.

"You can do it," he insisted, his voice muffled by the grass. "This is the water that has kept generations alive. Then, after that, the water that brought the first settlers to this hill. This is living history!"

I got on my knees reluctantly. I was not at all sure that I could manage to get my mouth close to the muck. I used my hand to bring some of it to my mouth. I took a tentative swallow, letting most of the rest dribble through my fingers. I couldn't imagine why anyone would make a stop for this stuff. But Clinkskill had. It had been, apparently, the perfect place to host horses and travellers overnight.

Richard was standing again, his pack on, enthusiastic. "That was great," he said and smiled. He sauntered downhill toward the others.

"Be there in a second!" I called. When I was alone, I rummaged deep in my pack. My wife, Sara, had surprised me by packing a tiny bottle of Scotch into my bag for my trip. I hadn't opened it yet, but this seemed to be the perfect occasion. I took a mouthful of the 40-percent alcohol, gargled, and spit it out. Then I swallowed a mouthful more, just to be sure.

I was clearly a settler to the core and a man of little faith. Nonetheless, it seemed to be wise, when post-settlement cattle were upstream, to take this bit of history with an antiseptic chaser. I hurried to catch up with the others.

THE RIGHT OF RESPONSIBLE ACCESS AND THE CANADIAN WEST

A key relationship is between events and interpretation, between a happening and the subsequent ways in which it is converted into a more generally comprehensible and perhaps persuasive and exemplary narrative.

—SIMON COLEMAN[96]

---

96   Simon Coleman, "Anthropological Tropes and Historical Tricksters: Pilgrimage as an 'Example' of Persuasion," *Journal of the Royal Anthropological Institute* 21 (2015): 144–61.

August 15, 2017. Swift Current to Battleford Trail. *Photo by the author.*

AT OTTER'S STATION, there was no need to ask who owned the place or if we had the right to be there. Hugh had planned the stop. He had contacted landowners and received permission for our presence. Local farmer Lorne Kelsey was with us and showed us the remains of Clinkskill's stagecoach stop. The day before we had been served water, cold drinks, and muffins by the Elliotts, whose farm was just east of where we stood. It was fair to guess that everyone within kilometres knew that we were there.

There was another reason for my lack of concern. Whether in downtown Montreal or in rural Saskatchewan, as a white man I am accustomed to travelling free of fear and apprehension. Bruce McIvor—author, academic, lawyer, and member of the Manitoba Métis Federation—writes that, in contrast,

> the threat and reality of violence is at the core of Indigenous experiences with non-Indigenous Canada. My clients live with the threat of violence their entire lives. Violence inflicted

on them and their loved ones by non-Indigenous people. From an early age they learn the cruel reality that being a visibly identifiable Indigenous person in Canada means they live with a heightened risk of being insulted, attacked, and killed by non-Indigenous people. From Colten Boushie to Tina Fontaine, to a grandfather and his granddaughter handcuffed outside a bank in downtown Vancouver, violence against Indigenous people is the Canadian reality.[97]

This is not a reality that I have lived. If a half-ton truck approaches while I am stopped in my car on a rural road, my first reaction is not terror. I move through the world with credit card, cell phone, passport, and relative ease that too often I assume is normal. The truth, of course, is that such "freedom" tends to apply most to people who look like me.

When it comes to talking about paths, then, it is also necessarily to talk about those factors that *restrict* paths. The trails that we walked have their opposites: fences and No Trespassing signs. Tragically, in the years in which we were rediscovering and rewalking historic trails that cross what is now south and central Saskatchewan, more and more landowners were beginning to limit access to the lands on which the trails sit. If this trend continues, then soon heritage paths such as the Traders' Road, the Battleford Trail, and the Carlton Trail will become casualties. They will be collateral damage of rural residents' fears for their safety and security. Too often, instead of the government effectively addressing such concerns, unscrupulous politicians stoke the fears for their political advantage. Indigenous persons, and their treaty rights, are among the casualties.[98]

Sadly, part of what the "No Trespassing" debate hides is the common cause between First Nations and non-Indigenous rural

---

97   McIvor, *Standoff*, 90.

98   See "New Trespass Legislation Coming into Force on January 1, 2022," Government of Saskatchewan, December 16, 2021, https://www.saskatchewan.ca /government/news-and-media/2021/december/16/new-trespass-legislation -coming-into-force-on-january-1-2022.

populations in contrast to the needs of those who live in cities.[99] Chelsea Vowel writes that

> rural Canada personifies "the two solitudes" of Indigenous and non-Indigenous peoples in a way that is difficult to understand from urban settings. These two solitudes exist on lands that supply the bulk of resources extracted to support the urban south, meaning they also experience the effects of resource extraction in ways urban residents do not. When gravel aggregate is strip mined, when fracking exploration is undertaken, when large scale pig feedlots are proposed, rural Indigenous and non-Indigenous people are living with the direct consequences including clouds of silica dust, damage to aquifers, smell, noise, run-off, and increased presence of shift workers unaffiliated with local communities (and the violence that brings). Rather than being a situation that unifies Indigenous and non-Indigenous peoples however, each community is accustomed to working in isolation from the other.[100]

I've walked paths in Norway, Finland, Austria, and Iceland, where the historical right of access to land is so ancient that it predates written laws. In the Norse countries, some limited and responsible public access, including to most private and rural land, is simply understood as an inalienable right. In Finland, it is called *jokamiehenoikeus* and in Norway *allemannsrett* (literally, "everyman's right"). The term "right" doesn't capture the concept completely—we tend to think about "rights" applying to individuals. In Scandinavian countries, such rights are collective in a way much closer to Indigenous conceptions of rights. Nor is the concept as much about rights as it is about shared responsibilities.

---

99   Roger Epp, *We Are All Treaty People: Prairie Essays* (Edmonton: University of Alberta Press, 2008), 127.

100   Chelsea Vowel, "Beyond Territorial Acknowledgments," 2016, http:// apihtawikosisan.com/2016/09/beyond-territorial-acknowledgments/.

In May 2019, naturalist and film producer Antti Huttunen met me at Haukamakki (Hawkhill), Finland, where we had arranged to talk about public access. He called the social principle of public access an "ancient understanding" in Finland. He struggled to describe how most Finns instinctively feel about the lakes, rivers, and forests of their country. He finally settled on the English word *contract*. Interestingly, given the context of treaties, he also frequently used the word *covenant*. "*Jokamiehenoikeus* is like an ancient covenant," he said, "one we Finns have with the land and it has with us." In a way somewhat similar to Indigenous thinking about relationality, Finns believe that they belong to the land as much as it belongs to them. Even as landowners, Finns are required to share the bounty of the land, whether mushrooms, berries, or paths.

In these countries, the principle of "every person's right" does not abrogate private property. But it does recognize that no one person's (or corporation's) private ownership should be to the detriment of the wider community. Importantly, it also means that some part of the richness of one's country exists for the good of all.[101]

Parts of England have "the right to roam," won by widespread public resistance to enclosed lands and long legal battles that took place from the 1930s to the early 2000s.[102] Scotland has similar, and more wide-ranging, laws under a title that I prefer: "The Right of Responsible Access." Landowners in many parts of Scotland, England, and Wales are required not only to allow access to those who wish to take historic paths on their properties but actually to build turnstiles and other aids for walkers so that they can easily pass.

In return, walkers are obliged to act responsibly and not to create damage or harm the interests of property owners. If I were to pitch a tent on private property in Scotland, I would have to make sure to do so responsibly, out of sight of the landowner's house, at a

---

101   Matthew R. Anderson, "Why Canadians Need the Right to Roam," *The Narwhal*, July 30, 2018, https://thenarwhal.ca/right-to-roam-canada/.

102   Dave Sissons, Terry Howard, and Roly Smith, *Clarion Call: Sheffield's Access Pioneers* (Sheffield, UK: North End/Clarion Call, 2017).

distance from outbuildings, and not disrupting animals or crops. The law—but more importantly the embedded social practice (the culture)—is not to leave garbage or damage property. Under such conditions of respect, one has the right to be there.

Western Canada is hardly the United Kingdom. There are few walkers' groups, no mass rambling movement, and no one anxiously waiting for weekends to escape grimy factories in Regina or Saskatoon. But there are historic, important, and public trails that stretch across the country and now sit on privately held territory. Keeping those trails alive requires some form of agreement and access. Moreover, Saskatchewan and other prairie provinces must deal with an important issue that the British and Scottish landowners and ramblers in the 1930s never faced—treaty rights, which guarantee ongoing Indigenous access. Additionally, the western provinces hold what are called Crown lands as part of Canada's treaty obligations.

History is often ironic. Few chapters of Canadian history are more ironic than the fact that the very settlers who forced Indigenous Peoples off the great "commons" that was Treaty 4 and Treaty 6 territory were often themselves descendants of people who had been forced off such commons in Scotland, Ireland, and England.[103] It was the enclosure movements of those countries that exiled thousands from fields, woods, and streams that had nourished their families for centuries. Many of the dispossessed Scots, Irish, and English ended up in the colonies. In Canada, their descendants eventually helped to remove one of the last great commons of North America.[104] As Silvia Federici and Peter Linebaugh point out, any discussion of land use must begin by acknowledging those who first held the Land as a commons, the Indigenous Peoples.[105]

---

103 Aldred and Anderson, *Our Home and Treaty Land*, 10.

104 For more on this, see Trevor Herriot, *Towards a Prairie Atonement* (Regina: University of Regina Press, 2016), 36.

105 Silvia Federici and Peter Linebaugh, *Re-Enchanting the World: Feminism and the Politics of the Commons* (Oakland, CA: PM Press, 2019), 79.

Rural Norway has just as scattered a population as rural Saskatchewan. I believe that per capita it has fewer police. Yet, for the most part, the principles of public access are well respected. There are always those who vandalize property, leave garbage, and commit theft. To address such "free riders," laws must be enforced.[106] But when a society is based upon principles of mutual respect, and upon beliefs that land must be to the benefit of all, there are fewer problems. When there is lifelong education that reinforces the value of seeing land as a commons, the resulting attitudes are generally beneficial to landowners and non-landowners alike and encourage a vibrant, outdoor culture.

We Canadians don't realize just how much the default position of settlers and Indigenous Peoples vis-à-vis land, established by the treaties, has been reversed ironically and tragically. It was settlers who were sequestered originally. It was settlers who were granted "the right of access" to the land by the numbered treaties. Not the other way around. As a non-Indigenous academic, I am suggesting that changing Canadian culture by remembering European conceptions of the commons can be a more positive way of finding common ground (literally) than claiming rights or jurisdictions. For those of us from a European background, it means finding resources from within our own ancient traditions that will help us in acknowledging ongoing Indigenous sovereignty. This change of attitude could help to prepare us for the fundamental societal changes needed to rectify the many wrongs committed by not living up to the treaties.

THE BAD HILLS

WE SPENT MOST of that morning crossing the Bad Hills. The old tracks ran especially deep along hillsides, evidence of heavy use a

---

106   Herriot, *Towards a Prairie Atonement*, 90–91, doesn't mince words: "In place of a useful set of customs and practices, or a system of local governance that might prevent or resolve such disputes, . . . we have a legal system with ham-handed laws devised in distant legislatures and rendered inept by underfunded government agencies and monitoring systems."

century and a half ago by long trains of carts and wagons. As Otter's column moved north, and as Battleford rebuilt after 1885, seventy or more carts and wagons in a group were not unknown. The squealing of that many loaded axles on such hilly terrain must have been a sound heard for kilometres. Ironically, even while the resistance blazed, it was often Métis freighters who hauled supplies up the Battleford Trail for the Canadian army. Many of the teams hauling military freight across the South Saskatchewan River were also led by Métis and First Nations drivers.[107]

We passed a bald hilltop where someone had piled stones in the shape of an inukshuk, a strange sight when there were no buildings within kilometres. We flushed a coyote from its den and came across a medicine wheel (proof of the continuous Indigenous presence that Richard had just suggested to me at Otter's Station). Finally, after hours of trudging beside sloughs matted with dark algae presided over by twisted aspens, we arrived at the Greenan Community Centre.

The evening sky was streaked with pink cloud. The Community Centre is a solitary building not far from a rail crossing. It still holds chalkboards and desks from its pre-retirement life as a schoolhouse. Linda Kelsey, Lorne's wife, drove up while we were tending blisters and removing spear grass from our socks. She was carrying a very much appreciated pot of chicken stew and a salad. We filled our plates and visited with her, Lorne, and a small group of locals. A reporter from the Kindersley newspaper dropped by and half-heartedly conducted interviews. There was an out-of-tune piano in one corner. That night was a full moon. After our visitors left, we watched the bright prairie through the wavy single-paned glass while Connie played old tunes, and we tried to remember verses to songs that we hadn't thought of in years. There's something special about a full moon: it doesn't surprise me that, for the nêhiyaw, wâhkôhtowin includes an especially important relationship with the moon.

The next day Hugh announced that we would get a break from walking roads. Instead, we would be stretching our legs on unbroken prairie grass, heading through a large community pasture. Stepping through patches of yarrow and many-flowered aster, we crossed a fence near a herd of cattle. Soon we lost each other in the endless hills and draws. I walked with Don and Harold. I was determined to keep up with Harold's long stride and with Don's slightly pigeon-toed, quick steps. Don and I chatted about Leonard Cohen, the Psalms, and our own attempts at poetry. Several times we paused for the others, but no one seemed to be close by. After not seeing anyone for some time, we ascended·a long crease between hills and arrived at a salt lick and a fenceline, the first human-made objects in hours. I lay down on the grass and had a nap, hat over my eyes, Harold-style. Wandering back and forth along the fenceline, Don eventually got a signal and called Hugh. As so often happened, the hills had separated us. It turned out that the rest of the group were gathered just to the west of where we had stopped.

That night we camped at an abandoned farmstead near Bad Lake. Leon White, a rancher responsible for the community pasture that we had walked through, arrived to pay a visit. As we cooked our suppers on the tailgate of Connie's truck, more half-tons pulled in. As the evening sky thickened, and the coyotes started to sing, we had a lively conversation on lawn chairs. Philip Brown, a local rancher and a special constable in several local rural municipalities, was there with an old NWMP uniform. I think that he was disappointed our walk was not a re-enactment. The next day we walked by some old farm equipment on which he had set the uniform up like a flag in the breeze—whether as a tribute to our walk, or as a critique of it, I was never able to tell. While Philip and Hugh talked history, Devona and Ron Capnerhurst asked me if coming through the pasture we had seen any wildlife. Apparently, several moose had recently been spotted and a bear two years before. We hadn't really been concerned about bears, although I admit that I pitched my tent somewhat closer to the group after that mention. In his humorous memoir of journeying through Saskatchewan along the Qu'Appelle Valley, Norman Henderson, only partly tongue-in-cheek, notes that a walker's concern about bears arises from the fact that

NWMP display on the prairie, August 2017. *Photo by the author.*

"like us they are adaptable, unpredictable, omnivorous, and fond of processed foods."[108]

"It's beautiful out here," I said to Leon.

He looked in the direction that we had come, thought a while, and finally said, "It was till all these farmers showed up."

Devona told us about her eighty-four-year-old mother, who remembered when it was illegal to lock one's doors because it was necessary to provide overnight shelter for people who might be passing on the Battleford to Swift Current Trail. Her mother had told her that sometimes the family would arrive home to find a traveller in the house, with dinner already made.

While we were talking, a great horned owl flew overhead. Ron mentioned that the abandoned farmyard that we were in had been owned by a family whose baby had died and who had buried the child

---

108   Norman Henderson, *Rediscovering the Prairies: Journeys by Dog, Horse and Canoe* (Victoria: TouchWood Editions, 2010), 114.

at the other end of the caragana and chokecherry bushes. Each of us walkers took time to visit the small grave before leaving the next day.

By this point, we were having to adjust to the temperature swings of the changing season. It had started to become much colder when the sun went down. By the time I rolled into my tent in the trees, the dew was already heavy on the nylon. I spent that night in the densest part of the overgrown hedges, their fingers scraping the tent fabric. I felt drawn and worn. Both heels were now blistered badly. For reasons that I didn't yet understand, my calves had started to ache. I was beginning to have trouble sleeping on my back.

For two more days we traced a line along the edge of the Bad Hills, a high ridge where the land drops to the east and the walker can see for kilometres. In several places, it was so clear that we could see the community of Rosetown in the distance. We had a good smudge one morning at a spot where the Battleford Trail crossed the road, a motionless hawk eavesdropping from a nearby birch, only the occasional twitch of its head showing its interest. Richard was leaving for a few days, so we spent more time than usual remembering all those who had walked before us, whether First Nations, Métis, Canadian army, or settler. I left tobacco for Richard and thought about my parents.

As his friend, I was sad to see Richard go, but as a pilgrim, I was doubly sad. The smudging that had started with our first walk in 2015 had become our usual and much-appreciated morning ceremony. I knew that I would miss his quiet and thoughtful reflections and his gentle way of bringing in the occasional farmer or rancher who happened to join us. Fortunately, just as he left, Sharon Pasula, an Elder and a community worker whom I had met in Vancouver, was joining us and was also prepared to take leadership.

WALKING ACROSS TREATY 6 territory allowed us to experience senses that city people sometimes forget to use. For me, one of the most fulfilling was scent. I discovered that canola is fragrant even from far away. Sage is everywhere—a perfume that fills one's nostrils and smells like a prairie welcome. As I walked, I picked sprigs of sage for my hat; it was a lovely odour and did the double duty of keeping insects away. Buffalo berries do not have a strong scent, but the green patches of bush that contain them do. The dry smell of prairie grasses as one walks through them in the early evening is a treat. In some smudges, I learned to get over my dislike of cigarette smoke and to appreciate the moist smell of good, clean tobacco free of chemicals. Caragana bushes smell like shade. Alkali sloughs stink, tickling the nose with the false promise of undrinkable water. And here and there the best: the smell of green dark earth, and poplar shadow, for when the prairie sun blazes.

Belatedly, I had smartened up enough to abandon my worn-out boots for a pair of running shoes. Unfortunately, my blisters were now the size of dimes and too many to count. They were constantly soaking blood and fluid through my bandages and into my socks. I was having an increasingly hard time keeping my feet clean. I began to worry that I might have an infection.

After another long day, we trekked into the hamlet of Herschel, population thirty. The ubiquitous Herschel backpacks were named after this hamlet by their designers in Vancouver, whose ancestors had lived for three generations in the village. Hugh had arranged for us to have a day off in Herschel, partly because he knew that we would be needing it and partly for the local interpretive centre, a treasure of rural Saskatchewan. We were booked to stay at a retreat centre set up by locals Sue and David Neufeldt. The retreat centre is a lovely old home, with interior finishing made from wood salvaged from the local grain elevator.

We reached Herschel's Ancient Echoes interpretive centre just as it was closing. The menu promised saskatoon berry pie, and I begged and wheedled a piece from the staff as they shut down. When our hosts found out that we liked it, that evening Sue showed up at our door with a freshly baked saskatoon pie for our supper. Don had brought watermelon and cold beer from Rosetown, and we had one of the best potluck meals of the walk.

On our day off, a guide from the Ancient Echoes centre led us across bristle-grass prairie, grasshoppers exploding beneath our feet. We headed toward the pride of Herschel—an ancient archaeological site beside Coalmine Ravine. Dozens of lodge rings, and a turtle effigy, sit undisturbed amid the horsehair grass and cactus. At their centre is the treasure of the Ancient Echoes site: three carved petroglyphs. The petroglyphs are images of bison together with other symbols that have never been deciphered. Related organic deposits at the site have been radio-carbon-dated to the first century. In other words, about the same time that Jesus walked in Galilee, some ancestor of the Niisitapi or Gros Ventre carved symbols into the dolomite. On the other side of the ravine is a bison jump, its sides dark with trees. It was a powerful reminder of just how deep, and how long, Indigenous culture is on the prairie. Excavations suggest that the location was occupied for millennia.

Bright and early at 6:30 the next morning, crop-dusting planes roared over the retreat centre. When I went downstairs, Connie was already putting on tea. Soon we were on the road again. We walked all day, after twenty-five kilometres passing from prairie into scrub brush, a landscape of patchy grasses over fine sand just soft enough to make walking difficult. We started to see more No Trespassing signs posted regularly at intersections. A surprising number of the signs were misspelled, but the intent was clear enough.

Northrop Frye once wrote that

> it took Canadians a long time to get imaginative possession of their own space. The early settlers simply felt overwhelmed and beleaguered. The physical forts of the seventeenth century had changed by the nineteenth into the cultural attitudes that I call the "garrison mentality." The garrison mentality is defensive and separatist. Each group walls itself off and huddles inside, taking warmth and reassurance

from numbers, but keeping its eyes fixed apprehensively on what's outside.[109]

I wish that Frye had lived long enough to meet Gina Starblanket and Dallas Hunt. I think that they would have had much to talk about.

Outside our "garrisons," walking at about five kilometres an hour, the prairie pilgrim notices what can be so easily missed otherwise: the deep green, black, and red garter snake, the length of a pencil, motionless in the middle of the gravel road. A Lilliputian, it was not afraid of me at all and snapped at my hiking stick. The red-tailed hawk that circled above, complaining about our presence. The golden fawn that bolted from the brush onto the road and, after three incredibly long bounds, disappeared back into the thick aspen and berry bushes. The badgers, the skunks, and the coyotes. The yellow butterflies that jumped from a wet depression in the dirt road to flutter around us, a cloud of colour. The deep purple chokecherries on their red stems, much too sour to be tempting in the city but on this walk a juicy mouthful for which I was immensely *grateful*. Maybe that last word is the best description of all for spending so many hours, and so many days, outside and unencumbered: I was grateful. No Trespassing signs gave me the opposite of that feeling.

That evening high banks of dark clouds threatened rain. We arrived, exhausted, at the farmyard that was our destination. No one was home. Two large dogs ran free, crisscrossing the edge of the spot where we had been told we could camp. They were barking at us and baring their teeth. We kept our distance. We could have set up somewhere else. But first one of us, then all the others, admitted that we were missing the creature comforts of Herschel.

Hugh called the retreat centre, and it was free that evening. Our decision was easy. I was happy once again to have an indoor toilet and a shower. My feet were not looking good, and the relative cleanliness of being indoors made my new routine of daily bandaging easier. That night, floating on a cloud of Advil, I sat with Connie and Fred on

---

109   Northrop Frye, *Northrop Frye on Canada, Volume 12*, ed. Jean (Mary) O'Grady and David Staines (Toronto: University of Toronto Press, 2000), 470.

Adirondack chairs in the middle of the field listening to the coyotes and watching for Perseid meteors, until finally I was too sleepy to keep my eyes open.

After some initial shock at seeing a troupe of walkers on the prairie, our group of mostly white Canadians most often was greeted with generosity and open spiritedness by farmers and ranchers alike. Before our final departure from Herschel, Lynn Hollick came by with chocolate chip banana bread. Not long after, we passed the second Hutterite colony along our route, Valley Centre. Some of the bearded, checked-shirted men saw us coming. Two drove out in an all-terrain vehicle to say hello. When they heard who we were, they were followed by a tractor pulling a wagonload of Hutterite women dressed in their black kerchiefs and long dresses. In heavily accented English, they pressed into our hands warm cinnamon buns, still smelling of yeast, and freshly dug carrots. I don't know if any of them realized that giving gifts to pilgrims is a long and honoured tradition in several cultures. In Japan, Shikoku pilgrims often receive alms from local islanders who believe that by so doing they are participating in the merits that the pilgrims receive.[110]

While we cracked just-dug carrots between our teeth, Connie chatted with the women about mutual acquaintances in southern Saskatchewan, where she had taught school on a Hutterite colony. Her knowledge of these important prairie communal groups, and her "goodwill ambassadorship," were invaluable. I wasn't the only walker who later peppered her with questions about the similarities, differences, and relations among the farms that we had visited.

As we left the colony, rain began. Clouds of mist cottoned around us. In our cocoon, we crunched along the gravel, our rain ponchos bright against the fields. Looking at Ken, six foot five and broad shouldered, sheathed in cherry red; Hugh, smaller and in lemon yellow; and Fred, in a fluorescent green cape that extended to his

---

110   Ian Reader, *Pilgrimage: A Very Short Introduction* (Oxford: Oxford University Press, 2015), 50.

Prairie Teletubbies. *Photo by the author.*

ankles, I realized that we probably looked like prairie Teletubbies, the once-popular children's show characters.

A few kilometres later Crystal Craig drove by, grinning at the sight. She told us that she would have lunch prepared for us. When we reached her farmhouse, hamburger soup and coffee were waiting. Crystal's husband, Liam, served the soup while offering bad puns with such an infectious sense of humour that it was impossible not to laugh. When we set out again, Crystal accompanied us. Her Labrador retriever trotted alongside, scooting off to chase creatures real or imagined in the fields, while Crystal paced beside Hugh, pointing out features of the soil and the crops.

That evening we set our tents in a line next to the thick hedges and service vehicles at the Dubreuil farm. Doreen Dubreuil, like Crystal, is one of those phlegmatic, competent, rural women who reminded me of my aunts. A light rain had started up again, and we had our work cut out keeping the Dubreuil dogs and cats from finding shelter with us under our tent flaps. Doreen let us dry our wet boots and socks inside and had coffee and tea waiting for us the next morning. Each night was becoming a bit cooler and each morning wetter. We had entered the Eagle Hills.

The next day we walked to the Lorraine and Bob Heather farm twenty-two kilometres away. By now, we were consistently crossing more brush belts and encountering more brackish sloughs. There was far less open prairie, and we had to walk east and then west in order to skirt sections of rough ground. This was a part of the trail mentioned in some of the nineteenth-century diaries as "the first trees." Following the historic trail at this point was almost impossible, so Hugh led us along roads in a zigzag pattern: first east and then west.

Our way followed a line between shelterbelts of trees. We trod fine dirt and sand roads with silty depressions—it felt a bit like walking along a beach. We passed birch trees and bushes laden with chokecherries and buffalo berries. Prairie rosebushes exploded with colour—on some, the rosehips were already swollen and red. Here and there we had to step over coyote scat packed with chokecherry pits and occasionally the scat of less easily identifiable creatures, perhaps bears. For the first time in days, there were no hawks. Three-quarters of the way west, we came across a clearing. By the side of the road, a bronze plaque, affixed to a granite boulder, indicated that we had arrived at Sixty-Mile Bush.

Sixty-Mile Bush, also called Half-Way House, was once the second stop southward on the stagecoach and freighter trail from Battleford. Clinkskill described Sixty-Mile Bush as having a "log house, fairly large, belonging to an old chap named Bernier, a French-Canadian." Given Clinkskill's generous description of the cave-like Otter's Station, there is no way to know what "fairly large" might mean. Clinkskill added, however, that Bernier's hostel had partitions with curtains "for the lady passengers."[111]

The stone monument that now marks Sixty-Mile Bush sits in front of a gently undulating field of prairie grass. There are no visible remains of buildings. Hugh hopped the fence. He looked briefly at a large depression in the earth that might mark where Bernier's house stood, which later became the community store. Perhaps the

---

Clinkskill, *A Prairie Memoir*, 73.

low earth indicated where the Roman Catholic church stood after it was built for the Métis settlers until the community was abandoned around 1911. Looking at the quiet field, ringed with wild roses, and with poplars swaying in the breeze, it was hard to imagine that 125 years ago it was home to an active hamlet. From 1886 to 1889, the North West Mounted Police maintained a post there with two constables. Their patrol route extended to Herschel (Eagle Creek) and probably partway to Battleford. Patrols from Battleford included Onion Lake, Bresaylor, and Sounding Lake.[112]

Listening to the insects, and looking at the depression in the prairie, brought home one of those lesser-known facts of prairie history that need to be included in this restorying. So many of the places that we encountered—such as Ten-Mile Crossing in the Cypress Hills, Chimney Coulee, and Wood Mountain—were NWMP posts or settlements *that relied on pre-existing Métis communities*. Canadian history, when it remembers these communities at all, too often remembers the police but forgets the Métis who were there first. Inevitably, it seems, colonial history omits how both the police and the Euro-Canadian settlers relied on prior Métis knowledge and presence.

For days, we had seen almost no one along the country lanes on which we were walking. It felt odd, then, that in the next few kilometres we had to move to the side of the dirt road to let a number of vehicles pass. One of the cars slowed down, and the passenger rolled down her window. It was Lorraine Heather. Hugh had arranged for us to spend some time with the Heathers. They had tired of waiting and finally had driven out to check on us and invite us for afternoon coffee. When we got to their farm, they had saskatoon cake, tea, and coffee ready. It was a relief to take my shoes off on their lawn and give my wounded feet some air.

That evening we headed to the Biggar Museum, where almost fifty people came for our presentation. Biggar is a highway town of

112   Walter Hildebrandt, *Views from Fort Battleford: Constructed Visions of an Anglo-Canadian West* (Regina: Canadian Plains Research Center, 1994), 20.

just over two thousand people[113] and the closest that we came to the farm where Colten Boushie was shot. We had a friendly crowd. If some were uneasy with our project, they voiced no objections. There were familiar faces and some old friends; people stayed afterward to chat and to pass on their own memories of the trail. As in other towns, it occurred to me that, although most folks heard what we were saying about the importance of understanding our history as Canadians, there were others in whose minds the past, represented by the North West Mounted Police and the Battleford Trail, was in no way linked to the trial going on just down the highway despite our attempts to make that connection.

Friends from Saskatoon had also come out for the talk. I had arranged with Pamela Giles to meet me with a copy of Bill Waiser's book *A World We Have Lost* so that our group could give it as a thank-you gift to Hugh. We pilgrims stayed late at the museum, then headed to a highway motel. Despite the indoor warmth, and the warm showers, the beds were far too soft and the highway too noisy. At breakfast, we compared notes and realized that, after so many nights in the quiet darkness of the country, the rumble of passing eighteen-wheelers had kept us all awake.

The next day we gathered to smudge by a line of trembling aspen at the edge of the Heather farm. Although Bob and Lorraine seemed to be uncomfortable at first, they soon joined in wholeheartedly. As we began to walk, we saw that No Trespassing signs had become the norm. And, for the first time in two weeks, we had someone say something to us that was less than welcoming: a man drove by, slowed down, and warned us from his truck not to stray onto his property, not even "just off the road for a picnic." (Typical of "my home is my castle" people, he didn't seem to know the law. Legally, the ditches of roads were not his to claim.)

---

113   David McLennan, *Our Towns: Saskatchewan Communities from Abbey to Zenon Park* (Regina: Canadian Plains Research Center, 2008), 32–33, gives a succinct but colourful history of the town, known to many for its "New York is big, but this is Biggar" highway welcome sign.

However, not long after his rant, a woman also stopped by in a half-ton, smiled at us, and told us that she had heard about our walk on two different television stations and in the local paper. She said that her husband might join us. At that, she stopped, as if checking herself, and frowned. "Then again," she said, "it might be too much for him—he's almost sixty!" Thankfully, our eighty-one year old was already out of earshot, walking alone ahead.

Had we been a group primarily made up of Indigenous women and men, instead of a group primarily of white Canadians, we could never have ventured on the routes that we did. As with many racialized individuals who have been shot at, reported, or harassed simply for getting something from their own cars or homes, we would have been *assumed* to be troublemakers and/or trespassers. The "authorities" would have been called on us or far worse. Instead, most local farmers seemed to think that we were a strange sight but not an offensive one. These are the components of the unacknowledged structural racism from which we who are non-Indigenous have always benefited.[114]

For the first time in over a week, our walk took us across two highways. They were busy with traffic, which felt odd after our deeply rural routes. Thankfully, we spent most of the rest of the day closer to the actual trail. We skirted the eastern end of Whiteshore Lake, a vast and silent alkali marsh, where we put down tarps and ate lunch on a small hillock overlooking the white, salt-rimed expanse. It was an eerie spot. In the far distance, we could just make out the remains of some kind of industrial building. Someone said that it had been a salt refinery; to me, it looked like a post-apocalyptic crash site. Perhaps there wasn't much difference.

We reached the end of the day's trail about 4 p.m. Our host that evening was Russell Affleck. He had been kind enough to give us permission to camp in an overgrown farmyard down the road from his house. By the looks of it, the house had been his parents' and grandparents'. It seemed that after their passing, with his own

---

114   Eva Mackey, *Unsettled Expectations: Uncertainty, Land and Settler Decolonization* (Winnipeg: Fernwood, 2016), 113.

modern house already built, and the old house not fit for or worth renovation, Russell had simply boarded it up "as is."

This is common enough on the Prairies; when my uncle near Simmie built his new house in the 1960s, he put the old family home on skids, complete with boxes of my mother's scrapbooks, and calendars still on the walls, and hauled the whole thing by tractor to the pasture. There he left it to slowly collapse into the earth.

The eulogies that the profoundly destructive Duncan Campbell Scott, flush with Canada's new century in the early 1900s, wrote for "the Indians" have now settled ironically on my own relatives and some of their material heritage: "The race has waned and left but tales of ghosts / That hover in the world like fading smoke."[115] Henderson notes that the abandoned farmhouses by which he tented on his journeys were characterized by an atmosphere "both peaceful and melancholic."[116] That was certainly true of the old Affleck farmstead.

Barn swallows swooped as we took stock of the buildings. This abandoned house was in better shape than my grandparents' house. Still, it was listing badly. Fred, Christine, and I peeked through the cracked and broken windows. We could see tilting floors and half-peeled linoleum. There were some gorgeous furniture pieces that, had they been in better shape, would have fetched a good price. Fashionable clothes fell from torn garment bags hung in the closets.

Anyone who has spent time on farms in Saskatchewan knows this phenomenon. Of course, what to do with patrimony is not just a rural problem. Nor do all farm properties contain such obviously decaying museums. Those that do simply have more space than the city folks who pack their aged or deceased parents' belongings into a storage unit and promise themselves to do something with them someday.

---

115   Duncan Campbell Scott, "Indian Place Names," in *A Critical Edition of the Poems of Duncan Campbell Scott*, ed. Leon Slonim (Toronto: University of Toronto Press, 1978), 116.

116   Henderson, *Rediscovering the Prairies*, 115.

Either way it seems to me that the Canadian ambivalence about the past is not unrelated to the insecurity about trespassing that we were witnessing in the surrounding farms. Especially in the wake of wave after wave of rural depopulation, those farmers who are left have been forced to "go big." They feel not only the burden of their huge, and often risky, investments but also the social weight of the communities that once filled the rural municipalities and have left so many grey-board buildings behind. The "waning race" that Scott wrote of is looking more and more like mid-twentieth-century settler prairie culture, not the people whom the government tried so unsuccessfully to be replaced. Yet the kindness, the good humour, and the sheer diversity of our rural hosts on our pilgrimages were proof that there is a diverse and lively rural society replacing those farmsteads.

Canada is a colonial nation, a "settler state." Abandoned farmhouses like the one that we tented beside, or like my relatives' old homes now decaying into the earth, show that the success or failure of colonialism can be powerfully symbolized by a pioneer building. Settler children or grandchildren like me who have moved to faraway cities do not have to face the ghosts of their ancestors in the same way as people like Russell Affleck. We city dwellers can talk about land abstractly. We can romanticize it in part because we are already the beneficiaries of cashing out the homesteads. Our privilege is evident in our social, educational, and physical mobility.[117]

We walkers stretched out on tarps in the late afternoon sun. The sky was smoky yellow from northern forest fires, the edges of the horizon indistinct against the crops. Someone handed me a cold beer brought from Biggar; I was having trouble keeping my thoughts straight. I thought that it was the heat, the sun, and the beer. What I didn't realize was that I was already beginning to suffer from a general infection moving from my foot into my leg. It was becoming nearly

---

117   Emma Battell Lowman and Adam J. Barker, *Settler: Identity and Colonialism in 21st Century Canada* (Winnipeg: Fernwood, 2015), 89.

impossible to sleep through the night, and I was having more and more trouble walking long days on such poor rest.

That evening the forest fire smoke gave us a glorious sunset across the fields. Russell came by to say hello and to see how we were doing. It was a small act of kindness typical of many of our hosts. As we stood chatting, I decided not to·ask questions about the house beside us. But I wondered. It must do something to the psyche to have one's own past falling to ruin so close by.

The next day we passed an extremely well-preserved country landmark, Rosemount Cemetery. Trees were now everywhere, and we found a suitable thicket of aspens where we set our tarps and shared food (although looking over our shoulders for irate farmers). It was a twenty-two-kilometre day, ending in Cando, population sixty-eight. We set up beside a repurposed Quonset (a half-cylindrical building) that serves as Cando's community centre.

I made the mistake of putting my tent up without pegging it and going to help Connie with hers. While I was busy threading one of her tent poles, Judy Erickson caught my eye. "Is that yours?" she asked, pointing over my shoulder. I turned. My tent had escaped and was rolling and bouncing in the wind, already a quarter-field away. I caught it just before it reached the paved road. After carrying it back, my leg aching from the unaccustomed running, I made sure to peg it down firmly.

When an old farmer dropped by to check on the newcomers in the hamlet, Fred was the first to lean against the back of his truck, look out over the prairie, and compare notes. Fred grew up in southwestern Ontario. Despite his decades of being a minister, he is still a farmer at heart. One of the older men who dropped by mentioned that his father had always said that they should keep some of the Battleford Trail intact on a corner of one of their fields, and not cultivate it, so that the historic tracks would always be visible. Among its other aims, our walk was a call to such civic mindedness. It was heartening to see some for whom the trail is still treated as a respected part of history. In Saskatchewan, there is no chance (and should be no fear) that hordes of trekkers will take to the Battleford

Trail. Rather, it, like the vanished hamlet at Sixty-Mile Bush, should be granted a spot in the commonwealth of history.

We made our evening meal on the long wooden tables in the Cando Community Hall. The hall itself was bright and welcoming. But as was true at several of the rural community centres where we stopped, the water from the taps was undrinkable. It was a sign of the difficulties that many small communities—and many more First Nations—face. Thankfully, we had purchased water in Biggar. Kristin Enns-Kavanagh, the executive director of the Saskatchewan History and Folklore Society, had joined us that morning with her mother-in-law, Joyce. They brought homemade bannock and grape jam from Saskatoon. Kristin presented the bannock on a traditional cloth, a treat for everyone.

Only eight people came out that evening for Hugh's presentation, which featured some new photos and a concluding section that he had just done up that included photos of us walkers. During the talk, I fell asleep. The fatigue and pain medication were taking their toll. If the locals noticed me dozing, no one said anything. It was another cold night; frost was in the air, and the temperature hovered near zero. The next morning broke cold and wet even as the sunrise slanted gold across our campsite. We could see our breath. Fred unpegged his tent and jammed it to dry in the concrete stairwell beside the hall. "It's my tent-escape-prevention mechanism," he teased me as I walked by.

For Further Reading

On the dependence of early settlers on Métis individuals and communities, see Trevor Herriot, *Towards a Prairie Atonement* (Regina: University of Regina Press, 2016), 46–49. Herriot also notes that, "from the outset of the fur trade in the seventeenth century, the long-term interests of local communities all over the northern plains have been sold down the river to industries serving distant markets."[118] The "Laurentian School" concept of western regionalism,

---

118 Herriot, *Towards a Prairie Atonement*, 21.

with nuances, sees the Prairies as an economic "hinterland" used by more metropolitan centres, usually in central Canada, to serve their economic needs, whether fur, grain, or oil, often with little regard for the people or environment of the region. See R. Douglas Francis, "Regionalism, W.L. Morton, and the Writing of Western Canadian History, 1870–1885," *American Review of Canadian Studies* (2001): 571, 576. At the same time, it is important to acknowledge the significant differences between the nineteenth-century emptying of the plains, with its attendant starvation and racism, and the more gradual and far less catastrophic rural changes in the twentieth century. It is also important to note that the (usually central Canadian) economic exploitation of the Canadian west has been used by settlers as a way to deflect attention away from their own colonial interests. See Eva Mackey, "'Death by Landscape': Race, Nature, and Gender in Canadian Nationalist Mythology," *Canadian Women Studies* 20, no. 2 (2000): 128.

MOSQUITO–GRIZZLY BEAR'S HEAD–LEAN MAN FIRST NATION

BOARDING SCHOOL

In the late fall
ice waited
outside our cabin.

Inside
crackling fire
licked the guts
of the woodstove.
The coal oil lamp
flickered in the
one-room shack.

Two white-skins
talked in tongues.

Father's long face
stretched further
to the floor.
Mother's crimson cheeks
turned like swirling ashes
in the stove-pipe.

Behind
mother's draping dress
a six-year-old sister.
Her small fist
white against
brown skin.

I sat behind a
thick home-made
wooden table,
trembling.
My stomach couldn't hold
the fresh cinnamon roll.

The air was
wrapped in
raven darkness.

Namōya māskoc.
It's a mistake.
Father's voice
shook.
Mother swayed.

The white-skins
left.
The cold seeped in the
cracks of the door,

its fingers wrapped
in silence.
The world
was silent.

The family gone.
The family not ever more.

—SKY DANCER LOUISE BERNICE HALFE[119]

A FEW STEPS from the Cando Community Hall put us back on open prairie, walking north. We kept the Battleford Trail to our west. After twenty-one kilometres of road walking, we passed a sign announcing Mosquito First Nation. There was a moment of awkwardness: Richard had suggested that we put down tobacco on entering the First Nation, but we were unsure where and when it would be appropriate. We put some down at the entrance and again later, thinking that doing so twice would be better than not at all. We passed through a fence, went down a long dirt road, and finally arrived. No one was at the Mosquito Band Hall. While Hugh tried to reach his contact by phone, the rest of us sat resting, our backs against the shady side of the building.

Occasionally, passing cars slowed down for their occupants to have a look at the group of strangers dozing against their packs. I felt like an alien. I thought about Samuel Anderson and the British surveyors in 1873, and the uncertainty expressed by the Nakota and Lakota whom they met, who'd been right to be so uneasy about the coming immigration. We talked quietly about the family of Colten Boushie, who'd lost their son to a white farmer not far from where we were sitting, and about the all-white jury finally selected for the trial after the defence had disqualified all unwanted—that is,

---

119   Sky Dancer Louise Bernice Halfe, "Boarding School," in *Bear Bones and Feathers* (Regina: Coteau Books, 1994), 63–64.

Indigenous—jurors.[120] I felt some of the same tension on Mosquito First Nation that we'd been feeling passing certain farms. But here it felt far less aggressive. No one at Mosquito stopped to ask if we had permission to be there.

Part of the reason that justice in relation to Indigenous Peoples must be repaired at the level of government policy is the long and sordid history of deal breaking by our governments. Not only must justice be done, but also it must be accompanied by education. One of the Saskatchewan farmers whom we met shook his head when talking about Battleford. "We're circled by reserves," he kept repeating. "Surrounded."

This man, and his choice of words, illustrate why learning history is important. Apart from the language of being "surrounded" (the garrison mentality again), separating the nineteenth-century nêhiyaw and Nakota into small groups and isolating them from one another on a ring of reserves around Battleford was in fact the *government's* idea. Mistahimaskwa had resisted signing Treaty 6 so long precisely because the nêhiyaw leader wouldn't give up the dream of a much larger commons of Indigenous territory, a true homeland such as the treaties promised, where all the people could hunt and farm together.[121] The farmer didn't know this rather basic fact of history.

Dishonouring the choices promised by the treaties, and breaking Indigenous groups up and mixing them, the government hoped to speed up the process of assimilation. This was clearly the rationale behind the Indian residential institutions. It also motivated "enfranchisement," the often enforced "invitation" to Indigenous individuals to become full Canadian citizens. The government wanted individual Indigenous men to take for their sole ownership a piece of property that would then be cut from the reserve. Of course, reserve land was not the government's to offer, and doing so was clearly against

---

120   See Kent Roach, *Canadian Justice, Indigenous Justice: The Gerald Stanley and Colten Boushie Case* (Montreal and Kingston: McGill-Queen's University Press, 2019).

121   Wiebe, *Big Bear*, 132.

both the spirit and the letter of the treaties. But this did not stop the encroachment of private settler property on reserve lands, whether in the Haldimand Tract, at Kahnawà:ke, or on Treaty 6 territory.

As it so often does, the assimilative urge came down to money. The government hoped to reduce both the territory held by Indigenous nations and the cost of support agreed to by treaty. It went against everything for Indigenous people to take land from the collective. And the presence of surveyors on reserves,[122] marking out individual real estate, went against the solemn promises that the government had just made to protect the meagre allotments.

When almost no one applied for enfranchisement, Canada sought another way out of the deal: the *Indian Act* was changed, once again, to make enfranchisement compulsory for any Indigenous person who obtained a university degree or became a member of the clergy. This amazingly racist law effectively kept Indigenous people from developing such leadership. In addition, Indigenous women who married non-Indigenous men were "enfranchised," meaning that they lost their treaty rights, as did their children. Even Indigenous men who fought for Canada in the Second World War, on their return home, discovered that they had lost their status.[123] This was all part of Canada's strategy to assimilate Indigenous Peoples and thus make the so-called Indian problem (which is to say, more honestly, *the Canadian obligation*) disappear.

A short while after we arrived at the Mosquito Band Hall, a man and a woman arrived in a truck, and two young women drove up in a car with several coolers in the back seat. They greeted us and invited us in for supper. Our Mosquito hosts smudged the table and the food. Hugh's contact, Tristan Bird, a band councillor, arrived, and I, Hugh, and others gave the gifts that we had brought for our hosts. As we ate around the long tables, the sun went down, and the temperature dropped. The raucous wind never abated. "Stay inside

---

122   Joseph, *21 Things*, 29.
123   Joseph, *21 Things*, 30.

the hall," Tristan said to us. "It's too cold to sleep outside. It's warm here and dry. Please be our guests."

I thought about Tristan's choice of word: *guests*. On that visit, we could reasonably say that we were "guests" of the Mosquito First Nation. The next morning we would have our breakfast, and then we would *leave*, unlike the first European "guests" who stayed, negotiated, forced their way in, and eventually took over, all while trying to ignore their debts.

During the meal, Steve dropped by. He lived next to the Band Hall. He told us that he's actually Assiniboine, even though he now speaks Cree, because that's what was taught in the local school. "Our ancestors were all just dumped here," he told us. "Now we're a mix. But that's not how it used to be."

Richard and his wife, Pat, drove up from Regina to join us. After our meal, Helen, another member of the Mosquito First Nation, arrived. She wrapped a shawl around her shoulders and complimented us on making the walk. It was interesting how without fail those in the Canadian communities where we stayed wanted to talk about the past, the history of the trails, whereas the Indigenous people whom we met immediately understood the contemporary purpose of our walks as acts of solidarity.

Helen told us her story of being taken from her parents and placed in a residential school. She laughed when talking of her childhood and cried as she began speaking about the abuse that she had suffered at the school and the suffering and death that she had witnessed. She told us how, as a young girl in the dormitory, she had promised herself that she would remember who she was, and who her family was, even while she was forbidden from going home to see them.

After Helen finished quietly telling us her story in the half darkness, all I could think about was the murder case before the courts. From Tristan, to those who served us our supper, to Steve, to Helen, no one had mentioned the trial.

For most of the nineteenth century, the situation of Indigenous Peoples and of European settlers on the prairie was the reverse of what we were experiencing. Then the nêhiyaw and Nakota roamed relatively freely, whereas most settlers lacked full mobility and stayed close to the few established villages or towns. The west was only sparsely settled by Europeans, and the usual language that one would hear outside the few villages was nêhiyaw, Michif, or Anihšinâpêk.

In western Canada especially, the earliest European visitors and intermittent colonists initially had to adjust to an Indigenous world and to rely on Indigenous populations not only for their business but also for their very survival.[124] Sarah Carter suggests that a better paradigm than "discovery" or "invasion" for understanding the relationships established between Indigenous and settler populations on the prairie in the nineteenth century is a term such as "encounter" or "exchange."[125] *Exchange* could still be a good word, I believe, since it expresses more accurately the meaning of the treaties. It reminds us Canadians, and our governments, what we should be living up to.

Even as Indigenous Peoples were being forced onto reserves, hints of the earlier model of exchange and cooperation survived. Our research indicated that early Battleford Trail travellers would plan an overnight stay on Mosquito First Nation. There, like us, they were happy to have a comfortable bed and a good meal. Clinkskill mentions the stop at Mosquito with obvious appreciation compared with the overnight stops farther south. Despite the overt racism contained in so many articles in the *Saskatchewan Herald* of the day, the newspaper couldn't help but tell another story, half hidden in its notices of contracts tendered and building projects. That story tells of how the town's inhabitants relied on Indigenous markets for their agricultural products and how they looked to Indigenous men and women for labourers, freighters, and other workers, even for the construction of the telegraph line that connected them to the rest of settler society. Battleford was established on a nêhiyaw site,

---

124   Carter, *Aboriginal People and Colonizers*, 33.

125   Carter, *Aboriginal People and Colonizers*, 33. See also Herriot, *Towards a Prairie Atonement*, 46.

and its prosperity continued to depend in large part on the people whom the settlers claimed to have "displaced."

FORT BATTLEFORD

> *Whether one is an educator, a policy maker, a negotiator, a*
> *church layperson, a professional or blue-collar worker, or an*
> *ordinary citizen committed to social justice, reconciliation*
> *as resistance involves accepting personal and political*
> *responsibility for shifting colonial attitudes and actions.*

—PAULETTE REGAN[126]

FOR A WEEK, whenever Fred, Hugh, and Connie found an object on the road or in the ditch—a bolt, a bit of glass, a piece of flat iron—they put it into the back of one of the trucks. Early the next morning after our stay at Mosquito First Nation, Fred set up an installation art piece made from the collection. It was a sharing of memories, one of the small ways in which we were beginning to realize that our days together were coming to an end. Following the "exhibit," we packed up our art, thanked our hosts, and set off again. Where the freighters would have done the trip from Mosquito to Battleford in one long day, arriving at night, Hugh had planned it for two so that we would have time on the second day for a celebration of arrival.

This last section of the trail paralleled a gravel road. We had good walking in cool weather. The path took us to the edge of the Eagle Hills, where we came over a ridge to find ourselves face to face with the majestic sweep of the North Saskatchewan River valley. After descending a short distance, we arrived at the Johnson acreage. The Johnsons have a well-kept spot, with manicured grass and several sheltered areas among the hedges. This was where our hosts kindly let us set our tents.

126   Paulette Regan, *Unsettling the Settler Within: Indian Residential Schools, Truth Telling, and Reconciliation in Canada* (Vancouver: UBC Press, 2011), 217.

Students at the Battleford Indian Industrial School depicted in a photo on a monument at the site of the school, 2017. *Photo by the author.*

We were all aware that this was our last night as a group. We made supper and shared our food amid a lot of laughter and the recounting of recent memories. When the sun set, the air instantly chilled. This time no one moved for shelter. We put on more clothes, and still more clothes, and kept sitting as long as we could in our little circle in the dark. We talked about what the walk had meant, laughed at our haikus, and did that thing that people do when they start to talk about an extraordinary, shared experience as if it is already over when it isn't. Eventually, despite wanting the evening to go on and on, it grew too dark, and too cold, to continue. We hugged each other and crawled into our tents. I listened for the coyotes. Maybe we were too close to Battleford. There was nothing but the wind.

Hugh had planned our arrival so that the last morning of our walk we had only about ten kilometres to finish. Once again we had walked about 350 kilometres. By this point, I could no longer stand on my left leg any length of time without lifting it to take pressure

Christine Ramsay, one of the walkers, at the remains of the Battleford Indian Industrial School, 2017. *Photo by the author.*

off my swelling ankle and foot. Before Richard's morning smudge, Ken read journal excerpts from one of Colonel Otter's troops as they marched north in 1885. The writer was a recruit from central Canada who probably had never seen either an Anihšinápēk or nêhiyaw person or the plains. He wrote that "we saw our first Indian today. He was within rifle distance."[127]

With the smudge, Richard shared a short and powerful teaching. "How do we measure the distance now?" he asked. "Do we still measure it like that unnamed soldier? Close enough to harm? Close enough to be defensive? Or have we learned to say 'the Indian' we meet is close enough to greet, to get to know, to invite to eat, to sit together, and learn from and with?"

---

127   "Excerpt of the Diary of an Unnamed Officer Who Was With Otter," entry for Wednesday, April 22, 1885, Canadian War Museum Archives, 58A 1 101.38.

The rest of the day passed in a blur. My main recollections of the arrival at Battleford are that it was educational but often troubling.

I remember the last few kilometres toward Battleford being particularly picturesque. Where the trail meets the Battle River, a local amateur historian waited for us. Stanley (I will call him) is a somewhat severe-looking older man with a thin face and a thick grey moustache. He took us a short distance south of Battle Creek up and into the trees so that we could see some of the surviving government buildings that had overlooked the town back in the 1870s and 1880s. Despite his cane and stoop, Stan set a quick pace. He kept pointing this way and that and voicing his frustration that younger members of the community "did not seem to care" about the history of Battleford. We saw the Land Registry building, built in 1878, the first registry office in the North-West Territories. As we peered through the windows of the locked site, we were told that Battleford's Government House had been abandoned during the resistance in 1885 and that the townspeople had been forced to take refuge inside the fort. In addition to facts with which one could quibble, our guide used highly charged vocabulary—words such as *natives*, *attacking*, *fear*, *safety*, and *siege*—without seeming to realize, or question, the bias that they carried.

In the next breath, his monologue turned to the present and how to protect these historic sites. Again we were seemingly enlisted as allies. Stan began with the news that a concerned local group—all settler descendants, mostly older men—were worried that there would be an arson attack against the Land Registry building. He spent considerable time detailing how the building needed to be protected. The former Government House, converted to the Battleford Indian Industrial School, run by the Anglican Church from 1883 to 1914, had been burned to the ground by arsonists in 2003. Our guide framed the conversation in "we-they" terms: "we" want to keep history intact, but "they" just want to see everything destroyed. "We" value the historic buildings; "they" don't have a sense of history. It became clear that the "they" were Indigenous people from First Nations around Battleford.

There followed an uncomfortable silence, in part because not all of us were "we," as Stan was putting it. Neither did the majority of our walking group, settler descended, want to be included in any blanket judgment about honourable or dishonourable actions. I spoke up to venture the opinion that, regrettable as it is, burning down a building that stands for oppression is a terrible sign, if nothing else, of caring, and caring *a lot*, about history. Stan interrupted, muttering statements of denialism that many Canadians have heard or spoken: how not all teachers at Indian residential schools abused children (as if the fact that so many did is excusable), that there had been many "good people" working there, and so on. "They were treated very well, better than at home. And they got a good education," the local contact concluded. Again "we" versus "they."

Richard tried, several times, to raise the larger significance of the residential school. He brought up the sheer number of children who had died and the systemic violence of assimilation. He said clearly how residential schools, viewed systemically, were how white society had tried to eradicate Indigenous presence.

Our guide wasn't listening. After a while, Richard gave up and sat by one of the stone memorials, hat in hand.

Eventually, Don Bolen sidetracked our guide by asking about one of the architectural features. The rest of us wandered over to the foundation stones and the brick chimney, all that is left of the residential school. As with most of the "schools," this one came with a cemetery. It is about 640 metres south on the open prairie. When the school closed, the principal, Reverend Edward Matheson, directed Indian Affairs to keep care of the cemetery, which he reported contained the remains of from seventy to eighty former students as well as members of his family.[128] Instead, the government ignored, and tried to forget, the site. It was only in 1975, six decades later, after an archaeological dig, that a chain-link fence, a memorial cairn, and

---

128   Josh Greschner, "Walk Commemorates Industrial School Cemetery," *Battlefords News-Optimist*, May 23, 2018, SaskToday.ca, https://www.sasktoday.ca/north /local-news/walk-commemorates-industrial-school-cemetery-4120647.

grave markers were finally erected. Battleford was an early example of the recovery of these children's memories, spearheaded in part by the same Indigenous groups whom our guide was complaining "had no respect" for history.

In disagreements such as we'd just had with our guide, a person might be right in a detail or two yet still terribly wrong. There was a horrific disregard for the lives of children torn from the hands of their families by illegally passed Canadian law. Of course, there might have been some well-meaning teachers. That in no way excuses the system or the systemic mistreatment of Indigenous children.

The history of Indian residential "schools" in Canada is simple in at least one sense. They were not schools. The purpose of the institutions was assimilation and cultural genocide. Most schools were run like internment camps. If there is anyone who doubts that their effects were murderous, then the recovery of thousands of undocumented or, worse, *de*documented (grave markers removed decades later) children's bodies should be proof. At the time of the founding of the schools, senior officials in Indian Affairs called the children "inmates." When the judge sentenced Big Bear in 1885, he reportedly told him about his son Mistatim Awâsis (Horsechild) that "I cannot sentence your son to prison, but I can sentence him to residential school," leaving little doubt how the judge viewed the institution.[129]

Fact after fact makes it abundantly clear that both the project of the residential schools, and how they were governed, supervised, underfunded, and mismanaged, amounted to an act of violence against Indigenous Peoples that is impossible to reconcile with any good whatsoever. The graves speak louder than words. And those who suggest that this awareness is somehow new don't know their history. Already in 1907 senior government health inspector Peter Henderson Bryce reported that 24 percent of the children entering the mission schools in western Canada died either while in the school or shortly thereafter. *One-quarter*. Would any parent willingly send a child to such a place? One school, the only one to give full statistics, reported *69 percent* mortality during that period.[130] Imagine being forced to send your child to a school where half or more of the children are expected to die because of starvation, sickness, and abuse. It seems to be unbelievable that this took place. But it did.

When Indigenous families resisted, in 1920 the *Indian Act* was amended again, just as the Spanish flu pandemic finished sweeping through the schools. This time the *Indian Act* gave police the power to go onto reserves and forcibly remove children from their homes when alarmed parents resisted sending their loved ones to the schools. Whistleblower Bryce was forced to retire and ended up publishing his alarming findings at his own expense. But the deaths continued.

In the first decades especially, Indigenous children were not only dying from mistreatment but also considered hostages. In his proposals for the Indian residential schools in Manitoba and the North-West Territories, J.A. Macrae wrote that locating the schools in "white" towns made it "unlikely that any Tribe or Tribes would give trouble of a serious nature to the Government whose members had children completely under Government control."[131]

After inviting the churches to be responsible for the schools, writes Charlie Angus, "the department set the transfer payments for students so low that it institutionalized the abuse and deprivation that followed."[132] Churches wanted to gain adherents and, if possible, skim money from their school subsidies for their other operations. The government wanted to assimilate Indigenous children and to do so as cheaply as possible. These twin aims made for a deadly combination. We have seen the thousands upon thousands of graves that Indigenous families and survivors have always told us were there. They are proof that the Canadian government and the churches wilfully ignored death rates from malnutrition-linked

---

130 Charlie Angus, *Children of the Broken Treaty: Canada's Lost Promise and One Girl's Dream* (Regina: University of Regina Press, 2017), 16.

131 E. Brian Titley, *The Frontier World of Edgar Dewdney* (Vancouver: UBC Press, 1999), 79.

132 Angus, *Children of the Broken Treaty*, 14.

disease, overcrowding, and abuse and created terrible situations precisely for children who could do little to protect themselves.[133]

It was a bit stunning to encounter an attitude that so willingly ignored such facts, especially from an amateur historian. Certainly not all Battleford history enthusiasts have shared it. Campbell Innes, an early-twentieth-century local historian, largely responsible for restoring the fort, wanted it to contain an "Indian Museum" to tell the stories of the Indigenous Peoples rather than, as he put it, simply to "valorize the NWMP."[134] Innes published a book in 1926 based in part upon interviews with local Indigenous groups, attempting to cast more light on the Thirst Dance of 1884 at Poundmaker's reserve and subsequent events during 1885 at Frog Lake and Battleford.[135] Innes argued a point since backed up by other historians: during the Riel Resistance, there was never any nêhiyaw-Métis alliance. Nor was there ever an "Indian rebellion" at Battleford. Innes argued that the nêhiyaw under Big Bear and Poundmaker never engaged in rebellion, and the later Frog Lake murders of nine settlers began as targeted killings of particularly hated Indian Agents.[136]

The Métis Resistance turned out to be the political tool that the government needed to finalize its subjugation of the Indigenous population of the prairie region. Tellingly, more than three times as many nêhiyaw and Nakota were prosecuted for "rebellion-related crimes" by the government as were Métis defendants.[137] Assistant

133   Joseph, *21 Things*, 54.

134   Hildebrandt, *Views from Fort Battleford*, 104.

135   Campbell Innes, *The Cree Rebellion of 1884, or, Sidelights on Indian Conditions Subsequent to 1876* (Battleford, SK: Battleford Historical Society, 1926); reprinted in Ross Innes, *The Sands of Time* (North Battleford, SK: Turner-Warwick, 1986), vi.

136   Daschuk notes that later reports also pointed to revenge, not just for starvation but also for sexual predation, as a motive that in part might have been responsible for the initial murders. James Daschuk, *Clearing the Plains: Disease, Politics of Starvation, and the Loss of Aboriginal Life* (Regina: University of Regina Press, 2013), 152–53.

137   Waiser, *A World We Have Lost*, 560.

Indian Commissioner Hayter Reed recommended the cessation of all rations to the reserves, except in exchange for work, and stated the convenient opinion that the treaties had been "entirely abrogated by the rebellion."[138] This despite the fact that there had been almost no action by any of the First Nations. In contrast, several chiefs had sent messages at the beginning of the resistance reconfirming their loyalty to the queen. Whether in the case of Mistahimaskwa (released from his sentence one year early so that he wouldn't die in prison and be an embarrassment to the Canadian government) or of Poundmaker or Payepot, the strategy of the government was clearly to break the traditional leadership. This it did, and brutally.

After our long and exhausting walk from Swift Current to Fort Battleford, it seemed to be an odd ending to have to speak up against the very person there to welcome us at the finish. Fortunately, the Battleford Indian Industrial School was not our last stop. However, perhaps for the other pilgrims, as for me, it was the most devastating.

Our guide departed. Richard and some others put down tobacco at the remains of the school, and our group sat and talked quietly. After some time for meditation and prayer, Hugh reminded us that we had a final appointment at the historic park where the reconstructed fort and interpretive centre were located. We walked from the hilltop to a plaque near Battle Creek commemorating the *Saskatchewan Herald* newspaper and its publisher, P.G. Laurie, as well as a sign marking the first telegraph office in the North-West Territories. Once we crossed Battle Creek, the final kilometre or so was uphill. We stopped briefly at the site where Otter's troops had dug in against an imagined foe, then jogged across a busy double-lane highway beside big-box furniture stores, feeling more than slightly out of place, to Fort Battleford Park.

At the park, we were met by Tammy Donahue-Basiuk, also of the Battlefords Historical Society. She took our orders and then returned with take-out sandwiches provided by the historical society. Two of my cousins were at the fort with my aunt, and we hugged and visited.

---

138   Stonechild and Waiser, *Loyal till Death*, 216.

I noticed that our guide, Stan, was back; although I never found out for certain, I believe that he had paid for our meals. I thought about how the surface ripples of his language implied such deep shoals of anxiety. The fear of so many settler descendants is often linked to uncertainties about our own identities. Remarkably, Richard took his sandwich and went to sit with Stan. They chatted quietly. More than once I heard them, eventually, laugh together.

Later, in his impact statement on the walk for the Saskatchewan History and Folklore Society, Ken Wilson wrote that "thinking about the different users of the Trail—the soldiers marching to Fort Battleford, for instance, or the Métis freighters who brought the Trail into being—helped me realize the stark divisions between the ways different groups view that history. [All] have their roots ... in the events of the 1870s and 1880s, and those events continue to shape our ways of seeing each other."[139] The day had turned sunny and warm, and we had hot coffee and proper bathrooms. For the first time in three weeks, we had no further steps to travel.

As had happened two years previously on the NWMP Trail, we ended our long prairie walk at a reconstructed fort. This time, however, there were no costumed summer constables. Instead, Hugh ushered us onto the open field inside the fort palisade, where the staff and Tami Conley-Blais had set up chairs in a line. Thanks to the local First Nations, and to the Saskatchewan History and Folklore Society, we were to be welcomed to our destination by nêhiyaw drummers and dancers.

The Battleford Trail trek ended in a way that the Traders' Road walk never could have. In Battleford, there is no way to forget the ongoing presence of the prairie's Indigenous Peoples. Farther south and west, the social evolutionary myth that required Indigenous Peoples to become a vanishing race was easier to hold on to in the absence of many nêhiyaw, Lakota, or Nakota on the land. However, 150 years after the events of 1885, Battleford is still a polarized town where Canadian and Indigenous communities struggle to live side by side.

---

139   Ken Wilson, "Impact Statement for the SHFS," September 4, 2017.

Simply put, the dance was a gift. It was extraordinarily beautiful. A more striking contrast to the residential school whose ruins we had just visited, and a more powerful symbol of resurgence, could never be found. A group of young nêhiyaw introduced themselves, set up, offered tobacco to their drum, and began to drum and sing. Several very young girls and their two adult teachers danced a "welcome dance" in colourful and ornately beaded dresses. Some of the dresses were jingle dresses. We watched, entranced by the drumming, the singing, and the quiet, sure movements of the children.

Traditionally, the jingle dress is used for healing, and I wondered if healing was what was needed on land as deeply troubled as these grounds. I'm sure that I wasn't the only walker who at that moment was mentally contrasting these dancers, so proud and confident in their culture and traditions, with the elderly white volunteer who sat with us, so clearly anxious and upset about whether his culture and traditions would be preserved. Looking at the Indigenous youth, and at the settler-descended historian, I wondered how they could possibly meet and find common ground.[140]

Watching the beatific smiles on Dallas Roan and the other nêhiyaw dancers, it was surreal to think that the largest mass hanging in Canadian history, of six nêhiyaw and two Nakota men, took place in this spot in November 1885. It, too, was a public spectacle. It was also an illegal one: at the urging of Edgar Dewdney and of Hayter Reed, the hanging was made public despite the law forbidding public executions.[141] The eight men were tried and convicted for the murders earlier that year of nine whites at Frog Lake. The only settler male to escape the Frog Lake killings was William Bleasdell Cameron, who eluded the guns when nêhiyaw women disguised him with blankets and bundled him away.

---

140   Perhaps Richard's chat made some difference. Years after the walk, I saw a photo of this local history volunteer behind a group of local nêhiyaw making a pilgrimage to remember the Indigenous children buried by the residential school.

141   Stonechild and Waiser, *Loyal till Death*, 221. See also Seesequasis, "The Stanley Verdict."

Traditional welcome dancers, Fort Battleford, August 20, 2017.
Photo by the author.

Cameron wrote *Blood Red the Sun* in 1921. During my writing of
this book, I spent an evening with my brother and sister in Regina
going through our parents' things after their funerals. In one of
my mother's boxes, I found Cameron's book. Momentarily, I was
confused: was it one of my research texts that had somehow slipped
into my mother's effects?

On opening the inside cover, I was surprised to find a dedication:
"To Mr. and Mrs. John Golling on the occasion of your Golden
Wedding. With the compliments of Ruth and Everett Baker." John
and Martha Golling were my mother's parents. Both died while I
was quite young. To my recollection, I never heard either of them
speak of prairie history or Baker, whose name I wouldn't have
recognized in any case.

Farther down the page was another note. "We spent ten days with
the author, William Bleasdell Cameron, on the old Frog Lake, Fort
Pitt, and Frenchman Butte Trails. Shaunavon Saskatchewan, July 3,
1966." There it was. Proof that Everett Baker, whom I had come to

know only through books about him, had known my grandparents. It helped to explain why he would have taken the photo of my mother when she was fifteen and on a school trip to Saskatchewan Landing. When I told Hugh about it, he laughed. "I guess western walking runs in your family."

THAT DAY AT Battleford my leg was throbbing badly while I watched the dance. To ease the pain, I kept it elevated. I had walked the distance, but on arrival I was finally able to admit that something was wrong. An hour or so later, after thanking the dancers and drummers, we pilgrims hugged and said our final goodbyes to each other. Hugh offered me a lift back to Swift Current. Once under way, I asked him if he'd mind if I took off my bandages to have a look at the blisters.

When I removed my bandages, there was a swampy, sour smell from my leg. I did what I could with topical antibiotics and water in Swift Current. Soon I was on a plane for Montreal, where my own doctor confirmed that I had a general infection and gave me a long lecture about letting it go untreated for so long. Fortunately, a serious round of antibiotics combined with more topical treatments eventually healed the skin and stopped the infection. It could have been much worse.

When I flipped through the book by Cameron, I saw that one of the Nakota men sentenced to hang in 1885, as he waited at the gallows, asked his wife to bring him new shoes—heavy moccasins—for his execution. He said that he wanted them "so that he could make the long walk to the Sand Hills after his death."[142]

---

142   Cameron, *Blood Red the Sun*, 212. Stonechild and Waiser, *Loyal till Death*, 222–23, identify Miserable Man as the source of this quotation.

Chapter 4

MORE PRAIRIE TRAILS

Walking focuses not on the boundary lines of ownership that break the land into pieces but on the paths that function as a kind of circulatory system connecting the whole.

—REBECCA SOLNIT[1]

COLONIALISM IS INVISIBLE TO MANY OF US ONLY because it is the norm. If colonialism is invisible to you, then it is probably because you (like me) are benefiting from it. Resources are still being extracted, Indigenous bodies are still a battleground for economic interests that do not care about treaties, and police violence against Indigenous Peoples did not end with the nineteenth-century history of our trails. Like Colonel William Otter did when he arrived at Battleford in 1885, police are still breaking down the doors of Indigenous people simply defending their homes.

As Raymond Aldred writes, "the Cree Elders say: 'If the land is not healthy, how can we be healthy? And how can we walk in a good way?'"[2] On our prairie pilgrimages, we tried to seek out truth, relation, and beauty: tawny-shouldered hills of mixed-grass prairie as far as the eye can see, a stag slowly turning, its antlers high above

1   Rebecca Solnit, *Wanderlust: A History of Walking* (New York: Penguin, 2000), 162.
2   Raymond Aldred and Matthew R. Anderson, *Our Home and Treaty Land: Walking Our Creation Story* (Kelowna: Wood Lake Books, 2022), 73.

bright yellow waves of canola, white-rimmed alkali flats, the dark purple of chokecherries against the palm, a Swainson's hawk hanging motionless against the wind, friends, newly made, offering food for our journey.

These are the basic ingredients of an identity rooted in this land through treaty. But land without healthy relationships turns toxic. If we who are Canadians learn anything from the nêhiyaw and Nakota, the Lakota and Niisitapi and Anihšināpēk who travelled freely until they were no longer allowed to do so, and who now return even stronger, from the Métis brigades that moved east and west with the hunt, and now celebrate their past with pride, and from the hopeful little farming and ranching communities that once dotted the Prairies and are now seeking new ways of being, then we should learn that identity in the land is identity that the *land* bestows, honouring *all* our relations.

At a convenience store in the Okanagan Valley, near Vernon, British Columbia, a clerk asked my wife and me where we were from. Even though she had lived in Montreal for fifteen years, Sara immediately answered that she was from New Brunswick.

"Montreal," I said.

Sara challenged me. "Is that so?"

"Of course!" I responded. "Where else? It's been over thirty years. Most of my adult life. My kids grew up in Montreal."

"But Montreal is not where you're *from*," Sara insisted. "Where are you *from*?"

The store clerk, somewhat nonplussed, the change still in her hand, looked on at the two of us.

"When you close your eyes and think of a landscape," Sara continued, "is it Montreal you see?"

"No," I admitted. When I close my eyes and think of "home," I see the golden hills, the coulees and the draws, the short grass, and the cottonwoods that I've been describing in this book.

IT WOULD BE a mistake to leave you with the impression that this story of prairie pilgrimage ends here. In the years since the walks that I've described, Hugh and the Saskatchewan History and Folklore Society have helped many others to discover the old ways on the prairie. Almost every year Hugh has planned a walk on historic tracks in danger of slipping from memory. The walks have evolved, bringing in more and more participants, more of them Indigenous.

It is important work. If we let the Traders' Road and the Battleford Trail, the Frenchman, the Carlton, and the other trails go, if we do not remember them and write about them, film them, travel them on foot or horseback or by car, recalling and retelling the Indigenous and settler stories that they represent, and maintaining our relationships with these paths, then we lose not only the trails but also a critical part of identities. These trails reveal not only the past but also who we still are in all our complexity. "The way story works," writes Aldred, "is that you have to repeat a story for it to continue to have power."[3]

Long-distance walking on the prairie will never have the pastoral feel of village-to-village meanderings in Alsace or the ease and comfort found along leafy country lanes in England. Although, to my surprise, there was a Welsh couple running the café in Mortlach who served wonderful fish and chips, none of our treks ended with a picnic served on a red-checked tablecloth, as one might encounter in Europe. The trails that we walked are as empty of people (*now*, it must be pointed out) as the remotest stretches of the Spanish Meseta. But none was empty of memory or meaning. They were not footpaths *through* the prairie so much as footpaths *of* the prairie. By walking them, we were made to be more of the prairie as well. Body, mind, memory, land, and spirit are related, and the land claimed us as we walked. We experienced that synthesis again and again.

Indigenous participants on the grassland walks expressed their feelings of recognizing home, spirit, and relation. Others are

---

3   Aldred and Anderson, *Our Home and Treaty Land*, 31.

starting to organize prairie walks for mixed Indigenous–settler-descended groups. Awàsisak (Our Future) walks, for instance, were organized in 2019 from Edmonton to Calgary, and in 2021 and 2022 to Fort Pitt, Saskatchewan, to mark the signing of Treaty 6.[4] For settler descendants like me, these treaty trails organized by the SHFS and others are as significant as, and arguably more so than, paths to Santiago, Jerusalem, Croagh Patrick, the Shikoku, Kumbh Mela, or Varanasi. The prairie paths provide learnings that are essential if the next chapters of Canadian life are to move forward. The trails remind us Canadians that our ancestors were recent arrivals in treaty territories, that they had indispensable help from the people for whom this is still their homeland, and that the arrangements made were only to share it.[5] As Allen Jorgenson writes, "the narrative of the land is one of welcome, but this is a narrative that has been undone by colonial design."[6] Despite how deep colonization went, the arrangements that placed settlers and original peoples in relation *are still in force*. We Canadians belong on this Land as treaty people, a fact that puts our sovereignty in its limited place. We need to call on our governments to implement treaties properly, to live up to the obligations made, and to return land that was never ours. When our governments don't do this, we need to push them to do the right thing, whether it concerns reparations, Crown lands, or policing. These are the right actions that, in our case, our walking called out in us.

---

4   Thandiwe Konguavi, "Five-Day Walk in Alberta, Sask. Aims to Build Relationships, Deeper Understanding of Treaties," CBC News Edmonton, September 6, 2021, https://www.cbc.ca/news/canada/edmonton/treaty-walk-to-build-relationships-deeper-understanding-1.6165940. See also the documentaries of these walks at https://www.treatytalk.com/.

5   Harold Johnson, *Two Families: Treaty and Government* (Saskatoon: Purich, 2007), 92.

6   Allen G. Jorgenson, *Indigenous and Christian Perspectives in Dialogue: Kairotic Place and Borders* (Lanham, MD: Lexington, 2021), 82.

Were the walks pilgrimages? Each felt holy in its own way. There are few words better than *pilgrimage* for what we experienced, even if the word is notoriously difficult to define. "We live in relationship with a spiritual world," writes Aldred. "That spiritual world is not abstract from the physical world in which we live. We need a shared spirituality of unity, that nonetheless still recognizes the differences between non-Indigenous and Indigenous life and experience."[7]

Our walks were unsettling. They were not tourism. We crossed territory that many of us thought we knew. But to *walk* it, rather than *drive* it, made the familiar into a strange country, a cartography mapped by stone piles and isolated stands of poplar, grandfather stones and black-centred glacial kettles, buckbrush and teepee rings, abandoned farmhouses and cow trails along undulating fencelines bordered by yarrow and cacti. There was nothing more exciting than coming to the far edge of a highland and seeing the prairie drop away like a golden rolling ocean. Or stepping carefully down a spray of gravel from a sun-blasted hilltop and feeling the embracing shade of a hidden coulee.

We learned that part of being on the walk meant needing our hosts. As pilgrims often have, we *needed* shelter and water. We appreciated electricity, food, and indoor plumbing when available! Our hosts were settler ranchers, farmers, townspeople, Hutterites, and First Nations. We learned from them about how rural communities are revitalizing in ways not always obvious to outsiders.

We also learned about the human capacity for generosity. Once, near Kyle, a man drove by as our group stretched out for a kilometre or more along the road. His question to the first trio of walkers was "Did you have a breakdown?" When he slowed down for the second group, he rolled down his window and asked "Why are you doing this?" By the time he had driven another few hundred metres, and met the stragglers, he asked them if he could do anything to help.

---

7   Aldred and Anderson, *Our Home and Treaty Land*, 26.

THE GOOD WALK ON THE PRAIRIES

Being a participant in Treaty means that your identity is
bigger than just you.

—RAYMOND ALDRED[8]

SINCE OUR FIRST trek, when at times Hugh and I were the only walkers, our numbers have grown with each new trail. People have joined our walks for hundreds of kilometres or only for an afternoon. Each individual brings some new way of seeing the prairie and contributing to the group. There is little uniformity: some eat alone and quietly, whereas some pool food. Some have wanted to end the day sitting in a circle with guitar and beer; others go off by themselves, meditating as the sun sets. The group aspect of the walk creates logistical problems, of course. But such issues are far outweighed by the richness of community that results in the sharing of laughter and occasionally tears, of knowledge both personal and nation-based, and of formal and informal ceremony.

At the outset of this book, I quoted Indigenous scholar Dwayne Donald, who states that "walking as a life practice . . . can teach kinship relationality and help reconceptualize Indigenous–Canadian relations on more ethical terms."[9] That is certainly how it has worked for us. I cannot speak for the others, but for me the walking was personal, political, and spiritual, all three at once.[10] Four walks and two funerals: it was an unexpected way to work through the grief of losing my parents. At the same time, it became cathartic, a way to understand better the place that raised them and me: the place that I call home.

---

8   Aldred and Anderson, *Our Home and Treaty Land*, 75.
9   Dwayne Donald, "We Need a New Story: Walking and the wâhkôtowin Imagination," *Journal of the Canadian Association for Curriculum Studies (JCACS)* 18, no. 2 (2021): 53.
10   Kathleen E. Absolon (Minogiizhigokwe), *Kaandossiwin: How We Come to Know* (Winnipeg: Fernwood, 2011), 121.

The coincidence of the timing was a gift, and the land turned out to be healing. But the walks were also a form of dissent: the dissent of following a sometimes-meandering human path across an artificial, and commercially drawn, world of legal squares, their precise lines marking township, section, and quarter. As Solnit has put it, "walking sews together the land that ownership tears apart."[11] Claims to exclusive "private property" negate a sense of our relationship to the land as belonging to it rather than it to us.[12] Ownership (without such relational responsibility) breaks ancient chains of reciprocity that make for good and healthy relationships with neighbours.

Even though we respected private property, the historic paths do not care about No Trespassing signs. These trails precede such claims and such divisions. They tell a story that too many of us have forgotten about a time when settlers had an understudy's relation to the land and learned from Indigenous Peoples how to live on it. There was a time when, not long ago, Indigenous individuals and groups were not automatically treated as interlopers by a racist society that has made the great outdoors "white space."

The parcelling of the prairies that began with the waves of surveyors of the late 1870s is only 150 years old (I'm glad that my brief stint on a survey crew had to do with making a roadway, not a property line). Hugh was careful always to get the permission of landowners for our walks. To the credit of most rural Saskatchewan ranchers and farmers, we (a mostly "white" group) had nearly unanimous cooperation. We were careful never to abuse the generosity of those who let us pass, and I am thankful to them.

Yet we were showing that there is *public* interest in what lies almost completely on what are now *private* spaces. That public interest must be safeguarded. Such safeguarding must happen not only for the sake of the historical memories but also for how the trails witness what should be safe spaces for *all* peoples, especially those who first walked them and are now excluded. The trails are living examples

---

11   Solnit, *Wanderlust*, 163.

12   Aldred and Anderson, *Our Home and Treaty Land*, 11.

of a common *contemporary* interest, whether one is nêhiyaw, Métis, settler descended, or a newcomer.

The trails that we walked were as old as the bison herds, the burial grounds that go back millennia, and the Bear Hills that now seem to be so empty. But the trails were also as new as the guard dogs that we met as we approached Battleford and the Lakota man who slapped my back and told me that he preferred to travel to the Cypress Hills in his Ford truck. The Battleford trek was about remembering how Métis, First Nations, and settlers all once used the same trail. It was about smudging with farm families who had never before participated in such a ceremony. It was about including Indigenous Peoples' concerns and historical corrections in our conversations naturally, neither preaching nor apologizing, just quietly and consistently recognizing the facts. It was about *not forgetting* but mentioning the government-broken treaties, the expulsions, and the injustices when discussing the histories—and the present realities—of rural and urban prairie life.

In this account, I have tried to highlight contemporary Indigenous writers, scholars, and issues. But this book is ultimately still the writing of a Canadian struggling with his settler-descended identity. Indigenous reality can be co-opted too easily as yet another settler-descendant "lens." Indigeneity becomes the "other" (again) against which people like me measure and evaluate what it means to be Canadian in this epoch of the country's history.

To avoid that, Canadians must deal with the legacy not only of Mistahimaskwa's life but also of Colten Boushie's death. The definition of being Canadian must address not only the ten thousand children's graves but also the fact that our churches and governments tried to cover over and silence their memory. Our national character must include not only the history of the forts but also the contemporary history of the Indigenous person who has been shot during a "wellness check," who has been murdered or gone missing, or who has been driven out of a city by police on a winter night and left to freeze to death trying to walk home to shelter. The definition of being Canadian must likewise include our unique relation, through treaty, to nêhiyaw podcasts, Mi'kmaw social media posts, Inuit art installations, Indigenous health-care specialists, Métis music, and Haudenosaunee businesses.

EPILOGUE: THE FRENCHMAN'S TRAIL

THE YEAR AFTER we trekked from Swift Current to Battleford, Hugh Henry led us once more onto the open grassland in Saskatchewan. This time he had mapped out the Frenchman's Trail, a route taken by settlers mostly from Quebec headed to homesteads around Gravelbourg and Ponteix. We were starting in the community of Mortlach and heading south.

For all my talk of pilgrimages, this was the first of our walks that actually qualified in the classic sense: the terminus of our walk happened to coincide with a real shrine, the Co-Cathedral in Gravelbourg. As we followed roads south from Mortlach, we passed near where Hugh grew up.[13] Don Bolen's childhood was spent near Gravelbourg; in fact, his grandparents had walked this trail on their arrival in Saskatchewan. Even though the Frenchman's Trail was our first path to have been primarily a route for settlers, more of our pilgrim group, ironically, were Indigenous than ever before, a trend that has continued in subsequent SHFS walks.

We humans are the canvas on which landscape works. It was always the land that occasioned the telling of tales and the surprise discovery of revelations. "It is ultimately the land that gives shape to the stories and to the spirituality that arises from them."[14] The evening of our arrival in Mortlach, a lone female moose greeted us from the fields. It seemed to be an omen: it was the first time in my life that I'd seen a moose on the open prairie.

I learned to be in a new relation to the land by walking on it with people who heard, saw, and felt different stories in the draws and

---

13   In 2021, with help from Richard Kotowich, Hugh built an "installation /reconciliation action" piece at Wiwa Hill, where his Marriott great-grandparents homesteaded and where they are now buried.

14   Aldred and Anderson, *Our Home and Treaty Land*, 88.

rises. Harold Steppuhn saw the advancing and retreating glaciers, the salinity and water tables,[15] Fred Ludolph the dry spell that had stunted a section of crop, Christine Ramsay the angles of light on canola fields and approaching clouds. In the prairie wind, Ken Wilson heard the author writing about grasses, Don Bolen the songs of Leonard Cohen and the prayers for repentance prompted by a thousand pastoral visits with the children of residential school survivors. Madonna Hamel, the desert mother mystic, heard women's strong voices, their calloused hands on farm implements, aprons, and crucifixes. Connie Sykes saw the meteor shower and the lark sparrow that sang as it flitted from fencepost to cottonwood at a safe distance from our passing.

There is the geography that we know and can trace topographically. It is made up of distance, terrain, and movement, for instance knowing that it is about twenty-two kilometres to the next town, that there is an alkali lake in the way, and that a night's rest, some good conversation, and a cup of tea await us. But there is another geography as well, one that exists off the maps, even though it overlaps them. This is a geography related to uncertainty, to bodily aches and pains, to imagination and discovery and time spent walking along a cattle trail alone. For me, it has been a wonder to see the land through the eyes of other pilgrims: city through the eyes of country, Canadian through the eyes of Indigenous. It has given me a taste of empathy, expressed in community, learned through walking in treaty territories.

On the Frenchman's Trail, there were new walkers and new ways to see what Denise Nadeau calls "the geographical contours" of our genealogy:[16] Larry Dudragne, quietly keeping one eye on the road, his other on the birds; Louise Million, as long and tough and lean as Harold, with whom I sheltered under a tarp against the sun;

---

15   In December 2022, Harold took me on a walk through southern Swift Current in sub-zero temperatures to point out how the "bench" referred to earlier in the book is actually the terminus, in his opinion, of the glaciation that accompanied the last ice age.

16   Denise M. Nadeau, *Unsettling Spirit: A Journey into Decolonization* (Montreal and Kingston: McGill-Queen's University Press, 2020), 228.

Dave Cyca, whose reedy voice when he picks up a guitar sounds so much like home. Barbara Anderson, determined and serene in her walking, and Tara Million of the quiet smile, who once measured the prairie against her decisions about the future. Judy Corkery, who laughed about family members as if they were walking beside her, and ReAnne Letourneau, facing the sunrise alone in prayers while the rest of us struggled to get down our morning tea and coffee. Louise Halfe, whose voice has been mixed forever in my mind and heart with her powerful nêhiyaw-English poetry, who took my arm and pretended to limp painfully, stuffing her giggles under her hand while she watched to see if her gentle, kind Peter Butt would fall for the ruse: "Sometimes when I walk," she once wrote, "my left ankle calls / buckles and I stumble / When I was young / stumbling was a frequent conversation / between my ankle and my heart."[17]

George Greenia points out that pilgrimage is an activity that brings solidarity, that "crafts consensus about symbolic gestures to express core values."[18] Maybe the most profound thing that we did on our walks was simply *being outside*, together on the land for long stretches of time. Indigenous Peoples were usually outside the stockade walls. Perhaps outside the walls of our spiritual and social "stockades" is where we who are prairie settler descendants might also find our identity.

AFTER FINISHING THE Frenchman's Trail walk, I met my brother and sister and their families, and we drove west to Shaunavon. Mark

17   Sky Dancer Louise Bernice Halfe, "āhkamēyahtamowin," in *Burning in This Midnight Dream* (Regina: Coteau Books, 2016), 7.

18   George Greenia, "The Lakota Future Generation Ride of the Lakota Sioux," in *Pilgrimage in Practice: Narration, Reclamation, and Healing*, ed. Ian S. McIntosh, E. Moore Quinn, and Vivien Keely (Boston: CABI, 2018), 144.

brought with him the two small urns that contained the reserved ashes of our parents.

It had taken some time to coordinate our schedules. Now, at last, we were making our trip to fulfill their final wishes. It was raining when we drove up the hill toward the cemetery south of town, a rain heavy enough that we had to take umbrellas to stand around the small grave and its crumbling concrete.

Once we were there, none of us quite knew what to do next. We talked a bit about a sister whom Mark and I had never known and whom our sister Kandace had been too young to remember. My brother has an incredibly dry sense of humour, and we had many laughs remembering our parents. We had a shovel and lots of time. When we left, the baby sister who had died so long ago finally had a part of her mother and father with her again. And our parents were with her again as all three were held in the embrace of the prairie.

As we drove away, my sister and I chatted in the back seat of the car. I thought about the prairie grass around the grave, the bits of straw against the old cement, the rusty lichen marking the name Anderson from the late 1950s. I thought about my parents and their ashes, this final resting place where the wind blows constantly from the west, where bison graze in a nearby pasture, and where moss and sage gradually take over anything in the ground.

The land is not "other." We who are settler descended need to learn once again to sit at the feet of those who, since time immemorial, have counted the prairie, the lakes, the forest, and the rivers among their relations. What a grand thing it would be if the term "settle" came to mean settle in the sense of particulates spread over a grave or buried beside it. Settle as in becoming, eventually, part of an ancient soil, giving rich nutrients to what in time might become new growth. How precious it would be if we learned that what is important is not making a claim on the land as much as learning how best to let it make a claim on us.

Perhaps, someday, if we walk the good walk, then this will be true, in this place that we wish so dearly to call home.

Hugh Henry taking GPS coordinates beside the Traders' Road tracks, August 6, 2015. *Photo by the author.*

ACKNOWLEDGEMENTS

WALKING OUR GOOD WALK ON THE PRAIRIE has taken many relations. I thank my friend Richard Kotowich, our first pilgrimage Elder, for his thoughtfulness, his attention to proper protocol on the land, his smudges and offerings of tobacco, his challenging and listening, and his guidance in community every morning. And for his theological chats with me over many walking kilometres! "The land makes the Elder," as does the community.

Thank you to Sky Dancer Louise Bernice Halfe and Peter Butt for their spiritual leadership on the Mortlach to Gravelbourg pilgrimage and the Humboldt to Fort Carlton walk and to Louise for her heart-breakingly tough, playful, and beautiful poetry. The excerpts from her poems are taken from the following: *Bear Bones and Feathers* (Coteau Books, 1994; Brick Books, 2022); *Blue Marrow* (Coteau Books, 2004; Kegedonce Press, 2020); *The Crooked Good* (Coteau Books, 2007; Kegedonce Press, 2021); and *Burning in This Midnight Dream* (Coteau Books, 2016; Brick Books, 2021).

I'm also thankful to Dr. Raymond Aldred, Treaty 8, for sharing so many good talks over breakfasts in Montreal, for inviting me to learn from the students of the Indigenous Studies Program at the Vancouver School of Theology, UBC, and for reminding me that I am a Treaty 4 person, no matter where I am.

My spouse, Dr. Sara Parks, read and commented on every word of this manuscript and offered space, time, and a home in England, Ireland, and Nova Scotia in which to write; I cannot thank her enough. Mark Anderson, my brother, kept a vehicle ready just for these projects and a closet full of camping gear for me. His generosity, together with that of my sister-in-law and fellow walker, Barbara, has been essential. My sister Kandace, and brother-in-law Vern Enslen, also provided moral and material support that was a daily surprise. My three children have consistently supported my urge to write and believed in me, and in part I wrote this book for Nathan, Daniel, Gabriel, and their families so that they could know their father that much better. During preparations for the walks, my cousins Jan, Karen, and Arlene, and my aunt Isabelle Swanson (may she rest in peace), fed and housed me, more often than I can mention.

Thanks to Ken Wilson, prairie walker extraordinaire, who—when not walking the Northern Great Plains—is often reading and writing about walking. Ken kindly looked at and commented on portions of this work and provided help from his encyclopedic knowledge of walking literature. Sometimes I just followed his trail.

Jim Daschuk met me before our first long trek and was kind enough to provide me with some of his notes, along with much valuable primary source material. His book, *Clearing the Plains*, remains a constant inspiration and a sourcebook to me, as to many others.

Thank you to Kristin Enns-Kavanaugh, and to the Saskatchewan History and Folklore Society, not only for believing in our crazy project but also for walking with us. Thanks to the society for sponsoring the NWMP Trail and the Battleford Trail walks, for having housed the Everett Baker slides, and for continually moving forward in specific acts and policies of remembrance, representation, and decolonization.

My thanks to Dr. Kenneth Atsenhaiaton Deer, Thomas Teiowí:sonte Deer, Orenda Konwowennontion Boucher, and many others in Kahnawà:ke for accepting us as pilgrims. Sara Terreault was my co-conspirator in setting up Concordia University's Old Montreal to Kahnawà:ke Kanien'kehá:ka Territory and in so many of our early ventures into the theory and practice of pilgrimage.

Thanks to Harold Steppuhn, who not only provided wise advice and encouragement while walking but also has been the source of much geographical information since (and is just so darned photogenic). Don Bolen did far more than walk with me. Having such a fine-souled poet bless a family grave is an honour that I will not forget. My thanks to Trevor Herriot for his encouragement, his courage in speaking out for the prairie, his books, and his mentorship, and to Branimir Gjetvaj for his photos. Thank you to Wood Mountain poet, author, and wise woman Thelma Poirier, who started us off, and to Métis Elder Cecile Blanke, who believed in our Battleford Trail walk and supported it. I thank Stew and Cyndi Tasche for walking with us but even more for the musical *The Cypress Hills Will Never Be the Same*.

Candace Savage's powerful *A Geography of Blood* first sparked my interest in the true, hidden, and bloody history of an area that I thought I knew; in many ways, her research and her beautiful writing started me walking on Treaty 4 land. Kristin Catherwood was gracious in her interviews and in providing the Heritage 150 spot on our walks; she continues to advocate for the land and its people. Thanks to George Tsougrianis for his documentary about our walk, James R. Page for his superb photos and his graciousness in sharing them, and Norris Currie for faithfully coming out to shoot footage at various points.

Thanks to Mette Ducan and the late Robert Ducan, my hosts at The Convent Inn, Val Marie, and to all the folks who make Prairie Wind and Silver Sage such an active artistic, historical, and community centre, including Diana Chabros and Joseph Naytowhow.

Christine Jamieson (Boothroyd-Nlaka'pamux First Nation), with whom I've shared so many meals and conversations about Indigeneity and identity, has been a dear friend and a support throughout our mutual learning. I'm thankful for the very active American and Canadian Studies department at the University of Nottingham, England, where I gave myself a sabbatical to write this book. Somehow, to my great benefit, the University of Nottingham has a surprisingly well-stocked collection of books about the history of Saskatchewan and the North-West Territories. Thank you also to the Concordia

University Part-Time Faculty Association, which provided funding for my participation in some of these walks.

Thank you to all those—especially Audra Hunwicks, Jim Murphy, Cathy Valenti, Eric E. Dyck, John and Cathy McPhail, Marla Berg, Ken and Jocelyn DeBoer, Joanne Carnegie, Lorraine Reinhardt, Daiva Jaugelis, Elise Moser, Darquise Charron, SpringLaw, Christine Jamieson, Lyndon Sayers, Wanda Gronhovd, Catherine Beatson, and Karin Neutel—who gave funds and encouragement to support the first NWMPT walk. Please accept my apologies that none of you got your GoFundMe rewards because of my faulty camera.

I owe a debt of gratitude to the University of Regina Press for taking on this book. I'm especially thankful to David McLennan, who worked hard to keep me up to date on the process and shared his love of the Prairies by keeping such a close eye on the manuscript and permissions, and to Dallas Harrison and Rachel Taylor for their thoughtful and detailed editing.

I cannot voice enough appreciation to my fellow walkers and our hosts.

On the NWMP Trail: Hugh Henry, Harold Steppuhn, Hayden Thomassin, Kathryn Scott, Richard Kotowich, Madonna Hamel, James R. Page, Don Bolen, Allen and Gwenanne Jorgenson, Trevor Herriot, Branimir Gjetvaj, Simone Hengen, Barbara Anderson, Kristin Catherwood, Norma Hain, Stew and Cyndi Tasche, and Randie Walker, as well as Dave and Esther Green on horseback.

Our hosts on the NWMP Trail: Chief Ellen Lecaine of Wood Mountain Lakota First Nation; Wood Mountain Lakota First Nation and especially Band Councillor Dave Ogle; Judy Fitzpatrick of Wood Mountain; the Assiniboia detachment of the Royal Canadian Mounted Police; Peter Huska (Ukrainian Orthodox Church); New Horizons Centre (Mankota); Bill and Audrey Wilson; Margaret and Keith Walker; Mike Sherven; Denis Duquette; Prairie Wind and Silver Sage; Terry Jensen and family; Judy and Alan Erickson; Rod Hammond and the Valley View Bible Camp; Curt and Lorie Gronhovd; Wade Duke and family; Robert Gebhardt, who guided us in a tour of Chimney Coulee; Ethel Wills; Candace Savage, guest speaker in Eastend; the Arnal family; Lois and Roland Lacelle; the Clinton Brost family; Roger and Lou Parsonage; Parks Canada and the Parks Canada staff at Fort Walsh; and last but certainly not least the Saskatchewan History and Folklore Society, which funded the Eastend program and provided support throughout.

The other walkers on the Battleford Trail: Connie Sykes; Richard Kotowich and Pat Erhardt; Fred Ludolph; Ken Wilson and Christine Ramsay; Hugh Henry; Harold Steppuhn; Don Bolen; and those who joined us for sections of the walk: Sharon Pasula; Judy Erickson; Sharon Enns and Kristin Enns-Kavanagh; Kristin Catherwood; Lorne Kelsey; Phil Brown; Lynn Hollick; Crystal Craig; and Joyce Tremmel.

Our hosts on the Battleford Trail: Tim and Patricia Orthner; Rennie and Henry Funk; the women of the Swift Current Hutterite Colony; Gord Nodge; Shirley Boyer, Kyle and District Museum; Rural Municipality of Lacadena (Sanctuary); Carl Sothmann (Otter Station); Doug Bone and others in Greenan; Marvin White; Ruth White (Cappie's trees); Fiske Community Hall (Trevor Cross); Lorne and Linda Kelsey; Herschel Retreat House (Jimmée and Devon Wiens); Ancient Echoes; Valley Centre Colony; Crystal and Liam Craig; Doreen (Kent) Dubreuil; Robert and Lorraine Heather; Biggar Museum and Gallery (Delta Fay Cruikshank); Russell Affleck; Cando Legion Hall; Mosquito–Grizzly Bear's Head–Lean Man First Nation (Tristan Bird); Robert Johnson; Tammy Donahue-Basiuk (Battlefords Historical Society); Don Light; Tami Conley-Blais; and the nêhiyaw dancers and drummers at Fort Battleford.

The walkers on the Frenchman's Trail: Hugh Henry; Judy Corkery; Sister ReAnne Letourneau; Harold Steppuhn; Connie Sykes; Louise Million; Tara Million; Simone Hengen; Ken Wilson; Laurent (Larry) Dudragne; Don Bolen; Madonna Hamel; Barbara Anderson; Dave Cyca; Louise Halfe and Peter Butt; Karen Clark; Kristin Enns-Kavanagh; and for the pre-walk archaeological tours: Norma Hain; Judy Knelsen; and Richard Kotowich and Pat Erhardt.

Our hosts on the Frenchman's Trail: Mortlach Golf Club (Dale Domeij); Mortlach Museum (Pam Speir and others); Garth Ferguson;

August 18, 2017, near Cando, Saskatchewan. *Photo by Kristin Enns-Kavanagh.*

Village of Coderre (Leonard Lepine); Shamrock Regional Park; Renaud Larochelle; the Gravelbourg Co-Cathedral; and Jeannette and André Moquin.

I appreciate the many individuals, First Nations, and institutions that allowed us to trek across their fields, pastures, coulees, and farmsteads on these journeys. Your welcome made *The Good Walk* possible.

Finally, my thanks to Hugh Henry, who helped me to fill out this list of names, and my deep apologies to anyone whom I missed—with this many people involved, there are probably several important people who have slipped by. It is not by chance that even in my acknowledgements I have had to ask for the aid of Hugh. He is the person without whom none of the walks outlined in the book would have taken place. He is the person who literally kept me, and the rest of us, on "the good walk." Over every hill and through every draw, it was Hugh who remained an inspiration for quiet, steady, thoughtful, and low-tech journeying, both physical and intellectual. This book is dedicated to him.

BIBLIOGRAPHY

ARCHIVAL SOURCES

Alexander Morris to a Party of "Sioux from Wood Mountain," n.d. Library and Archives Canada [hereafter LAC], RG 10, VOL. 3613, file 4049.

Augustus Jukes to Edgar Dewdney, October 21, 1882. LAC, RG 10, reel C-10134, vol. 3744, file 19506-2.

Edgar Dewdney to John A. Macdonald, October 21, 1882. LAC, RG 10, reel C-10131, vol. 3744, file 19506-2.

"Excerpt of an Unnamed Officer Who Was with Otter," April 14–16, 1885, Canadian War Museum Archives, 58A 1 101.38.

James Morrow Walsh Fonds. Glenbow Archives, M 8065, file 11b. https://searcharchives.ucalgary.ca/index.php/james -morrow-walsh-fonds.

Report from D[r]. Kittson of the Northwest Mounted Police Stationed at Fort Macleod, Concerning the Insufficiency of the Rations Issued to the Indians in the Northwest Territories. LAC, RG 10, vol. 3726, reel C-10126, file 24 811, Mikan 2059165.

"The *Saskatchewan Herald*." Saskatchewan Historic Newspapers, University of Saskatchewan. http://sabnewspapers.usask .ca/islandora/search/dc.title%3A%28Saskatchewan%5C%20 Herald%29.

Sessional Papers of the Dominion of Canada, 3rd Parl, 5th Sess (1878), vol. 5. http://www.canadiana.ca/view/oocihm.9_08052_11_5/605?r=0&s=1.

WEB MATERIALS

Hamel, Madonna. "Pop 89: Deep Scribe Preserve." Your West Central Voice. https://www.yourwestcentral.com/articles/pop-89-deep-scribe-preserve.

Maskêgon-Iskwêw, Âhasiw. "Talk Indian to Me #1." Ghostkeeper, 1995. http://ghostkeeper.gruntarchives.org/publication-mix-magazine-talk-indian-to-me-1.html.

McConnell, R.G. Geological and Topographical Map of the Cypress Hills—Wood Mountain and Adjacent Country. Montreal: Burland, 1885.

Soggie, Joan. "Lost in the Red Ochre Hills." https://www.yumpu.com/en/document/view/53016697/lost-in-the-red-ochre-hills-part-ii-saskatchewan-archaeological-.

Truth and Reconciliation Commission of Canada. *Honouring the Truth, Reconciling for the Future: Summary of the Final Report of the Truth and Reconciliation Commission of Canada.* http://publications.gc.ca/collections/collection_2015/trc/IR4-7-2015-eng.pdf.

Vowel, Chelsea. "Beyond Territorial Acknowledgments." 2016. http://apihtawikosisan.com/2016/09/beyond-territorial-acknowledgments/.

BOOKS AND ARTICLES

Abley, Mark. *Conversations with a Dead Man: The Legacy of Duncan Campbell Scott.* Madeira Park, BC: Douglas and McIntyre, 2013.

Absolon, Kathleen E. (Minogiizhigokwe). *Kaandossiwin: How We Come to Know.* Winnipeg: Fernwood, 2011.

Ahenakew, Edward. *Voices of the Plains Cree.* Edited by Ruth M. Buck. Regina: Canadian Plains Research Center, 1995.

Aldred, Ray. "A Shared Narrative." In *Strangers in This World: Multireligious Reflections on Immigration*, edited by Hussam S. Timani, Allen G. Jorgenson, and Alexander Y. Hwang, 193–206. Minneapolis: Fortress Press, 2015.

Aldred, Raymond, and Matthew R. Anderson. *Our Home and Treaty Land: Walking Our Creation Story*. Kelowna: Wood Lake Books, 2022.

Alfred, Gerald R. (Taiaiake). *Heeding the Voices of Our Ancestors: Kahnawake Mohawk Politics and the Rise of Native Nationalism*. Toronto: Oxford University Press, 1995.

———. *Peace, Power, Righteousness: An Indigenous Manifesto*. 2nd ed. Oxford: Oxford University Press, 2008.

Andersen, Chris. "Critical Indigenous Studies: From Difference to Density." *Cultural Studies Review* 15, no. 2 (2009): 80–100.

———. *"Métis": Race, Recognition and the Struggle for Indigenous Peoplehood*. Vancouver: UBC Press, 2014.

Andersen, Finn. "A Glimpse into the Past through the Eye of Everett Baker (1893–1981)." In *Plain Speaking: Essays on Aboriginal Peoples and the Prairie*, edited by Patrick Douaud and Bruce Dawson, 89–92. Regina: Canadian Plains Research Center, 2002.

Anderson, Alan B. *Settling Saskatchewan*. Regina: University of Regina Press, 2013.

Anderson, Frank W. *Fort Walsh and the Cypress Hills*. Self-published, 1989.

Anderson, Ian. *Sitting Bull's Boss: Above the Medicine Line with James Morrow Walsh*. Victoria: Heritage House, 2000.

Anderson, Matthew R. "'Aware-Settler' Biblical Studies: Breaking Claims of Textual Ownership." *Journal for Interdisciplinary Biblical Studies* 1, no. 1 (2019): 42–68.

———. "Luther's Failed Pilgrimage and the Body of Christendom." *International Journal of Religious Tourism and Pilgrimage* 7, no. 1 (2019): 52–61.

———. "Pilgrimage and Challenging a Canadian Foundational Myth." In *Pilgrimage in Practice: Narration, Reclamation, and Healing*, edited by Ian S. McIntosh, E. Moore Quinn, and Vivian Keely, 148–64. Wallingford, UK: CABI Press, 2018.

———. "'Settler-Aware' Pilgrimage and Reconciliation: The Treaty Four Canadian Context." In *Peace Journeys: A New Direction in Religious Tourism and Pilgrimage Research*, edited by Ian S. McIntosh, Nour Farra Haddad, and Dane Munro, 98–120. Newcastle upon Tyne, UK: Cambridge Scholars, 2020.

———. "Strangers on the Land: What 'Settler-Aware' Biblical Studies Learns from Indigenous Methodologies." *Critical Theology* 1, no. 2 (2019): 10–14.

———. "Walking to Be Some Body: Desire and Diaspora on the St-Olaf Way." *International Journal of Religious Tourism and Pilgrimage* 7, no. 1 (2019): 62–76.

———. "Why Canadians Need the Right to Roam." *The Narwhal*, July 30, 2018. https://thenarwhal.ca/right-to-roam-canada/.

Angus, Charlie. *Children of the Broken Treaty: Canada's Lost Promise and One Girl's Dream*. Regina: University of Regina Press, 2017.

Asch, Michael, John Borrows, and James Tully. *Resurgence and Reconciliation: Indigenous-Settler Relations and Earth Teachings*. Toronto: University of Toronto Press, 2018.

Asher, Lila, Joe Curnow, and Amil Davis. "The Limits of Settlers' Territorial Acknowledgments." *Curriculum Inquiry* 48, no. 3 (2018): 316–34.

Baker, Everett. "There's a Long, Long Trail A-Winding." In *Fort Walsh to Wood Mountain: The North-West Mounted Police Trail*, edited by Mike Fedyk, 84–89. Regina: Benchmark Press, 2010.

Barrett, Matthew. "'Hero of the Half-Breed Rebellion': Gabriel Dumont and Late Victorian Military Masculinity." *Journal of Canadian Studies* 48, no. 3 (2014): 79–107.

Beahen, William, and Stan Horrall. *Red Coats on the Prairies: The North-West Mounted Police 1886–1900*. Regina: Centax Books, 1998.

Bednasek, C. Drew, and Anne M.C. Godlewska. "The Influence of Betterment Discourses on Canadian Aboriginal Peoples in the Late Nineteenth and Early Twentieth Centuries." *Canadian Geographer* 53, no. 4 (2009): 444–61.

Bentley, D.M.R. "'Set Forth as Plainly May Appear': The Verse Journal of Henry Kelsey." ARIEL: A Review of International English Literature 21, no. 4 (1990): 9–30.

Bhabha, Homi. "Of Mimicry and Man: The Ambivalence of Colonial Discourse." October 28 (1984): 125–33.

Black, Norman Fergus. History of Saskatchewan and the Old North West. Regina: North West Historical Company, 1913.

Blanke, Cecile. Lac Pelletier: My Métis Home. Saskatoon: Gabriel Dumont Institute, 2019.

Cameron, William Bleasdell. Blood Red the Sun. 1927; reprinted, Calgary: Kenway Publishing, 1970.

Cardinal, Harold. The Unjust Society. Toronto: Douglas and McIntyre, 1999.

Carey, Jane. "On Hope and Resignation: Conflicting Visions of Settler Colonial Studies and Its Future as a Field." Postcolonial Studies 23, no. 1 (2020): 21–42.

Carter, Sarah. Aboriginal People and Colonizers of Western Canada to 1900. Toronto: University of Toronto Press, 1999.

———. "'An Infamous Proposal': Prairie Indian Reserve Land and Soldier Settlement after World War I." Manitoba History 37 (1999): 9–21.

Chambers, Ernest J. The North-West Mounted Police: A Corps History. Montreal: Mortimer Press, 1906.

———. The Queen's Own Rifles of Canada: The History of a Splendid Regiment's Origin. Toronto: E.L. Ruddy, 1901.

Cianca, Jenn. "Written by the Body: Early Christian Pilgrims as Sacred Placemakers." International Journal of Religious Tourism and Pilgrimage 7, no. 1 (2019): 11–21.

Clinkskill, James. A Prairie Memoir: The Life and Times of James Clinkskill 1853–1936. Edited by S.D. Hansen. Regina: Canadian Plains Research Center, 2003.

Coleman, Daniel. White Civility: The Literary Project of English Canada. Toronto: University of Toronto Press, 2006.

Coleman, Simon. "Anthropological Tropes and Historical Tricksters: Pilgrimage as an 'Example' of Persuasion." *Journal of the Royal Anthropological Institute* 21 (2015): 144–61.

———. "Do You Believe in Pilgrimage? Communitas, Contestation and Beyond." *Anthropological Theory* 2, no. 3 (2002): 355–68.

Collins-Kreiner, Noga. "Dark Tourism As/Is Pilgrimage." *Current Issues in Tourism* 19, no. 12 (2016): 1185–89.

Coues, Elliott. *New Light on the Early History of the Greater North-West: The Manuscript Journals of Alexander Henry and of David Thompson, 1799–1814.* New York: Francis P. Harper, 1897.

Cowie, Isaac. *The Company of Adventurers: A Narrative of Seven Years in the Service of the Hudson's Bay Company during 1867–1874.* 1913; reprinted, Lincoln: University of Nebraska Press, 1993.

Crane, Lyz. "Artists as Revitalization Agents." *Communities and Banking* 22, no. 3 (2011): 10–12.

Cresswell, Tim. *Maxwell Street: Writing and Thinking Place.* Chicago: University of Chicago Press, 2019.

———. "Place." In *International Encyclopedia of Human Geography: Volume 8,* edited by Nigel Thrift and Rob Kitchin, 169–77. Oxford: Elsevier, 2009.

———. "Toward a Politics of Mobility." *Environment and Planning D: Society and Space* 28, no. 1 (2010): 17–31.

Cumming, Carman. *Sketches from a Young Country: The Images of* Grip *Magazine.* Toronto: University of Toronto Press, 1997.

Danysk, Cecilia. "'A Bachelor's Paradise': Homesteaders, Hired Hands, and the Construction of Masculinity, 1880–1930." In *Making Western Canada: Essays on European Colonization and Settlement,* edited by Catherine Cavanaugh and Jeremy Mouat, 154–85. Toronto: Garamond, 1996.

Daschuk, James. *Clearing the Plains: Disease, Politics of Starvation, and the Loss of Aboriginal Life.* Regina: University of Regina Press, 2013.

Dempsey, Hugh A. "Jerry Potts: Plainsman." *Montana: The Magazine of Western History* 17, no. 4 (1967): 2–17.

Denny, Cecil E. *The Law Marches West*. 1939; reprinted, Toronto: J.M. Dent and Sons, 1972.

den Otter, Andy. *Civilizing the Wilderness: Culture and Nature in Pre-Confederation Canada and Rupert's Land*. Edmonton: University of Alberta Press, 2012.

Di Giovine, Michael A. "A Higher Purpose: Sacred Journeys as Spaces for Peace in Christianity." In *Pilgrims and Pilgrimages as Peacemakers in Christianity, Judaism and Islam*, edited by Antón M. Pazos, 9–37. Compostela International Studies in Pilgrimage History and Culture. Farnham, UK: Routledge, 2013.

Di Giovine, Michael A., and J.-M. Garcia-Fuentes. "Sites of Pilgrimage, Sites of Heritage: An Exploratory Introduction." *International Journal of Tourism Anthropology* 5, nos. 1–2 (2016): 1–23.

Dillard, Annie. *Pilgrim at Tinker Creek*. New York: Harper and Row, 1974.

Dippie, Brian W. "One West, One Myth: Transborder Continuity in Western Art." *American Review of Canadian Studies* 33, no. 4 (2003): 509–41.

Donald, Dwayne Trevor. "Forts, Curriculum, and Indigenous *Métissage*: Imagining Decolonization of Aboriginal-Canadian Relations in Educational Contexts." *First Nations Perspectives* 2, no. 1 (2009): 1–24.

——. "We Need a New Story: Walking and the wâhkôtowin Imagination." *Journal of the Canadian Association for Curriculum Studies (JCACS)* 18, no. 2 (2021): 53–63.

Douaud, Patrick, and Bruce Dawson, eds. *Plain Speaking: Essays on Aboriginal Peoples and the Prairie*. Regina: Canadian Plains Research Center, 2002.

Dyck, Noel. "Cultures, Communities and Claims: Anthropology and Native Studies in Canada." *Canadian Ethnic Studies* 22, no. 3 (1990): 40–55.

Eade, John, and Michael Sallnow. *Contesting the Sacred: The Anthropology of Christian Pilgrimage*. London: Routledge, 1991.

Eades, Gwilyma Lucas. *Maps and Memes: Redrawing Culture, Place, and Identity in Indigenous Communities.* Montreal and Kingston: McGill-Queen's University Press, 2015.

Elliott, David. *Adventures in the West: Henry Ross Halpin, Fur Trader and Indian Agent.* Toronto: Natural Heritage Books, 2008.

Epp, Roger. *We Are All Treaty People.* Edmonton: University of Alberta Press, 2008.

Erasmus, Peter. *Buffalo Days and Nights.* Edited by Henry Thompson. Calgary: Fifth House, 1999.

Fanning, Soren. "Forging a Frontier: Social Capital and Canada's Mounted Police, 1867–1914." *American Review of Canadian Studies* 42, no. 4 (2012): 515–29.

Federici, Silvia, and Peter Linebaugh. *Re-Enchanting the World: Feminism and the Politics of the Commons.* Oakland, CA: PM Press, 2019.

Fedyk, Mike. "History, Memory, and the NWMP Trail." In *Fort Walsh to Wood Mountain: The North-West Mounted Police Trail*, edited by Mike Fedyk, 1–14. Regina: Benchmark Press, 2010.

———, ed. *Fort Walsh to Wood Mountain: The North-West Mounted Police Trail.* Regina: Benchmark Press, 2010.

Francis, R. Douglas. "Regionalism, Landscape, and Identity in the Prairie West." In *Challenging Frontiers: The Canadian West*, edited by Lorry Felske and Beverly Rasporich, 29–50. Calgary: University of Calgary Press, 2004.

———. "Regionalism, W.L. Morton, and the Writing of Western Canadian History, 1870–1885." *American Review of Canadian Studies* 31, no. 4 (2001): 569–88.

Freud, Sigmund. "The Uncanny: A New English Translation." *Dialogues in Philosophy, Mental and Neuro Sciences* 11, no. 2 (2018): 84–100.

Frey, Nancy Louise. *Pilgrim Stories: On and Off the Road to Santiago.* Berkeley: University of California Press, 1998.

Frye, Northrop. *The Educated Imagination.* Toronto: Hunter Rose, 1963.

——. *Northrop Frye on Canada, Volume 12*. Edited by Jean (Mary) O'Grady and David Staines. Toronto: University of Toronto Press, 2000.

Gazan, Leah. "Will You Walk?" In *Unsettling the Word: Biblical Experiments in Decolonization*, edited by Steve Heinrichs, 104–06. Maryknoll, NY: Orbis, 2018.

Ghobashy, Omar Z. *The Caughnawaga Indians and the St. Lawrence Seaway*. New York: Devin-Adair, 1961.

Goeman, Mishuana. *Mark My Words: Native Women Mapping Our Nations*. Minneapolis: University of Minnesota Press, 2013.

Grand Coteau Heritage and Cultural Centre. "Everett Baker of Shaunavon." In *Fort Walsh to Wood Mountain: The North-West Mounted Police Trail*, edited by Mike Fedyk, 76–83. Regina: Benchmark Press, 2010.

Greenfield, Bruce. "'Now Reader Read': The Literary Ambitions of Henry Kelsey, Hudson's Bay Company Clerk." *Early American Literature* 47, no. 1 (2012): 31–58.

Greenia, George D. "The Lakota Future Generation Ride of the Lakota Sioux." In *Pilgrimage in Practice: Narration, Reclamation, and Healing*, edited by Ian S. McIntosh, E. Moore Quinn, and Vivien Keely, 137–47. Boston: CABI, 2018.

Groening, Laura Smyth. *Listening to Old Woman Speak: Natives and AlterNatives in Canadian Literature*. Montreal and Kingston: McGill-Queen's University Press, 2004.

Halfe, Sky Dancer Louise Bernice. *Bear Bones and Feathers*. Regina: Coteau Books, 1994.

——. *Blue Marrow*. Regina: Coteau Books, 2004.

——. *Burning in This Midnight Dream*. Regina: Coteau Books, 2016.

——. *The Crooked Good*. Regina: Coteau Books, 2007.

Hanson, Aubrey Jean. *Literatures, Communities, and Learning: Conversations with Indigenous Writers*. Waterloo: Wilfrid Laurier University Press, 2020.

Heinrichs, Steve. *Unsettling the Word: Biblical Experiments in Decolonization*. Maryknoll, NY: Orbis, 2018.

Henderson, Norman. *Rediscovering the Prairies: Journeys by Dog, Horse and Canoe*. Victoria: TouchWood Editions, 2010.

Hendriks, Robert W. *William Bleasdell Cameron: A Life of Writing and Adventure*. Edmonton: Athabasca University Press, 2008.

Herriot, Trevor. *The Road Is How: A Prairie Pilgrimage through Nature, Desire, and Soul*. New York: Harper Perennial, 2014.

———. *Towards a Prairie Atonement*. Regina: University of Regina Press, 2016.

Hildebrandt, Walter. *Views from Fort Battleford: Constructed Visions of an Anglo-Canadian West*. Regina: Canadian Plains Research Center, 1994.

Hiller, Chris. "Tracing the Spirals of Unsettlement: Euro-Canadian Narratives of Coming to Grips with Indigenous Sovereignty, Title, and Rights." *Settler Colonial Studies* 7, no. 4 (2017): 415–40.

Hogue, Michel. "Disputing the Medicine Line: The Plains Crees and the Canadian-American Border, 1876–1885." *Montana: The Magazine of Western History* 52, no. 4 (2002): 2–17.

———. *Metis and the Medicine Line: Creating a Border and Dividing a People*. Regina: University of Regina Press, 2015.

Hryniuk, Margaret, and Frank Korvemaker. *Legacy of Stone: Saskatchewan's Stone Buildings*. Regina: Coteau Books, 2008.

Hubbard, Tasha, and Jane Tootoosis. "Foreword." In *Storying Violence: Unravelling Colonial Narratives in the Stanley Trial*, Gina Starblanket and Dallas Hunt, 9–13. Winnipeg: ARP Books, 2020.

Hunt, Dallas. "Nikîkîwân: Contesting Settler Colonial Archives through Indigenous Oral History." *Canadian Literature* 230–31 (2016): 25–42.

Innes, Campbell. *The Cree Rebellion of 1884, or, Sidelights on Indian Conditions Subsequent to 1876*. Battleford, SK: Battleford Historical Society, 1926. Reprinted in Ross Innes, *The Sands of Time*. North Battleford, SK: Turner-Warwick, 1986.

Johnson, Harold. *Two Families: Treaty and Government*. Saskatoon: Purich, 2007.

Jorgenson, Allen G. *Indigenous and Christian Perspectives in Dialogue: Kairotic Place and Borders*. Lanham, MD: Lexington, 2021.

Joseph, Bob. *21 Things You May not Know about the Indian Act: Helping Canadians Make Reconciliation with Indigenous Peoples a Reality*. Port Coquitlam, BC: Indigenous Relations, 2018.

Kaye, Frances W. "An Innis, not a Turner." *American Review of Canadian Studies* 31, no. 4 (2001): 597–610.

Kennedy, Dan (Ochankugahe). *Recollections of an Assiniboine Chief*. Edited by James R. Stevens. Toronto: McClelland and Stewart, 1972.

King, Thomas. *The Inconvenient Indian: A Curious Account of Native People in North America*. Toronto: Doubleday, 2012.

Kovach, Margaret. *Indigenous Methodologies: Characteristics, Conversations, and Contexts*. Toronto: University of Toronto Press, 2009.

Krasowski, Sheldon. *No Surrender: The Land Remains Indigenous*. Regina: University of Regina Press, 2019.

Ladner, Kiera. "Proceed with Caution: Reflections on Resurgence and Reconciliation." In *Resurgence and Reconciliation: Indigenous-Settler Relations and Earth Teachings*, edited by Michael Asch, John Borrows, and James Tully, 245–64. Toronto: University of Toronto Press, 2018.

Larson, Margaret. *From Basket to Bridge: 1905–1980*. Kyle, SK: Kyle Heritage Committee, 1981.

Laurie Barron, F. *Walking in Indian Moccasins: The Native Policies of Tommy Douglas and the CCF*. Vancouver: UBC Press, 1997.

Lilburn, Tim. *Desire Never Leaves: The Poetry of Tim Lilburn*. Edited by Alison Calder. Waterloo: Wilfrid Laurier University Press, 2007.

Lowman, Emma Battell, and Adam J. Barker. *Settler: Identity and Colonialism in 21st Century Canada*. Winnipeg: Fernwood, 2015.

Macdougall, Brenda. "Speaking of Metis: Reading Family Life into Colonial Records." *Ethnohistory* 61, no. 1 (2014): 27–56.

Macdougall, Brenda, and Nicole St-Onge. "Rooted in Mobility: Metis Buffalo-Hunting Brigades." *Manitoba History* 71 (2013): 21–32.

Macfarlane, Robert. *The Old Ways*. London: Penguin, 2013.

Mackey, Eva. "'Death by Landscape': Race, Nature, and Gender in Canadian Nationalist Mythology." *Canadian Women Studies* 20, no. 2 (2000): 125–30.

———. *Unsettled Expectations: Uncertainty, Land and Settler Decolonization*. Winnipeg: Fernwood, 2016.

Massey, Doreen B. *For Space*. London: SAGE, 2005.

McCrady, David G. *Living with Strangers: The Nineteenth Century Sioux and the Canadian-American Borderlands*. Lincoln: University of Nebraska Press, 2006.

McDougall, John. *George Millward McDougall: The Pioneer, Patriot and Missionary*. Toronto: W. Briggs, 1888.

———. *On Western Trails in the Early Seventies: Frontier Life in the Canadian North-West*. Toronto: W. Briggs, 1911.

———. *Pathfinding on Plain and Prairie: Stirring Scenes of Life in the Canadian North-West*. Toronto: W. Briggs, 1898.

McGowan, Don C. *Grassland Settlers: The Swift Current Region during the Era of the Ranching Frontier*. Regina: Canadian Plains Research Center, 1975.

McGuire, Mollie C., and Jeffrey S. Denis. "Unsettling Pathways: How Some Settlers Come to Seek Reconciliation with Indigenous Peoples." *Settler Colonial Studies* 9, no. 4 (2019): 505–24.

McIvor, Bruce. *Standoff: Why Reconciliation Fails Indigenous People and How to Fix It*. Gibsons, BC: Nightwood Editions, 2021.

McLennan, David. *Our Towns: Saskatchewan Communities from Abbey to Zenon Park*. Regina: Canadian Plains Research Center, 2008.

McQuillan, D. Aidan. "Creation of Indian Reserves on the Canadian Prairies 1870–1885." *Geographical Review* 70, no. 4 (1980): 379–96.

Merriman, Peter, Mimi Sheller, Kevin Hannam, Peter Adey, and David Bissell. *The Routledge Handbook of Mobilities*. London: Routledge, 2014.

Meyer, David, and Henri Liboiron. "A Paleoindian Drill from the Niska Site in Southern Saskatchewan." *Plains Anthropologist* 35, no. 129 (1990): 299–302.

Mikaelsson, Lisbeth. "Pilgrimage as Post-Secular Therapy." *Scripta Instituti Donneriani Aboensis* 24 (2014): 259–73.

Moor, Robert. *On Trails: An Exploration.* New York: Simon and Schuster, 2016.

Moreton-Robinson, Aileen. *The White Possessive: Property, Power, and Indigenous Sovereignty.* Minneapolis: University of Minnesota Press, 2015.

Morton, Arthur S. *History of Prairie Settlement.* Toronto: Macmillan, 1938.

Morton, Desmond. *The Canadian General Sir William Otter.* Toronto: Hunter Rose, 1974.

———. "Cavalry or Police: Keeping the Peace on Two Adjacent Frontiers." *Journal of Canadian Studies* 12 (1977): 27–37.

Mouat, Jeremy. "'The Past of My Place': Western Canadian Artists and the Uses of History." In *Making Western Canada: Essays on European Colonization and Settlement,* edited by Catherine Cavanaugh and Jeremy Mouat, 244–66. Toronto: Garamond, 1996.

Nadeau, Denise M. *Unsettling Spirit: A Journey into Decolonization.* Montreal and Kingston: McGill-Queen's University Press, 2020.

Needler, G.H. *Louis Riel: The Rebellion of 1885.* Toronto: Burns and MacEachern, 1957.

Nevitt, Richard Berrington. *A Winter at Fort McLeod.* Edited by Hugh A. Dempsey. Calgary: Glenbow-Alberta Institute, 1974.

Okimâsis, Jean L. "As Plain(s) as the Ear Can Hear." In *Plain Speaking: Essays on Aboriginal Peoples and the Prairie,* edited by Patrick Douaud and Bruce Dawson, 35–54. Regina: Canadian Plains Research Center, 2002.

Padbury, G.A., Donald F. Acton, and Colette T. Stushnoff. *Ecoregions of Saskatchewan.* Regina: Canadian Plains Research Center, 1998.

Poelzer, Greg, and Ken S. Coates. *From Treaty Peoples to Treaty Nation: A Road Map for All Canadians.* Vancouver: UBC Press, 2015.

Poirier, Thelma. *Rock Creek.* Regina: Coteau Books, 1998.

———. *Rock Creek Blues.* Regina: Coteau Books, 2011.

Porter, Brian. "James Walsh of the North-West Mounted Police." In *Fort Walsh to Wood Mountain: The North-West Mounted*

Police Trail, edited by Mike Fedyk, 23–36. Regina: Benchmark Press, 2010.

Pratt, Mary Louise. *Imperial Eyes: Travel Writing and Transculturation*. London: Routledge, 1992.

Razack, Sherene H. "When Place Becomes Race." In *Race, Space, and the Law: Unmapping a White Settler Society*, edited by Sherene H. Razack, 1–20. Toronto: Between the Lines, 2002.

Read, Geoff, and Todd Webb. "'The Catholic Mahdi of the North West': Louis Riel and the Metis Resistance in Transatlantic and Imperial Context." *Canadian Historical Review* 93, no. 2 (2012): 171–95.

Reader, Ian. *Pilgrimage: A Very Short Introduction*. Oxford: Oxford University Press, 2015.

Regan, Paulette. *Unsettling the Settler Within: Indian Residential Schools, Truth Telling, and Reconciliation in Canada*. Vancouver: UBC Press, 2011.

Reid, Gerald F. *Factionalism, Traditionalism, and Nationalism in a Mohawk Community*. Lincoln: University of Nebraska Press, 2004.

Reid, Jennifer. *Louis Riel and the Creation of Modern Canada: Mythic Discourse and the Postcolonial State*. Albuquerque: University of New Mexico Press, 2008.

Roach, Kent. *Canadian Justice, Indigenous Justice: The Gerald Stanley and Colten Boushie Case*. Montreal and Kingston: McGill-Queen's University Press, 2019.

Robertson, David A. *Black Water: Family, Legacy, and Blood Memory*. Toronto: HarperCollins, 2020.

Savage, Candace. *A Geography of Blood: Unearthing Memory from a Prairie Landscape*. Vancouver: Greystone, 2012.

Scott, Duncan Campbell. *A Critical Edition of the Poems of Duncan Campbell Scott*. Edited by Leon Slonim. Toronto: University of Toronto Press, 1978.

Sharanya. "A Manifesto to Decolonise Walking." *Performance Research* 22, no. 3 (2017): 85–88.

Simmons, Matt. "RCMP Were Planning Raids while in Talks with Wet'su-
        wet'en Hereditary Chiefs about Meeting." *The Narwhal*, May 12,
        2022. https://thenarwhal.ca/rcmp-wetsuweten-meeting/.

Simpson, Leanne Betasamosake. *As We Have Always Done: Indigenous
        Freedom through Radical Resistance*. Minneapolis: University
        of Minnesota Press, 2017.

———. *Dancing on Our Turtle's Back: Stories of Nishnaabeg Recreation,
        Resurgence and a New Emergence*. Winnipeg: Arbeiter Ring, 2011.

Simpson, Leanne, and Kiera L. Ladner, eds. *This Is an Honour Song:
        Twenty Years since the Blockades*. Winnipeg: Arbeiter Ring, 2010.

Simpson, Patricia. *Marguerite Bourgeoys and the Congregation of Notre
        Dame, 1665–1700*. Montreal and Kingston: McGill-Queen's
        University Press, 2005.

Sissons, Dave, Terry Howard, and Roly Smith. *Clarion Call: Sheffield's
        Access Pioneers*. Sheffield, UK: North End-Clarion Call, 2017.

Smyth Groening, Laura. *Listening to Old Woman Speak: Natives and
        AlterNatives in Canadian Literature*. Montreal and Kingston:
        McGill-Queen's University Press, 2004.

Solnit, Rebecca. *Wanderlust: A History of Walking*. New York:
        Penguin, 2000.

Sperlich, Tobias, and Lace Marie Brogden. "'Finding' Payepot's
        Moccasins: Disrupting Colonial Narratives of Place." *Cultural
        Studies ↔ Critical Methodologies* 16, no. 1 (2016): 7–17.

Starblanket, Gina, and Dallas Hunt. *Storying Violence: Unravelling
        Colonial Narratives in the Stanley Trial*. Winnipeg: ARP
        Books, 2020.

Stegner, Wallace. *Wolf Willow: A History, a Story, and a Memory of the
        Last Plains Frontier*. Lincoln: University of Nebraska Press, 1980.

Stevenson, Allyson. "'Men of Their Own Blood: Metis Intermediaries
        and the Numbered Treaties." *Native Studies Review* 18, no. 1
        (2009): 67–90.

Stonechild, Blair. *The Knowledge Seeker: Embracing Indigenous Spir-
        ituality*. Regina: University of Regina Press, 2016.

Stonechild, Blair, and Bill Waiser. *Loyal till Death: Indians and the
        North-West Rebellion*. Calgary: Fifth House, 1997.

Suknaski, Andrew. *Wood Mountain Poems*. 1976; reprinted, Regina: Hagios, 2006.

Talbot, Robert J. *Negotiating the Numbered Treaties: An Intellectual and Political Biography of Alexander Morris*. Saskatoon: Purich, 2009.

Tauranac, John. "Subway Maps: Getting from A to D." *Focus* 41, no. 4 (1991): 30–36.

Terreault, Sara, and Matthew Anderson. "De Vieux-Montréal à Kahnawa:ké." *Room One Thousand* 3 (2015): 52–84.

Thompson, John Herd. *Forging the Prairie West*. Toronto: Oxford University Press, 1998.

Tinker, George E. "Tink." *A Native American Theology*. Maryknoll, NY: Orbis, 2004.

Titley, E. Brian. *The Frontier World of Edgar Dewdney*. Vancouver: UBC Press, 1999.

Tolton, Gordon Errett. *Prairie Warships: River Navigation in the Northwest Rebellion*. Victoria: Heritage House, 2007.

Touchie, Rodger D. *Bear Child: The Life and Times of Jerry Potts*. Victoria: Heritage House, 2005.

Tuan, Yi-Fu. *Space and Place: The Perspective of Experience*. 1977; reprinted, Minneapolis: University of Minnesota Press, 2001.

Tuhiwai Smith, Linda. *Decolonizing Methodologies: Research and Indigenous Peoples*. 2009; reprinted, London: Zed Books, 2012.

Veracini, Lorenzo. *Settler Colonialism: A Theoretical Overview*. Cambridge Imperial and Post-Colonial Studies Series. Houndmills, UK: Palgrave Macmillan, 2010.

Vowel, Chelsea. *Indigenous Writes: A Guide to First Nations, Métis, and Inuit Issues in Canada*. The Debwe Series. Winnipeg: HighWater, 2016.

Waiser, Bill. *Everett Baker's Saskatchewan: Portraits of an Era*. Calgary: Fifth House, 2007.

———. "Say It Ain't So: Henry Kelsey Was a Passenger, not a Pathfinder." *StarPhoenix* [Saskatoon], April 7, 2020. https://thestarphoenix.com/opinion/columnists/say-it-aint-so-henry-kelsey-was-a-passenger-not-a-pathfinder.

———. *A World We Have Lost: Saskatchewan before 1905.* Calgary: Fifth House, 2016.

Warkentin, John, ed. *The Kelsey Papers.* 1929; reprinted, Regina: Canadian Plains Research Center, 1994.

Weekes, Mary. *The Last Buffalo Hunter: As Told to Her by Norbert Welsh.* 1939; reprinted, Saskatoon: Fifth House, 1994.

Wiebe, Rudy. *Big Bear.* 2008; reprinted, Toronto: Penguin, 2011.

———. *The Temptations of Big Bear.* Toronto: McClelland and Stewart, 1973.

Wilson, Garrett. *Frontier Farewell: The 1870s and the End of the Old West.* 2007; reprinted, Regina: University of Regina Press, 2014.

———. "Jimmy Thomson." In *Fort Walsh to Wood Mountain: The North-West Mounted Police Trail,* edited by Mike Fedyk, 57–61. Regina: Benchmark Press, 2010.

———. "The NWMP Trail Fort Walsh to Wood Mountain." In *Fort Walsh to Wood Mountain: The North-West Mounted Police Trail,* edited by Mike Fedyk, 37–42. Regina: Benchmark Press, 2010.

Wilson, Ken. "Wood Mountain Walk: Afterthoughts on a Pilgrimage for Andrew Suknaski." *International Journal of Religious Tourism and Pilgrimage* 7, no. 1 (2019): 123–34.

Wilson, Ken, and Matthew R. Anderson. "The Promise and Peril of Walking: Indigenous Territorial Recognitions Carried Out by Settlers." *International Journal of Religious Tourism and Pilgrimage* 9, no. 2 (2021): 46–54.

Younging, Gregory. *Elements of Indigenous Style: A Guide for Writing by and about Indigenous Peoples.* Edmonton: Brush Education, 2018.

INDEX

MATTHEW ANDERSON was born to settler descendants on Treaty 4 territory. He holds the Gatto Chair in Christian Studies at St. Francis Xavier University in Antigonish, Nova Scotia/Mi'kma'ki, and teaches part time at Concordia University, Montreal/Tio'tiá:ke. Matthew is the author of *Prophets of Love: The Unlikely Kinship of Leonard Cohen and the Apostle Paul*, *Our Home and Treaty Land* (with Raymond Aldred), and *Pairings: The Bible and Booze*. His podcast is "Pilgrimage Stories from Up and Down the Staircase," and his websites are SomethingGrand.ca and UnsettledWords.com.